WILL ROGERS SPEAKS

**Over 1,000
Timeless Quotations
for Public Speakers
(and Writers, Politicians,
Comedians, Browsers . . .)**

**Bryan B. Sterling and
Frances N. Sterling**

M. Evans and Company, Inc.
New York

M. Evans and Company, Inc.
216 East 49th Street
New York, New York 10017

Library of Congress Cataloging-in Publication Data

Rogers, Will, 1879–1935.
    Will Rogers speaks : 2,000 timeless quotations for public speakers
/ [compiled by] Bryan Sterling, Frances Sterling.
        p.   cm.
    Includes index.
    ISBN 0-87131-771-0 (cl) : $18.95
    1. American wit and humor.   2. Quotations, American.
I. Sterling, Bryan B.   II. Sterling, Frances N.   III. Title.
PN6161.R664425   1994
818'.5202—dc20   94-42880
                                                                          CIP

Design by Charles A. de Kay

Typeset by Classic Type, Inc.

Manufactured in the United States of America

9   8   7   6   5   4   3   2   1

WILL
ROGERS
SPEAKS

Other books by Bryan and Frances Sterling:

The Will Rogers Scrapbook

The Best of Will Rogers

A Will Rogers Treasury

Will Rogers in Hollywood

Will Rogers' World

Will Rogers & Wiley Post: Death at Barrow

Authors' Preface

A superior power has seen fit to fling into the world, for once, a truly fine specimen—fine in body, fine in soul, fine in intellect.

The reference is to Will Rogers; the date: Sunday, July 25, 1926; the writer: James Agate, preeminent critic for Britain's most prestigious newspaper, *The Times* of London; the occasion: Will Rogers' opening as an added attraction in Charles Cochran's revue at the Pavilion, London.

As so many opportunities in Will Rogers' life, this London engagement came unexpectedly. He, his wife Betty, and their three children had come to Europe on what was to be a working vacation. Will had just completed a lengthy, strenuous lecture tour and Betty had hoped that Will might get some rest away from his usual surroundings. But there were interviews planned with Italy's dictator Mussolini, Spain's dictator Miguel Primo de Rivera and Spain's King, Pope Pious XI, and the Prince of Wales at York House. Will also had wanted to look in on the Disarmament Conference at Geneva. While traveling around Central Europe, Will and an American film crew shot enough footage to be later edited into a dozen travelogues. These short films, being silent, of course, would be annotated by Rogers' humorous titles and comments. In addition to his well established 1,500-word weekly newspaper article, which was internationally syndicated, Will had committed himself to a series of feature articles for the Saturday Evening Post. These articles would later be collected and published in the book *Letters of a Self-Made Diplomat to His President*.

While in Paris it was suggested that Will might want to take a trip to the Soviet Union, to observe first-hand the workings of the

Communist system. His astute findings were also first published in the Saturday Evening Post and later in book form as *There's Not a Bathing Suit in Russia & Other Bare Facts.*

Will also had a commitment to star in the British film *Tip Toes*, co-starring Dorothy Gish and Nelson ("Bunch") Keyes. If Betty had needed any further proof after 18 years of marriage, Will's "working vacations" meant much work with very little vacation.

News came of a tragic fire in Dromcolliher, an Irish village about thirty-six miles from Limerick City. Forty-seven men, women and children burned to death. Will Rogers immediately wired Dublin that he would like to appear in a fund raising benefit. He not only flew to Dublin but added a substantial personal check to President Cosgrave's fund for the survivors.

Charles Cochran, often called Britain's Ziegfeld, persuaded Rogers to step into his faltering show to add an international flavor. Will agreed to help his friend. Will opened on Monday, July 19th and *The Times*' regular theatre reviewer duly attended and wrote:

> Mr. Will Rogers, the American comedian and film actor, appeared on Monday night in Cochran's Revue at the London Pavilion. He is presenting each night for a season of at least six weeks, the "turn" that has earned him such popularity in America. He walks on to the stage in an ordinary, shabby suit—and just talks. At the first performance on Monday night, he talked a little too much, but that mistake can be rectified. At the beginning, Mr. Rogers seemed a little timid. He need not have been. Humour of the kind in which he delights, is international, and in a very few days he will be attracting all London to the Pavilion.

Intrigued by *The Times*' description of Will Rogers' opening in Charles Cochran's Revue earlier that week, James Agate had decided to attend a performance and judge for himself. As the reviewer's article had predicted, crowds indeed came to the Pavilion. Among them was Mr. Agate who then reported his impression in hyperboles.

The review of this 1926 London engagement might be viewed as a high point in Will Rogers' career, but it was only one more step in his climb to become America's first international multi-media super-star. Born November 4, 1879, near Oologah, in the Indian Territory that was to become the state of Oklahoma, Willie grew up as the youngest child and last surviving son of Clement Vann and Mary America Rogers. Both parents had Cherokee ancestry and

sely proud of his Indian heritage. From early age
e interested in leading the life of a cowboy than
dies his parents planned for him. Long before his
, Will was a competent rider, practicing rope tricks
nch hands. When formal tuition began, the con-
e-room schoolhouse seemed like punishment to

her died when he was ten, and he was sent to stay
lder, married sister, Sallie McSpadden, who lived
ea. Still, schooling went on. Over the years there
ols, each in succession more advanced, yet none
Will's attention. Finally a concerned father sent
mper Military School in Boonville, Missouri. After
uit "the school business for life."
onville, and not wishing to face his father, Will
Higgins, Texas, where he hired on as a ranch
ttle to far away rail heads for shipments east. The
dollars a month. This was the life Will enjoyed.
returned home. If Clem Rogers had hoped that
prepared to settle down, he was disappointed. An
h was to prod Will Rogers all his life, would not
er. Shortly he was off to the Argentine.
in the Argentine, a broke and hungry Will Rogers
rk tending a cattle transport across the Atlantic to
helped drive the herd into the interior to its new
e horses for the British Army. Drifting into Johan-
scovered Texas Jack's Wild West Show. Years of
tricks now came to the rescue. Billed as "The
Vill starred nightly; thus a career was born.
al months, Will left South Africa and joined cir-
ia and New Zealand, finally booking third-class
America. While still a long way from stardom, show
braced Will Rogers and he was forever "ruined as
k was concerned."

Engagements followed at the St. Louis Fair of 1904, vaudeville engagements in Chicago and finally the Horse Fair in New
York's Madison Square Garden. When the Fair closed, Will stayed
on, determined to break into Vaudeville. The novelty of his act, the
display of lariat tricks, including the lassoing of a galloping horse
and rider on stage, was something never seen in cities. It assured
Will bookings across the country. Vaudeville became Will's home
for the next ten years. In 1908 he married Betty Blake of Rogers,

Arkansas, the girl he had courted for many years, mostly from afar. Their honeymoon was along the vaudeville circuit but their love affair continued for the rest of their lives. "The day I roped Betty, I did the star performance of my life," Rogers later wrote.

Over the seasons Rogers' roping act changed. Horse and rider had long ago been eliminated from the performance. He now relied mostly on his own dexterity and added humorous comments, some about fellow acts, some about political events, some about local conditions. Playing on a vaudeville circuit, where the performer moved weekly from city to city, it was possible to perfect a certain routine and never change it.

Brief appearances in Broadway shows followed, until a call came from Gene Buck, Florenz Ziegfeld's assistant, asking Will to join the cast of The Ziegfeld Frolic. The Frolic was an entirely different show than the Ziegfeld Follies. It started at the stroke of midnight on the roof of the New Amsterdam Theatre, which had been transformed into the most luxurious nightclub. The Frolic attracted the elite of society with its excellent food and drinks, and New York's most sophisticated show. What was a cowboy, fully equipped with chaps, kerchief, stetson, and western twang, doing among the country's most beautiful girls? Why, stealing the show! Now commenting on the days's events both at home and abroad, the audience came as much to listen to Will Rogers as to look at the scantily clad beauties.

When Florenz Ziegfeld first heard that in his absence, Gene Buck had hired some rough westerner and placed him amidst his carefully selected Girls, he ordered Rogers fired. Buck tried to reason and asked for a week to prove his point.

"Flo," as he was called by those very close to him, simply did not like comedians. But in the case of Will Rogers he was soon convinced to make an exception. Not only was he most pleased with this cowboy's performance in the late night show, but he asked Will to join the Follies, in the theatre downstairs. Since many patrons were repeat visitors, who would attend the Follies first and then adjourn to the roof, Will Rogers had to change his routine for each show. No one could be expected to laugh twice at the same joke. Rogers would buy the latest newspaper editions before every show, and give each audience a different routine. On matinee days, he prepared three different acts.

In 1918 Sam Goldwyn offered Will the starring role in a motion picture to be filmed in Ft. Lee, New Jersey. "Movies" had as yet no voice, and Will Rogers could not use his greatest asset, his verbal wit. Nevertheless, Will's first film, "Laughing Bill Hyde" was well received by both, critics and audiences. Goldwyn offered Rogers a contract, on condition that he move to California. Will discussed this with Betty, and the Rogers family (now enlarged by Will, Jr., Mary, Jimmy, and Fred) moved west.

Goldwyn picked up the contractual option for a second year at an increase in pay, but he did not offer Will a new contract. In the following two years, Will made a dozen two-reel shorts for Hal Roach. When there was no further offer for his service, Rogers invested his money to produce his own films. While working on his third film, he found himself practically broke when he could not obtain distribution for his earlier films. Now in serious financial difficulties, Will went back to New York, to Ziegfeld and the Follies.

The McNaught Syndicate signed Will to write weekly columns at a salary of $500 per week. As the number of subscribing newspapers grew rapidly, the syndicate raised the payment to $1,000. Will's words, now in print in hundreds of papers, reached into every section of America. In New York, Will became the most requested after-dinner speaker. No convention banquet—whether it was for the corset manufacturers of America, or the international police chiefs—was considered a success, unless it could claim Will Rogers as its main speaker. Each speech he delivered was original and fitted only to the occasion. When asked to speak at a Jewish benefit featuring Eddie Cantor, Will hired a rabbinical student who worked with him for two weeks on the delivery of an address in Yiddish.

Will Rogers' fame and influence rose with each new field he entered. In 1925, Charles Wagner, an established tour promoter offered an entirely new idea: Why not go out on a lecture tour with the famous De Reszke Singers, a male quartet? Will discussed the offer with Betty and they decided that he should try it for a limited time, say—three months. The experiment proved so satisfactory for both parties, that Will—later without the quartet—continued these personal appearances until July 1928. Of course there were breaks for Christmas and New Years, as well as summer vacations.

In the summer of 1926, while touring Europe with his family, Will began sending cables, which *The New York Times* published on the first page of its second section. On his return to the United States, the now daily telegrams grew into the most popular feature of Rogers' writing career. These squibs, also internationally syndicated by McNaught, soon appeared in 600 newspaper in the United States and Canada. With his weekly articles and the daily telegrams Will reached 40 million readers, at a time when the entire population of the United States—men, women and children—was 120 million. His incisive, humorous comments on the day's news, delighted his readers. Will's columns was usually the first item read over morning coffee, whether it was in the White House or in White Sulphur Springs, West Virginia.

Will Rogers' position was unique in American history. Though claiming to be a Democrat, his arrows punctured the pompous of either party with equal accuracy. He was a favorite on either side of the political aisle. Two Presidents invited him to be their overnight guest: Republican Calvin Coolidge and Democrat Franklin Roosevelt. Each wanted to hear his reports on recently completed European tours.

Rogers knew personally nearly every member of Congress. He addressed many state assemblies and was on intimate terms with their governors.

In 1927, with the Mississippi River flooding vast areas, Will Rogers, on his own, began a tour of the area to raise money for the victims. Plane, pilot and gasoline were provided by private sponsors. Will Rogers flew from town to town, performing some days in half-a-dozen locations, raising vast sums of money, and beginning each collection with his personal generous check. It was said that Rogers would beat the Red Cross to any disaster site, where his appearance gave hope and support to the sufferers. In recognition of his service, the Red Cross made him an honorary Life Member.

In 1929, Will Rogers entered a new medium—sound films. The advent of talking pictures was ideally suited for Will Rogers' major talent—expressing his own wit. Most of the lines he speaks in the twenty-one sound films Rogers made for Fox Film, are his own. "No one could write for Will Rogers," said John Ford, who directed three of those films.

Will did not think of himself as a movie star. He claimed only two distinctions in the movies: "being the ugliest man in 'em, and still having the same wife I started out with."

Now past 50, Will Rogers made the list of the top ten screen stars; by 1933 he was Hollywood's top male star, beating such favorites as Clark Gable, James Cagney, Bing Crosby, and Fred Astaire.

In 1930 Rogers began a series of Sunday radio broadcasts and immediately became the most popular commentator. America loved Will Rogers; he spoke its language and expressed the country's fears and hopes. He was everybody's spokesman, he was their friend, who helped in times of need. And the country, now in the first stages of a rapidly deepening Depression, needed just such a reassuring voice. This was a kindly friend, perhaps a favorite uncle, perhaps a gentle grandfather. This was not a faceless columnist or commentator, this was the most recognizable person in the country.

In his daily telegram, on September 3, 1931, Will warned of the danger of pessimism: "If we did pass out as a great nation, our epitaph should read: 'America died from fright.'" In his Inaugural address, President Roosevelt expressed the same thought in his famous: "All we have to fear is fear itself."

Will clearly foresaw World War II and repeatedly warned his countrymen. When politicians proclaimed that "Prosperity is just around the corner!" Rogers cautioned: "War is closer around the corner than prosperity."

He accurately predicted Germany's build-up and attack on France and England; he foresaw Japan's attack on American holdings, foretold the fall of the Philippines, and repeatedly pointed out the vulnerability of Hawaii's installations. He was an advocate of greater military strength, and especially an independent Air Force.

Rogers' international views were shared by some, but the country was primarily concerned with its internal problems. But Will sounded the alarm, while helping to buoy up the sagging spirits of his country. He was loved and admired, respected and totally believed. Will Rogers had established himself in the minds and hearts of his countryman as an honorable man, a philosopher of the people. He sought no position, he wanted no title, no honorary doctorate. Once, nominated in his absence as Honorary Mayor of Beverly Hills, he spent his own funds to build recreational facilities for the police department.

The National Press Club in Washington, D.C., "elected" Will "Congressman-at-Large," while a leading magazine named him America's "Unofficial President." The appointments were, of course, in jest, but the implied recognition of Will's power was real. This potential for evil in the hands of a less principled man could have been easily perverted. Will never abused the influence entrusted him.

On August 15, 1935, Will Rogers died in a plane crash with famed aviator Wiley Post. They were on a trip around the world, when their lives ended near Barrow, Alaska. America mourned Will's death as no private individual had ever been mourned before—or since. Memorials from coast to coast still bear his name, testimony to his place in America's history. His words, though written or spoken some 60, 70 or even 80 years ago, could have been voiced this day. Of the sources of the most frequently used quotations in today's speeches and writings, Will Rogers' material is firmly secured in the number three position, topped only by the Bible and Shakespeare.

As you look through this book, you will find the truth of Will Rogers' words, and if you listen carefully, you just might hear the chuckle in his voice as he chides Congress, or expresses your own thoughts against the waste of your tax money.

I use only one set method in my little gags and that is that I try to keep to the truth. Of course, you can exaggerate it, but what you say must be based on truth. Personally I don't like the jokes that get the biggest laughs, as they are generally as broad as a house and require no thought at all.

I like ones where, if you are with a friend, and hear it, it makes you think and you nudge your friend and say: "He's right about that." I would rather have you do that than have you laugh—and then forget the next minute what it was you laughed at.

—*Will Rogers*

A

ACCIDENTS

Ah, the good old days. Then you lived until you died, and not until you were just run over.

May 14, 1933

★　★　★

About all we get in our Sunday papers is Saturday's auto casualties and the football scores.

That's one thing that the panic didn't hurt. No matter how hard times are, you can always get hit by an automobile.

November 23, 1930

★　★　★

Automobile prosperity is based on what they call "quick turnover." Well, with all these cheap make cars developing sixty and seventy miles an hour, and our improved roads and many sharp turns, you are going to see the greatest turnover in the automobile business this country ever witnessed. Undertaker shares will go higher than General Motors.

Yours for the airplane, where it's safe.

March 9, 1928

★　★　★

I have the Chicago Tribune in front of me and it says: "Annual Auto bill of U.S. is $14 Billion." In another part of the paper it says that 22 thousand met their deaths last year by auto and that we are well on our way to beating that record.

Fourteen billion we paid to kill 22 thousand. About $635,000 a piece, with no charges for the wounded and they must run at least two or three times as many as the killed. And they call all these accidents PROGRESS.

Suppose around 25 years ago, when automobiles were first invented, that a man, we will say it was Thomas A. Edison, had

15

gone to our government and he had put this proposition up to them: "I can, in 25 years, have every person in America riding quickly from here to there. You will save all this slow travel of horse and buggy. Shall I go ahead with it?"

"Why sure, Mr. Edison."

"But," says Mr. Edison, "I want you to understand it fully. When it is in operation it will kill 15 to 20 thousand a year of your women and children and men."

"What! You want us to endorse some fiendish invention that will be the means of taking human life? How dare you talk of manufacturing something that will kill more people than a war? Why, we would rather walk from one place to another the rest of our lives than be the means of taking a single child's life."

Now that is what would have happened if we had known it. But now it don't mean anything. It's just a matter of fact. Too bad.

April 4, 1926

Seven people were killed in the whole of America over the weekend in airplanes, and the way the newspapers headlined it you would have thought Nicaragua had invaded us. Yet in New York City alone, fifteen was killed and seventy wounded with bootlegged liquor, to say nothing of Chicago.

So it's safer to take a flight than a drink.

October 8, 1928

ACTORS

If you have ever been an actor, why, it just about ruins you for any useful employment for the rest of your natural life.

November 4, 1928

Actors are like politicians, they never grow up.

August 28, 1932

An actor has as much right as anyone else to have his political beliefs. He pays his taxes and is a good citizen. But I don't think he should carry any propaganda into his stage work. He has no right to use his privilege as an actor to drive home his political beliefs. We are paid by an audience to entertain them, not instruct 'em politically.

Then, if you want, as a citizen, go hire yourself a hall and tell 'em what you want to. You're a citizen then, not an actor.

November 9, 1924

ADOPTION

A man started out to adopt a little girl as a companion for another little foster daughter. The advertised age was from 10 to 12 years. Applicants began coming. One tramped in about 19 or 20. He got one flash and raised the age limit.

August 16, 1925

ADVERTISING

I defy even a Congressional investigating committee (you certainly can't pick a more useless body of men than they are), I defy them to say that a bathing suit on a beautiful girl don't come under the heading of legitimate advertising.

April 8, 1923

P.T. Barnum come nearer having a true slogan than anybody. He said: "There is a sucker born every minute," and Henry Ford was right there to take care of him the minute he come of age.

April 12, 1925

In my more or less checkered career before the more or less checkered public, I have been asked to publicly endorse everything from chewing gum, face beautifiers, patent cocktail shakers, Mah Jongg sets, even corsets, cigarettes and chewing tobacco, all of which I didn't use or know anything about. But I have refused.

You never heard me boosting anything, for I never saw anything made that the fellow across the street didn't make something just as good.

July 29, 1933

This country sure is organized and this country sure is advertised. When we arrive at the Poor House, we will be the best organized and the best advertised nation that was ever admitted.

In fact, it's paying dues to organizations and advertising that will put us there.

November 11, 1930

Let advertisers spend the same amount of money improving their product that they do on advertising, and they wouldn't have to advertise.

Notes

We toil and we struggle to maintain what is left of our beauty and manliness. Of course the radio helps us. At any hour somebody is begging and imploring us to go to the drug store and buy something that will take the wrinkles out of our ears, lift our eye brows, bring back that ruddy complexion.

There are as many gadgets on the market to overhaul men, as there is for women. I doubt if women have got much on men, when it comes to trying to outlook themselves.

February 24, 1935

ADVICE

Advice can get you into more trouble than a gun can.

August 20, 1933

I don't suppose there is any business with as many unemployed as the "advising" business.

May 23, 1934

We can see our friends or neighbors go out, make bad investments, do fool things, but we never say a word. We let him risk his life and his money without any advice. But his vote? We got to tell him about that, for he is kinder ignorant and narrow-minded and don't see things our way. So we advise him.

He ain't going to pay any attention to you anyhow, but it's a great satisfaction to think you are advising him anyhow.

November 1, 1934

AFGHANISTAN

They finally stopped us from sending Marines to every war we could hear of. They are having one in Afghanistan.

The thing will be over before Congress can pronounce it, much less find out where it is located.

December 19, 1928

It seems the King of Afghanistan thought he was adopting modern ideas by limiting his subjects to one wife per each. No wonder they threw him out. He was just old-fashioned and didn't know it. He wasn't modern.

December 19, 1928

AGRICULTURE

We are living in a peculiar time. You get more for not working than you will for working, and more for not raising a hog than for raising it.

February 3, 1935

The Secretary of Agriculture has got a tough job. It's by far the toughest job in the Cabinet.

The Secretary of the Navy only has to deal with an admiral; the Secretary of the Army with the Generals; the Postmaster General with the politicians, but when you deal with the farmers, you are dealing with a man who is a dealer himself.

May 28, 1934

Walking Monday afternoon through one of the most famous of the historical California missions, San Juan Capistrano, and who should I find in meditation before a wonderful old picture depicting the joy of the harvest, and the merrymaking at the sale of the crops?

It was the Secretary of Agriculture. Tears were in his eyes and he kept murmuring: "Oh, what have I done Father, that I couldn't have been Secretary of Agriculture in days like those?"

May 29, 1934

President Hoover is about finished appointing the committee that is to bring milk and honey to the famished agrarian. It looks like an awful simple problem they have to solve. All they have to do is to get the farmer more money for his wheat, corn and cotton without raising the price to the man that buys it.

June 30, 1929

Cattle are so cheap that cowboys are eating beef for the first time in years.

March 4, 1932

★ ★ ★

They have a course in those schools called Animal Husbandry. I asked a boy what it was and he told me. I had followed cows all my life and didn't know what it was.

March 28, 1926

ALABAMA

In a filibuster, Senator Heflin of Alabama held up all Senate business yesterday for five hours. That's a record for narrow views.

February 18, 1927

Last spring traveling down in Alabama, I had a chance to go by the great Negro school of Tuskegee, founded by Booker T, Washington. Had a great time there. Heard eighteen-hundred trained voices sing Negro Spirituals, AND HOW.

Why, it's the best run place you ever saw. Wonderful buildings, beautiful grounds. Why, it's bigger than Harvard and got a better football team.

January 27, 1929

ALASKA

This Alaska is a great country. If they can just keep from being taken over by the U.S., they got a great future.

August 13, 1935

★   ★   ★

I was never up in Alaska, but I know there is a lot of real guys up there, that can do something besides drink whiskey and recite "The Shooting of Dan McGrew."

February 8, 1925

ALBERTA, CANADA

Up in Alberta, Canada, there is only six on a jury, and they tried their Premier of that province for an affair with his secretary. (These foreigner courts do have some of the most Puritan notions.) The jury convicted him, but the judge said the jury was haywire. So now they don't know which one to try, the judge or the jury.

July 22, 1934

ALCOHOLIC BEVERAGES CONSUMPTION

While giving tremendous publicity to men and industries for assisting in "maintaining prosperity," let's don't overlook the part some states are playing.

Florida, Alabama and Georgia during this return to normalcy are the largest producers of distilled liquors, while New York, Pennsylvania and little Maryland lead the consumers.

The statistics also show that prosperity from this industry would have been greater was it not for the fact that in order for the product to go from Southern producer to the Northern consumer, it had to pass through Washington, D.C. and that it was almost impossible to get liquor past Washington.

December 11, 1929

ALEUTIAN ISLANDS

There is nothing on 'em, they are barren. Being in that state, of course, we own 'em.

January 17, 1932

★   ★   ★

The captain kept telling us that we were "off the Aleutians." This kept on for days. "We're off the Aleutians," till I thought he was off his Aleutian.

But he was right, we were.

January 17, 1932

ALIENISTS (PSYCHIATRISTS)

There are two things that I don't care how smart you are, you will never understand. One is an alienist's testimony, and the other is a railroad time table.

August 24, 1924

AMBASSADORS

At one time we were in wrong with the world. We were getting soldiers to enlist, but we had to draft Ambassadors to go to any foreign country.

May 25, 1930

★   ★   ★

I have always maintained that there was something the matter with Ambassadors, as none of them ever seemed to ambass properly. They are all right as long as nothing important shows up for them to do, but when it does they seem to flop miserably.

May 4, 1924

AMERICAN BAR ASSOCIATION

Pestilence finally caught us, the boll weevils descended on us in trainloads, 3,500 lawyers of the American Bar Association are here, eating us out of house and home. They are here, they say, "to save the Constitution, to preserve State Rights."

What they ought to be here for, that would make this convention immortal, is to kick the crooks out of their profession. They should recommend a law that every case that went on trial, the lawyer defending should be tried first, then, if he comes clear, he was eligible to defend. As it is now they are trying the wrong man.

July 14, 1935

The American Bar Association, that's a gang of lawyers who think that if you are not one of them you are in rompers, intellectually.

May 1, 1926

AMERICAN FEDERATION OF LABOR (A.F. OF L.)

Samuel Gompers has been for 40 years at the head of the largest organization of men in this country. He has done more for the working man than any man living. The reason the American Federation of Labor has been so successful is because when they found a good man, they kept him. They didn't go off electing some new fellow every four years.

December 21, 1924

Samuel Gompers spent his whole life trying to keep Labor from working too hard, and he has certainly succeeded beyond his own dreams.

December 28, 1924

AMERICANS

The American people are a very generous people and will forgive almost any weakness, with the possible exception of stupidity.

February 24, 1924

One-third of the people in the United States promote while the other two-thirds provide.

October 14, 1923

We are the only fleas weighing over 100 pounds. We don't know what we want, but we are ready to bite somebody to get it.

June 20, 1935

Half the people in the United States would rather collect one dollar from the Government than get $10 from an individual.

March 22, 1925

In schools they have, what they call, intelligence tests. Well, if nations held them, I don't believe we would be what you would call a favorite to win it.

There is still a lot of monkey in us. Throw anything you want into our cage and we will give it serious consideration.

June 25, 1935

If Americans are going to stop and start worrying about whether they can afford a thing, or not, you are going to ruin the whole characteristic of our people.

There wouldn't have been a dozen automobiles sold last year, if that was the case.

March 5, 1935

★   ★   ★

There is one rule that works in every calamity, be it pestilence, war, or famine: The rich get richer and the poor get poorer. The poor even help arrange it.

October 31, 1929

★   ★   ★

Just look at the millions of us here that haven't done a thing today that helps the country, or that helps anybody.

We have just gone along and lived off the country and we are just "lousy" with satisfaction of ourselves. We can't just laugh it off. We have prospered for years on nothing but our natural resources.

July 19, 1931

★   ★   ★

There is one trait that I don't believe any other people in the world have developed to the extent that our folks have. It's almost impossible to show the American folks something, that if you turn your head, they won't try to carry it home.

May 19, 1928

★   ★   ★

Americans have one particular trait that they need never have any fear of some other nation copying, and that is, we are the only people that will go where we know we are absolutely not wanted.

January 8, 1927

★   ★   ★

You give an American a one-piece bathing suit, a hamburger and five gallons of gasoline and they are just as tickled as a movie star with a new divorce.

September 4, 1933

AMMUNITION

Nations may not buy anything to eat, or anything to wear from you, but if you got a gun, they will buy it—and more than likely shoot it back at you.

Looks to me if every nation made their own ammunition, it would relieve their unemployment.

December 6, 1934

ANTI-TRUST LAW

You remember a few years ago this country had to pass a special law called the "Anti Trust Law," aimed primarily at two Trusts—The Oil and the Steel!

Now if you have to pass a law to curb businesses like that, they are not exactly the businesses to give confidence to the rest of our nation in regard to keeping the law.

February 1, 1935

APPENDIX

A convention is the only thing in the world, outside of the appendix, that no one has ever found a reason for.

Notes

ARBITRATION

Be sure you are right, and then go ahead, but don't arbitrate!

January 23, 1927

If American Labor would work while their case is being arbitrated, instead of striking, they would have the gratitude of our President and the sympathy of everybody.

October 13, 1933

Don't it look like in a case of a wage dispute, it would be compulsory for a man to keep on working but the workers send, say two representatives, the owners send two and the government send two and they confer. Then, if they were months settling this, and Labor won, their increase would go back to the time when the first protest was made.

That way nobody would be hurt very much and the Labor leaders and management could cuss each other in a room, the same way they do now in newspapers, yet nobody would have to be idle, listening to either side.

March 21, 1934

ARGUMENTS

You give us long enough to argue over something and we will bring you in proof to show that the Ten Commandments should never have been ratified.

April 15, 1930

ARIZONA

I would rather have Arizona's record as a state than New York with her numbers, Massachusetts with her intellect, or California with her modesty.

Arizona prolongs the life of the afflicted as well as makes perpetual the lives of the well.

July 4, 1933

★　★　★

You know that Arizona is really going to be understood and get somewhere some day. It and New Mexico, they are similar in lots of respects, but they are different from all the other states. They have great climates; almost any kind you like. They have a romance in history that outdates anything we have in our whole country, and there is just enough Indians to keep the whole thing respectable.

January 1, 1933

★　★　★

The trip across Arizona is just one oasis after another. You can just throw anything out and it will grow there. I like Arizona. She is a real cattle country and the old big stock pens along the railroad sho look good.

January 9, 1927

ARKANSAS

Any time you tangle with an Arkansaw hillbilly or hillbillyess, you are going to run second.

July 30, 1935

★　★　★

Arkansas took the literacy test just this week with an evolution bill. They just did make it.

Tennessee and Texas couldn't pass.

February 21, 1927

★　★　★

Arkansas voted last Tuesday against Evolution and Republicans. They don't want anything taught about either subject in their schools.

November 11, 1928

ARMAMENTS

A country is known by its strength and a man by his check book.

April 7, 1929

You give Ecuador England's Navy and right away Ecuador's ambassador would be seated next to the President at official functions, and England would go to the foot where Ecuador is now.

April 7, 1929

ARMENIA

Over in Armenia the rugs are made by the wives and lady friends of all these rug manufacturers and dealers. Over here they are bought by all the wives and lady friends of the men. Over there they sometimes take as long as 5 years to make one rug. Over here we sometimes take as long as ten years to pay for one.

April 15, 1923

ARMISTICE DAY

The day I am writing this is no doubt one of the greatest days in all world history, Armistice Day. When you think that half a dozen men could sit down and casually sign a pact to stop millions of men from killing each other.

But if they don't stop guys from making speeches on Armistice Day, why, we are liable to have the same war over again, only worse.

November 11, 1929

ART

Art is when you do something just cockeyed from what is the right way to do it, then it's art.

October 2, 1932

★   ★   ★

No matter how you built anything, and how you painted anything, if it accidentally through lack of wars or rain happened to live a few hundred years—why, it's art now.

August 21, 1926

ASIA

I tell you what the Orient needs. Don't bring a lot of clothes. You can get anything here, toilet articles, cigarettes, shoes, Scotch, and all America's standard equipment.

But for mercy sakes, bring a pillow with feathers in it. These out here are stuffed with rice, which wouldn't be so bad if they had cooked it first.

December 22, 1931

ATHEISTS

I was just thinking, if it really is religion with these nudists colonies, they sure must be Atheists in the Winter time.

March 15, 1934

All you would have to do to make some men Atheists is just to tell them that the Lord belonged to the opposition Political Party. After that they could never see any good in Him.

March 29, 1925

★ ★ ★

The basic foundation of the Communist Party is to be a non-believer—in other words, they are all Atheists.

Nobody knows what the outcome in Russia will be, or how long this Government will last. But if they do get by for quite a while on everything else, they picked the only one thing I know of to suppress that is absolutely necessary to run a Country on, and that is Religion. Never mind what kind; but it's got to be something or you will fail at the finish.

December 4, 1926

ATLANTIC OCEAN

On the Atlantic I generally get seasick just as they are pulling up the anchor.

February 27, 1932

★ ★ ★

We ought to set by a day of Thanksgiving, blessing the Atlantic and Pacific Oceans for their splendid judgment in locating where they did.

June 24, 1932

★ ★ ★

Nobody's ever found any particular good use for salt water. We've never found out what salt water was for, but I'll tell you it's awful handy when they've got three or four thousand miles of it between you and an enemy.

You let somebody sneak up some night and take all the water out of the Atlantic and Pacific oceans, and brother, by noon the next day we'll be beating our Fords into muskets, I'll tell you that.

February 11, 1934

ATOM

I see where two English scientists were able, the headline

said, to "split the atom." The world was not bad enough as it was; now they go and split the atom. That's the last straw.

May 3, 1932

AUSTRALIA

Australia is a fine place. It's beautiful, the people are congenial and hospitable, and no one making a tour of any length should miss it. There is only six and a half million people there, but that's enough people. Who wants more people than that?

March 5, 1933

I was in Australia many, many years ago, and I have always maintained that they had the best horses, I mean horse for horse all over the country, that they had the best horses in the world.

April 24, 1932

AUTOMOBILES

It's getting so a man that has a car now walks further than he ever did in his life, walking back from where he parked it at.

This is liable to bring walking back among grown people.

December 27, 1925

The automobile has changed the mode of living and the habits of more people than Caesar or Mussolini or Chaplin or Daniel Webster or Clara Bow or Xerxes or Amos 'n' Andy or Bernard Shaw. Why, they have run over more people in one month than either Washington or Lincoln disposed of in both their wars.

June 1, 1930

I unconsciously broke an American record of five years' standing yesterday. I bought a new car and didn't trade an old one in.

If I just had paid cash for it, I would have broken a real record, but I didn't.

October 1927

I see where one of our automobile manufacturers announced that his car was going to be four inches wider. It's the most revolutionary idea that has hit us since Southern Senators first appeared in socks and neckties.

Anyhow, how many times have you missed somebody by less than four inches? Well, from now on you will hit him.

September 6, 1925

The mass-produced automobiles are responsible for more buildings than any man living. There is more garages and filling stations built than there is homes, churches or schools.

If there was a single bed in every filling station in America, it would give every homeless man, woman and child a home to themselves.

June 1, 1930

It is the mass-produced automobile that alone is responsible for this great era of transportation in which we half-way live. The boys that make those cars know our problem. Our problems is paying for one of their problems—that is our problem.

They have drove more men into the debt than war has.

June 1, 1930

Mr. Ford is a good friend of mine, and I was at his home. I happened to ask him in case of stiff competition, how cheap he could sell his car.

He said: "Why, Will, by controlling the selling of the parts, I could give the cars away. Why, those things would shake off enough bolts in a year to pay for themselves, and the second year, that's just pure profit."

1923

★   ★   ★

A back seat driver can do more harm with the voice alone, than the one in front can do with a steering wheel.

Notes

★   ★   ★

The big thing about automobiles is still "accessories." You price a car nowadays, and the salesman gives you a figure. It sounds pretty reasonable. Then you say: "That includes everything?"

"Well, no, if you want wheels on it, that will come extra. Then come the bumpers, front and rear, and the lights. Of course you will want lights, in case you might want to use the car at night. And the mirrors are extra, in case you want to see what's going on in the back seat."

"Well," you wonder, "just what does go with the car at the original price you quoted me?"

"Well, the name and the good will."

January 20, 1929

★   ★   ★

In 1914, the Ford Company passed its first 1,000 cars a day production. So Americans woke up and said we got to have somewhere to put these things, and somebody thought of the idea to build roads to store them on.

And as fast as they would make roads, these things would clutter them up. I don't care where you try to hide a road, one of those road-fillers will find it.

January 25, 1925

★   ★   ★

Everything is sold on credit anyhow. Even the most experienced can't tell by looking at a car how many payments are still to be made on it.

December 1929

★   ★   ★

In most cities they use cars to drive, but in Los Angeles they just park 'em. Some men leave their cars there all night in order to hold the space for the next day.

1920

★   ★   ★

Headline says: "Five Autos Held Up!" Didn't say whether it was a bandit or a garage.

1920

★   ★   ★

Any day between now and the end of the year you can find me standing in line, waiting to get my automobile license. There's a hundred policemen keeping you in line and ten thousand out in the street looking to arrest you, and there are two people inside issuing licenses.

By the time I get to the window I am going to fool 'em. I'm going to get *next year's* license; this year's is a total loss now anyway.

Notes

Automobile Race

When you see a horse race, the horse that's in front is the winner, but when you see a fifty, or a hundred, or a five hundred mile automobile race, why, the fellow that is in front may be thirty laps behind. You don't look at the race, you look at a big score board to see who is ahead.

No sir, there is no kick in the world like a nose and nose finish of the old bang tails.

September 24, 1933

★   ★   ★

That Englishman, Malcolm Campbell sure deserves a lot of credit. 276 miles an hour in an automobile! All the credit we get out of it, we furnished the beach.

It seems strange the we Americans don't hold the automobile speed record, for we have millions trying to break it every day.

March 8, 1935

Automobile Show

The big National Automobile Show was in town last week. They showed a steam car that would run by building a fire in it out of hay, old shoes and newspapers. Why, the man told me you could get 100 miles out of a William Jennings Bryan speech.

The manufacturers say that in ten years there will be an auto to every man, woman and child in the U.S. They are making preparations to build them. Now all they got to do is control the birth rate.

January 14, 1923

★　★　★

The automobile show has just been held here in New York. They hold it every year. They have the same cars, only painted different.

This year the cigar lighters lay flat in a little compartment, instead of being placed up and down. They don't work any better, but they lay different.

January 18, 1925

AVIATION

We spend a billion dollars on good roads. Why not a subsidy to commercial aviation?

Congress is waiting two more wars to see if planes are practical.

April 14, 1927

★　★　★

Don't say "aviation is not safe or not practical" just because of an accident caused by an act of nature. There are certain things nature can do to you, whether it's an earthquake in California, a flood in Mississippi, a tornado in Ohio, or a drought in Arkansas. When nature enters into it, don't criticize.

April 5, 1933

★　★　★

Airlines have flown a million miles and no injuries to anyone. Then get the record of automobiles that run 50 miles a day and you will find they have got more accidents than they have cars.

You don't have to stop to figure out which is the safer. All you have to do is to compare the intelligence of the men that pilot planes with the intelligence of everybody that drives a car.

January 28, 1928

★   ★   ★

It looks like the only way you can get any publicity on your death is to be killed in a plane. It's no novelty to be killed in an auto any more.

October 31, 1927

★   ★   ★

We are going to fly to New York. First thing we have to do is to get to the aviation field. It took us just an hour and a half to drive through the traffic to the field. Ain't autos grand? What would we do without them?

If we had had a dirt road, with no expense to the tax payers, we would have got over there with a horse and buggy in about forty minutes.

January 21, 1928

AZTECS

The Aztecs and the Cliff Dwellers existed and had a civilization before the Meades and the Persians and the Gauls (by the way, the Gauls are still there) had even taken out their citizenship in Rome or Greece.

March 13, 1927

★   ★   ★

If Columbus had landed in Galveston and marched inland to Santa Fe, New Mexico, he would have been met by a delegation of modern "Redmen of the World," and the Aztec Rotary.

March 13, 1927

B

BALDNESS

The International Beauty Congress met in New York yesterday and they figured out that this rubbing something on your head to prevent baldness, is really what causes it. They claim that you got to take the stuff internally for it.

So from now on if you see a bald-headed bird reach for his flask, don't ask him for a swig. It's only irrigation juice for his roof.

March 12, 1931

BANKERS

When a banker fails, he fails in splendor.

February 7, 1933

★ ★ ★

I tell you borrowing money on what's called "Easy Terms" is a one-way ticket to the poorhouse.

March 18, 1923

★ ★ ★

You can't break a man that don't borrow.

March 18, 1923

★ ★ ★

The banker, the lawyer and the politician are still our best bets for a laugh. Audiences haven't changed at all, and neither have these three professions.

August 11, 1935

★ ★ ★

I guess there is no two races of people in worse repute with everybody than the international bankers and the folks that put all those pins in new shirts.

August 26, 1932

If you think borrowing ain't a sucker game, why is your banker the richest man in town? Why is your bank the biggest and finest building in your town?

March 18, 1923

★   ★   ★

The American Bankers' Association is holding their annual benefit! It's their biggest benefit yet. The government has contributed permission for them to consolidate and freeze out the little fellow and the public, of course, will contribute everything else.

October 25, 1927

★   ★   ★

At their convention in Houston, every banker that could afford a failure in the last year is there!

October 25, 1927

★   ★   ★

The Bankers' Institute, who call themselves the Educational end of banking, are holding a big convention out here in California. Every one of 'em carries American Express money orders—there is not a checkbook in a carload.

June 8, 1932

★   ★   ★

An old country boy banker from Colorado slicked the city slicker bankers out of one-half million bucks and they give him fifteen years so fast that you would have thought he had assassinated a big government official.

You let a city banker slick an old country boy out of something and before night he will merge with another bank and finally wind up as a member of the Federal Reserve.

October 11, 1929

★   ★   ★

We are a good natured bunch of saps in this country. When a bank fails, we let the guy go start another one.

Everything is cockeyed, so what's the use kidding ourselves.

June 30, 1930

★   ★   ★

The Farm Board destroying every third row of cotton is the nub of a great idea. There's too many banks, bump off a third.

August 16, 1931

★   ★   ★

If a bank fails in China, they behead the men at the top of it that was responsible. If one fails over here, we write the men up in the magazines as how: They started poor, worked hard, took advantage of their opportunities (and Depositors) and today they are rated as "up in the millions."

If we beheaded all of ours that were responsible for bank failures, we wouldn't have enough people left to bury the heads.

February 6, 1927

See where Congress passed a two billion dollar bill to relieve bankers' mistakes. You can always count on us helping those who have lost part of their fortune, but our whole history records nary a case where the loan was for the man who had absolutely nothing.

Our theory is to help only those who can get along, even if they don't get a loan.

January 22, 1932

★   ★   ★

The good old U.S.A. still holds one international record: our international bankers have loaned more of other people's money to foreign countries on less security than was ever loaned before, even with security.

Now there is a record we want to see beat, but no other bankers in the world are dumb enough to beat it.

March 21, 1932

★   ★   ★

I hope the Bankers' Institute goes to Canada and sees how it is that Canada has only had one bank failure in ten years. This idea evidently is not copyrighted.

June 8, 1932

★   ★   ★

Banking and After-Dinner Speaking are two of the most nonessential industries we have in this country. I am ready to reform if they are.

March 18, 1923

★   ★   ★

Another big bank failure. Suppose the Fire Department was run like a bank. A fire examiner finds a small fire and goes back from time to time to see it getting bigger.

Then, just as there is nothing left but the chimney, he notifies the Department: Hey, we better see what we can save for those people!

January 22, 1933

Water goes downhill and moistens everything on its way, but gold or money goes uphill. The Reconstruction Finance Corporation loaned medium and small banks money, and all they did with it was pay off what they owned to New York banks.

You can drop a bag of gold in Death Valley, which is below sea level, and before Saturday it will be home with papa J.P. Morgan's bank.

February 1, 1933

Franklin Roosevelt closed all the banks. That's one thing you would never get a Republican administration to do, voluntarily close a bank. Their theory was to leave 'em open till they folded.

March 9, 1933

Will you please tell me what you do with all the vice-presidents a bank has? I guess that's to get you more discouraged before you get to see the president. Why, the United States is the biggest business institution in the world and they only have one vice-president, and nobody has ever found anything for him to do.

1923

There's talk of opening seven thousand closed banks. That will put over a half-million bank vice-presidents back on the payroll.

September 25, 1933

One fellow paid his bank the interest on his mortgage the other day, and the police heard about it and followed him and sure enough, he had been in some of the late robberies.

May 17, 1931

★   ★   ★

I see where Jesse Jones and his Reconstruction Finance Corporation are not satisfied with the way the banks are just sitting counting their money. So, to make the banks ashamed of themselves, the R.F.C. is going to make loans to industry.

Jesse, you been a banker yourself, you ought to know you can't shame a banker, especially a big one.

December 18, 1933

★   ★   ★

I can't figure whether we made any progress in the last one hundred years, or not. For instance, I've been looking back and there was only two bank failures that year, and they hung both of them.

May 14, 1933

★   ★   ★

Instead of passing bills to make borrowing easy, if Congress passed a bill that no person could borrow a cent, they would go down in history as committing the greatest bit of legislation in the world. You will say, what will the banker do? Well, let him go to work, if there is any job any of them could earn a living at.

March 18, 1923

You'd think I am going to put these bankers out of business right away; well, I am not.

You see, it's not from a personal view that I am for abolishing banks. It's just that I don't think these boys realize what a menace they are. And as far as being good fellows, personally, why, I have heard old-timers talk down home in the Indian Territory, and they say that the Jesse James gang, and the Dalton Boys, were the most congenial men of their day, too.

March 18, 1923

There is two things that can disrupt business in this country. One is War, and the other is a meeting of the Federal Reserve Bank.

April 2, 1929

No wonder the Republican Party in this country is careful to do nothing to interfere with big banking interests. Big money only goes to the Party that supports big money.

August 28, 1931

Did you know that a hundred years ago no country in the world owed us anything? We were smart enough to owe them! I tell you, the older we get the dumber we get.

May 14, 1933

We can't alibi all our ills by just knocking the old banker. First he loaned the money, then the people wanted it back and he didn't have it; now he has it again and is afraid to loan it, so the poor devil don't know what to do.

June 8, 1932

★ ★ ★

Loan Sharks and Interest Hounds! I have addressed every form of organized graft in the United States, excepting Congress. So it's naturally a pleasure for me to appear before the biggest. You bankers are without a doubt the most disgustingly rich audience I ever talked to, with the possible exception of the Bootleggers

Union, Local No. 1, combined with the enforcement officers.

I see where the convention was opened by a prayer and you had to send outside your ranks to get somebody that would pray. You should have had one creditor here, he would have shown you how to pray. I noticed that in the prayer the clergyman announce to the Almighty that the bankers were here. Well, it wasn't exactly an announcement, it was more in the nature of a warning. He didn't tell the devil, he figured the devil knew where you were all the time.

1923

★   ★   ★

You bankers have a wonderful organization. I understand you have ten thousand here, and with what you have in the various Federal prisons that brings your membership up to around thirty thousand. So, goodbye paupers, you are the finest bunch of Shylocks that ever foreclosed a mortgage on a widow's home.

1923

BANK ROBBERS

Branch banks are all the go now. They realize they have got to bring the banks nearer the robbers. That way he won't be annoyed by having to drive through traffic just to rob one bank.

The branch bank is the robber's only salvation.

October 25, 1927

★   ★   ★

The future of bank robberies is to arrange some way to charge admission. So many people seeing robberies for free is what's killing the business.

June 20, 1934

BASEBALL

From politics to baseball is quite a jump upwards. Not only financially, but morally.

April 26, 1925

★   ★   ★

The baseball season opened on Wednesday, matinee day; everything of any importance always happens on a day when we have to work in the theater.

I'll bet you when the world comes to an end, it will be on a matinee day and I will miss it.

April 29, 1923

They have three umpires, one to correct the other two.

April 25, 1926

★ ★ ★

It's a joke to see a homer in some of the ball parks, it ruins the whole interest of the game. It does look like as big a game as base-ball is, and as much money as they make, they would have a regu-lation playing field, the same size all over. You don't see them cutting off the end of a tennis court, to put in more stands.

Then, if a man got a home run, he would know he deserved it, and everybody would have an equal chance on every field.

October 12, 1924

★ ★ ★

Most all the men are in good shape when they go down south for spring training. But those teams stay there till they get 'em hurt, even if it takes all spring.

April 26, 1925

★ ★ ★

Baseball requires more brains, more practice and more real skill than all others put together. It's the only game when you see it played, you know whether the ones playing it are paid or not.

October 14, 1929

★ ★ ★

Baseball is our national game and will always be our national game.

From an old first baseman of the Oologah (Oklahoma) Giants.

April 17, 1934

★ ★ ★

Baseball is the greatest game in the world, for the greatest number of people. It's the least crooked sport ever invented. And I am going to it, and believe in it, and admire the type of men that play it, till I get so old that my whiskers will get caught in the turnstiles.

January 23, 1927

BEAN SOUP

If I happen to have some bean soup, I want to be able to locate, at pretty prompt intervals, some little objects that look to me like beans.

I don't want a bowl of it where the beans have just been dri-ven through there at low tide.

July 17, 1927

BEAUTY PARLORS

Beauty parlors are thicker than filling stations. But more power to the people that run 'em, for they have to listen to people with nothing on their minds but wanting to look better.

April 30, 1929

BEER

They make beer nowadays so light, that you have to take a glass of it for a chaser after drinking water.

Notes

Europeans are raised on beer and wine. They have it at their tables at every meal. Europeans have been accustomed all their lives to drink all they want, sometimes for hours at a time, and then get up and walk home, even in narrow streets.

1919

BELGIUM

Belgium is just an unfortunate country geographically. No country has it in for Belgium personally. They just like to use their grounds to fight on. It's really not a country, it's just a Military Highway.

If I was Belgium, I would rent the country out to say, France and Germany, move out till the they got through with it, and then come back and get it in shape for the next war.

September 13, 1925

BEVERLY HILLS, CALIFORNIA

I love to stroll down in the old parts of Beverly Hills because I know of old places that have been built for four or five years.

September 25, 1932

If I had known that as mayor of Beverly Hills, I was ruling in a city of the "sixth class," I would never have taken the thing in the first place; why, I will be years living that down.

August 28, 1927

As mayor of Beverly Hills, I just sit at my desk day in and day out, taking care of the worth while things that come up. I have found out that it don't pay to interfere officially with any kind of sex problems. I just figure if both sides was not slick enough not to get caught, they are too commonplace for me to waste my official time on.

My constituents, I don't claim that they are all good, but the most of them is at least slick.

June 19, 1927

BIBLE

You can't get far ridiculing a man for upholding the Bible, or even a Dictionary, if it's his sincere belief.

August 9, 1925

The Bible is not read more than it is, because it is not in the picture section. If they could see David in his training quarters getting ready to slay Goliath with the jawbone of a Senator, people would stop and look at it.

December 21, 1924

Director Cecil B. DeMille, in a moving picture, parted the Red Sea, and more people have seen it in the pictures than ever heard of it outside of pictures. I have had more people ask me where DeMille got that idea, and they say it certainly was original.

December 21, 1924

★ ★ ★

If some preacher was just smart enough to put the Bible into a crossword puzzle, the entire United States would know it by heart.

December 21, 1924

★ ★ ★

That's one wonderful thing about the Bible. There was no censorship in those days. Of course, now some of our churches hold conferences and cut out certain parts they think don't belong in there, or change them to what they think should be said instead of what was said.

In other words, we are always having somebody improving on the words of the Lord. That's even worse than a scenario writer brightening up Shakespeare.

June 22, 1930

BIOGRAPHERS

The trouble with a lot of these biographers is that they go and lower the moral of the character with a lot of facts. Nothing will spoil a big man's life like too much truth.

October 29, 1933

BIRTHS

I went to get a passport to go to Europe. A lady said: "Here is the application and you will have to produce a birth certificate or someone will have to swear that they know of your birth.

"Well," I told her, "I have no birth certificate and as far as someone that was present at my birth and can swear to it, I am afraid that will be rather difficult. You know, the old-time ladies, of which I am a descendant, they were of a rather modest and retiring nature, and being born was a rather private affair and not a public function."

April 29, 1926

★   ★   ★

In the early days of the Indian Territory, where I was born, we had no birth certificates. You being there was certificate enough.

We were rather trusting that way. But if my folks had had at least a premonition at my birth that I would some day wander any further than a cow can stray, they would have made provisions for a proof of my birth.

April 29, 1926

★   ★   ★

Never mind that Birthday thing! I am pretty sore today and am looking for the ones that reminded me that on November 4, 1879, I was born at Oolagah, Indian Territory.

Boy, you get as old and look like an old badger as I do, you want nobody reminding you of that. When I was born, say, I was the prettiest baby that had been born there. But don't go around bragging on good-looking babies. You never know what they're liable to become. Anyhow, I played a game of polo and roped calves all day, so there is life in this old nag yet.

November 4, 1934

BOLL WEEVIL

It's not my place to tell people what to do. That's what we pay the President a lot of money per year for. I'm not getting paid for looking after the nation's affairs, so it's not for me to settle the boll weevil.

How about the South finding some way of using them after they mature. Get some famous New York chef to frame up a dish made of them. Just tell those New Yorkers it was eaten in Paris and they would go wild and pay any price.

Or get some breakfast food company to use them. They are using everything else. Just think what wonderful advertising pos-

sibilities the name has: "Eat a Bowl of Boll Weevil for Breakfast!"
September 2, 1923

BOOKS

We used to be worried about one of our public men when we hadn't heard anything of him in a long time. Now we don't worry. We know he has just been writing a book.
Notes

So many books are being published that you couldn't possibly remember 'em, so you just got to read the titles. Then, books nowadays are not written to be remembered, anyhow, they are written just to be sold, not even to be read.
December 25, 1932

Say, here is a list of the latest best selling books: "Jesse James Would Have Been an Amateur Had He Lived Today!" And "How I Made Agriculture Pay and How!" by the Farm Board.
February 27, 1932

BOOTLEGGERS

You can pick an American bootlegger out of a crowd of Americans every time. He will be the one that is sober.
August 19, 1927

The booze they sold was so strong, they had to dilute it with alcohol.
1919

Speaking of the high cost of liquor, the poorer people will have to go to Europe this summer to escape the high prices over here.
1919

People are going to use it and somebody has to supply it. It was originally a small business but it grew and grew far beyond even the expectations of its most optimistic boosters, till today it's no longer a business, it's an industry.

There is no such thing as a small supplier, no more than there is a small banker. Each is a subsidiary of some big concern, he just makes delivery, and it's for a chain.
July 6, 1930

President Harding canvassed Denver on "The Enforcement of the Law!" The bootleggers all agreed with him that the stricter the Law is enforced, the better it will make prices.

If there is one thing that will starve out bootlegging, it is cheap prices.

July 15, 1923

BOSTON, MASSACHUSETTS

Boston just looks like an old town that had been hit by a state capitol.

Notes

★   ★   ★

I am here in Boston helping them to celebrate their 300th anniversary, or something. I've got to be honest with you, I don't know what you are celebrating the 300th of, but I drove down here in a car tonight and the ruts we hit must have been 300 years old.

June 15, 1930

★   ★   ★

The biggest Marathon race we have in this country finished here today, and an old boy from Canada won it, because he never owned a Ford and didn't know how to run one. Outsiders won everything.

We ride good, but we get out of wind walking to the garage.

April 19, 1929

★   ★   ★

One thing they do have here in Boston, and that's the old fighting ship Constitution—the only ship that has withstood every disarmament conference.

June 17, 1930

★   ★   ★

Last night I stayed all night at Gilroy, California, and over 90 per cent of all the garlic in the United States is raised there. But here is the big astonishment. Boston is one of the greatest consumers of garlic in America.

May 17, 1935

★   ★   ★

Can you imagine me appearing at Symphony Hall in Boston? From the Stock Yards at Claremore, Oklahoma, to Symphony Hall, Boston! Me, with my repertoire of 150 words (most of them wrong), trying to enlighten the descendants of the Cod.

January 3, 1926

BOXING

Sporting News will embrace everything except Heavyweight Boxing Championship battles. They will be found in the Financial Section.

December 16, 1923

★   ★   ★

How present day prize fighting ever got mentioned in the category of sports will always remain a mystery to most people.

August 23, 1925

★   ★   ★

I tell you, those big purses at prize fights sure make a man think. I certainly kick myself I didn't learn to box.

But I am making up for it. I am having my oldest boy drop all his studies and just specialize on boxing, and when he becomes champion, I hope he can find some good partner to fight with every year or so.

Then the hardest part is to carry the money away.

And to think that crazy kid of mine wanted to be a lawyer.

September 25, 1927

★   ★   ★

A smart prize fight manager or a smart race horse trainer make great prize fighters and great race horses simply by knowing what race to put 'em in, or who to fight, and what race to keep 'em out of, and what fighters not to let 'em meet.

October 29, 1927

BRAILLE, LOUIS (BRAILLE SYSTEM)

I got the finest letter tonight. It was from a blind girl, and she sent me one of my Sunday articles and it was all written out in Braille.

I don't know how long that system of writing has been out. It may have been before the Nobel Prize was given out for outstanding achievement. But Braille, or whoever he was, should have had that prize. It undoubtedly stands out as the greatest benefit to a handicapped people.

Gosh, think of helping the world like that.

January 15, 1933

BRAVERY

Cowardice or bravery is never racial. You find both in every country. No country has a monopoly on bravery; great deed of heroism is liable to break out in the most unexpected places.

March 12, 1932

It was a dark, rainy, cloudy day on the New York end of the air mail run. No planes through in two days. I wanted to get home to my family in California. I insisted on going. It wasn't bravery—it was dumb ignorance and an unlimited confidence in all air mail pilots.

October 19, 1928

BRAZIL

Why, Brazil is bigger than England, France, Italy and Japan and has more natural resources than all of them combined. Yet she couldn't get to a Chamber of Commerce membership rally. Same old answer: No Navy!

March 16, 1930

BRITISH COLUMBIA, CANADA

Did you read about a bunch of women up in British Columbia as a protest against high taxes, sit out in the open naked, and they wouldn't put their clothes on?

How far is it to British Columbia?

April 5, 1931

BUDGET, UNITED STATES

The Budget is a mythical beanbag. Congress votes mythical beans into it and then tries to reach in and pull real beans out.

February 24, 1933

Here it is, right here in the paper, a whole financial statement of how we stand. Now I know a lot of you don't pay much attention to our Government finances. We read 'em and we look like we are doing fine, and then, there is another bunch of figures on the other side, that deny what the ones on this side say.

It's like a publisher with both a morning and an evening paper. They have one to keep the other out of a law suit.

December 16, 1928

★   ★   ★

The President said: The Politicians have overdrawn our bank balance, so that it now has the record for an overdraft. What we need is cheaper preparedness.

'Course, as soon as we get used to this overdraft, why, it won't be so bad, but now everybody's attention is focused on it. Besides, we got to get this thing hushed up before the next election.

May 31, 1931

We will never get anywhere with our finances till we pass a law saying that every time we appropriate something, we got to pass another bill along with it, stating where the money is coming from.

February 12, 1932

★ ★ ★

They sent the budget to Congress. It took the head man of every department in Washington 6 months to think up that many figures. Now, you have a budget like you have a limit in a poker game. You're not supposed to go beyond it till at least an hour after the game started. When we do, it just makes another department in Washington.

December 16, 1928

★ ★ ★

Congress has had quite a time with the Budget. There's things on there that you had no idea existed. Take, for example, the Department of Justice, it costs us billions of dollars. In fact, Justice is about the cheapest thing we got on our list. Maybe that's why we don't get any more of it.

I'm in favor of paying more for Justice and naming some of the people that ought to have what's coming to 'em.

December 16, 1928

★ ★ ★

There is only one unpardonable thing you can say—either in the Navy, Army or in politics—and that is to propose to cut down its expenditure. You can accuse them of negligence and even laziness, but to suggest spending less money, well, he just lost his compass in mid-ocean!

October 26, 1927

BUFFETS

Most buffet suppers, or dinners either, are a kind of excuse for not having much to eat. There is something about a "Buffet" that suggests that it's only going to be a couple of sandwiches and some potato salad.

April 9, 1933

★ ★ ★

These days, when you visit a friend's newly finished home you will be shown all the bathrooms and when you leave you couldn't, to save your soul, tell where the dining room was. Most of the eating, if one happens to be entertaining at home, is done off the lap. This custom of slow starvation has shown vast improvement of late. Instead of the napkins being of paper, they have been supplanted by almost-linen ones—that's to try and get your mind off the lack of nourishment. Why, in the old days they couldn't have fed you on your lap 'cause you couldn't have held all they would give you. Nowadays you have to feel for it to find it.

April 1, 1923

BUSES

I have never made a long bus trip, but I am going to some of these days. I hope they don't scare me as bad to ride in one as they do when they fly by me on the highway.

May 21, 1933

BUSINESS

Big Business got big according to law. But not according to Hoyle.

May 30, 1933

Big business—we're always hearing about big business, see? Big business has got a plan. Theirs is—they talked to the President: "Quit trying to reform us and give us a chance to recover."

The President says: "Can't you reform and recover, too?"

But big business' answer is: "No, we can't do anything with a cop on every corner watching everything we do. Give us a chance, and then, honest, when we're able, we'll reform. And besides," they asked the President, "We never—Mr. President—we never know what you are going to do next."

The President says: "Neither do I."

April 21, 1935

Big business wasn't entirely responsible for getting us into this Depression, and they are not going to be entirely responsible for getting us out as lots seem to think.

April 21, 1935

Business says to the President: "Look how England has recovered, for they're being let alone. Their business is being let alone and nobody is bothering them!"

The President says: "Yes, you pay as big an income tax as England does, then we'll recover too.

April 21, 1935

The day of the little guy working for himself is passing. My sympathy is naturally with the little fellow that has struggled along all these years and given the best he could for the money. He must have given pretty good value, for none of them got rich, so that shows that he didn't cheat anybody.

March 23, 1930

C

CAESAR, JULIUS

Caesar was kinder the Head Man. There was two political factions in Rome then, the Republicans and the Christians. Caesar was of course, a Republican and contributed generously to their campaign funds, and would kindly furnish Christians for the Sunday afternoon affairs at the arena.

In that ingenious way he kept the Christians the minority party.

February 2, 1930

Brutus, being a learned man, far beyond the knowledge of other Senators, was the first person to have no confidence in investigations. So instead of investigating Caesar, he just procured a Bowie knife and just stabbed the gentleman, practically ruining him. It was a rather crude way of arriving at the facts, but you must remember that Brutus was an honorable man.

February 2, 1930

CALIFORNIA

We took California away from Mexico the next year after we found it had gold.

When the gold was all gone, we tried to give it back, but Mexico was too foxy for us.

September 9, 1932

California is a great old state; we furnish the amusement to the world; sometimes consciously, sometimes unconsciously; sometimes by our films, sometimes by our orators, but you can't beat it.

September 9, 1932

I never saw California looking more beautiful. The tremen-

50

dous rains out here have washed away all the real estate signs.
March 14, 1927

Well, here in California, people were thinking and voting on whether to keep a governor four years or eight. I think a good, honest governor should get four years, and the others life!
November 8, 1927

We have our fun out here in California day in and out joking about the East mired down in snow and galoshes, while we bask in sunshine, roses and fine football. But let's be good sports and admit it, boys, we need rain. It's not just an admission, I will make it a motion that it be called a prayer—take it from a tax payer that still has vacant lots to sell.
January 3, 1930

★ ★ ★

California acts a good deal like a dog pound does in any town. It gets the undesirable strays off the streets. We are the human pound of America. Some of their own communities even go so far as to catch 'em and send 'em out here.

But being good humanitarians, we just take 'em right in, and in a week they are as big liars as the natives. Which shows they are not without some genius at that.
April 30, 1933

★ ★ ★

California is happy today. It's raining! It's raining!

That might mean just another mud hole to some places, but brother, when you haven't seen a drop of water that hasn't come through a faucet in ten months, why rain looks like a miracle from the government. Give California two months of rain in the year and nothing can stop us but a lack of adjectives.
January 16, 1933

★ ★ ★

The other day I visited one of our old California missions. One should never pass any of these missions without stopping and going in. They are among the great historical spots of our country. This one was built in 1776. That's the year our World Series was over with England.

An old priest had come up into the country, Father Junipero Serra, and he built missions and schools and he taught the Indians. He was a greater humanitarian than all the Pilgrims combined, including the three million that came over on the Mayflower. He civilized with a Bible, and the old Pilgrims did it with a blunder-buss.

June 10, 1934

★   ★   ★

We had a very exciting weekend out here in California, this land of sunshine and second mortgages. You know, I never saw people moving around so much. Every one of us hustling from bank to bank, trying to renew our notes.

But driving from bank to bank a man has got to be careful nowadays, for at the price of gas he will burn up more gasoline trying to get a loan than the loan is worth.

May 17, 1931

★   ★   ★

Everything is in California, all the great sights of nature, and along with all the wonders we have out here is the world's greatest collection of freak humans on earth. We maintain more freak religions and cults than all the rest of the world combined. Just start anything out here and if it's cuckoo enough you will get followers.

December 8, 1929

★   ★   ★

"Did the earthquake do as much damage as was reported?" Of course, the minute I got back east, every guy you meet would ask. You see, there is lots of jealousy of California by lots of communities all over the land, but we in California are a real boon to humanity, for you don't know how glad they are to get rid of some of the people we are able to take off their hands.

April 30, 1933

★   ★   ★

You take a Southern Californian and put him in a snow drift or anywhere else where he can't see a filling station or a cafeteria, and he is ready to write out his will.

January 31, 1933

CAMERA

The newspaper camera has made more criminals than bad environment.

December 30, 1927

★   ★   ★

Personally I think the camera has done more harm for politics than any other one faction. Everybody would rather get their picture than their ideas in the paper.

July 8, 1928

CAMPAIGN BUTTONS

You can get your name easier on a button than you can get it on the letter box in front of the White House.

October 4, 1931

CAMPAIGN FUNDS

I read where one fellow was nicked for 75 thousand berries for the Campaign Fund! And here the President was elected by the biggest majority of any President.

What would these boys spend on an election if it happened to be close?

April 6, 1924

CAMPAIGNS

The "Promising Season" ends next Tuesday, and at about 8 o'clock that same night, the "Alibi Season" opens and lasts the next four years.

October 31, 1928

We can get all lathered at the time over some political campaign promise, but if the thing just drags along long enough, we forget what it was that was originally promised.

The short memories of the American voters is what keeps our politicians in office.

April 7, 1930

There wasn't any more truth in over half of what any so-called orator said. If it wasn't a "Deliberate Lie," why, it was an "Exaggerated Falsehood."

November 13, 1932

Politicians just ain't equipped to conduct anything on a high plane. They got their minds set on the tail end of Pennsylvania Avenue—and they will promise anything short of perpetual motion, just to have senators eat breakfast with 'em.

July 26, 1928

Now this is one year the more a man promises, the less he will be believed. Voters are not going to vote for a man this year with any hope of him helping 'em, anyway. They are just going to vote for him for—well, I don't believe they will even go to the trouble of voting.

June 19, 1932

★   ★   ★

Well, here goes that radio again: "If I am elected, I will pledge myself to relieve the farmer. I will enforce the law and . . ."

Oh, applesauce! I will be glad when it's all over.

October 21, 1928

★   ★   ★

Most men that emerge from a political campaign with any spoils were more lucky than competent. A good campaign manager can do more than an able candidate. "Trades" makes presidents, more than ability.

July 10, 1932

★   ★   ★

The less a voter knows about you, the longer he is liable to vote for you.

October 26, 1928

★   ★   ★

I think you will find that campaigns have ruined more men than they ever made.

October 26, 1928

★   ★   ★

The old voter is getting so he wants to be saved before October every election year.

September 26, 1932

★   ★   ★

It's been a clean campaign. A clean campaign is one where each side cleans the other of every possible vestige of respectability.

November 6, 1932

★   ★   ★

Why do these candidates go to Omaha, or Denver, or Wildcat Junction, Tennessee, to speak? This thing of meeting your hero, and getting acquainted with him is awful liable to make you start hunting another hero.

October 26, 1933

★   ★   ★

You can always tell a poor business year by the number of candidates. When nobody else will give you employment, you feel like the state should.

July 29, 1930

★   ★   ★

Well, the campaign is degenerating into just what I thought it would. It started out to be honorable, but honor in politics seems out of place.

There is so many scandals being whispered about, but in politics practically everything you hear is scandal, and besides, the funny thing is that the things they are whispering about ain't half as bad as the things they have been saying out loud.

October 12, 1928

With the election coming on, you are going to be fed a lot of hooey about a lot of things. Naturally both sides are going to put their best side forward.

They are now trying to figure out which side is their best.

May 29, 1932

You may wonder "Just when does a campaign really start?" Well, they usually start about 15 minutes after the official returns are in from the last election, on about the fifth drink after the counting is over and the radio has announced that 'So-and-So concedes the election to his honorable opponent!' That is the first hooey of the following campaign—right then is when the boys start laying their traps for the open office-holding season and they start soaping the tracks right away.

October 23, 1932

It don't take much political knowledge to know that a man can get more votes running on the people's request, than he can running on his own request.

August 3, 1927

If you have a radio, the next three months is a good time to have it get out of fix. All you will hear from now until election will be: "What I intend to do is . . ."

What he intends to do is to try and get elected. That's all any of them intend to do.

August 3, 1924

You can't beat an administration by attacking it. You have to show some plan on improving it.

July 26, 1928

What's happened to the "Dignified High Type Campaign" that was to take place this year? If all the charges that's been made in regard to both the candidates were laid end to end, it would take 'em over two hours to pass a given point.

And if all the "Denials" were heaped in a pile, Lindbergh couldn't fly over them. You know, it's a funny thing about a denial is that it takes twice as many words to deny it as it did to make the accusation.

October 19, 1928

Look at the campaign plea of my old friend, Governor Bulow of South Dakota, who is out for the Senate seat and who says: "There is no issue in this election; the other fellow has got the job, and I want it!"

October 31, 1930

Let's raise the amount any man can contribute to another man's election campaign. When you regulate the price that a man can spend for votes, you are flirting with the very backbone of American Liberty. If we can't be a good nation, let's at least not be accused of being a cheap nation.

May 20, 1926

I don't know of any quicker way in the world to be forgotten in this country than to be defeated for President. A man can leave the country and people will always remember that he went some place. But, if he is defeated for President, they can't remember that he ever did anything.

July 6, 1924

CANADA

George Washington whipped England to try and get us freedom. Canada stayed with England and got it.

December 1929

I was a-reading in the papers here lately where Canada was having a sort of tough time. I have always had such high regards for the way they generally handle their affairs, that I just naturally thought they were going good.

July 21, 1935

Canada, they truly have been a good companion; I won't call them neighbors, for they haven't borrowed enough from us to be called neighbors. I would prefer to still call 'em Friends. They are a fine tribe of people. They are hardy—they got to be to live next to us and exist; they have made a great showing with a few people over a tremendous area.

The whole of New York City, where 80 per cent of our wealthy people are in storage, if you turned 'em loose in Canada on their own resources, it would be fifty years before one would get far enough away from Toronto to discover Lake Erie. No, Canadians are built of sturdier stock; they have suffered more than their share; they furnished more than their share of men and money in the Great War. Their example was a cause of real admiration to all our Country.

February 27, 1932

The big boss in Washington said he wished me, if I had time, to go up into Canada and see what kind of a deal I could make in the way of annexation. Now from what I can see, there don't seem to be any demand in Canada to join in with us and be murdered or run over with us. They strike me as entirely too sane a nation to fit in our scheme of things down home.

October 17, 1926

I have no doubt that we could make Canada a paying proposition, for that country is now supplying about everything we use in the way of raw material. So, if we can just keep from annexing them, and keep from loaning them anything, why, we ought to be friends for years to come.

October 17, 1926

I can't see any reason for annexing Canada except to use part for a skating rink in the winter, but we got such a poor class of skaters we couldn't afford to maintain it just for that, unless we could trade in Wisconsin on it in some way.

What we need is some good country to annex us.

October 17, 1926

★   ★   ★

After looking over Canada last week and reporting to you in regard to taking it under the auspices of the United States, well, that's all off. We don't want more people in this country. What we want is to try and improve the mob we have here now.

Canada couldn't help us out. They couldn't even learn us English; they speak it just as bad as we do.

October 24, 1926

★   ★   ★

When it comes to running their own business, Canada don't need any great advice from us. She is a mighty good neighbor and a mighty good customer. That's a combination that is hard to beat.

We agreed to buy from each other, and we will—till somebody comes along and sells cheaper.

August 28, 1932

CANDIDATES FOR PUBLIC OFFICE

It don't take nearly as good a man to be a candidate, as it does to hold the office, that's why we wisely defeat more than we elect.

May 31, 1928

★   ★   ★

I not only 'don't choose to run' I will say I won't run—no matter how bad the country will need a comedian by that time!

June 28, 1931

★   ★   ★

I am not a candidate for any office, whether President, Vice-Presidential, Senator or Justice of the Peace. I couldn't run anyhow because I can't make up my mind which side to run on. I don't know which side of the issues the most votes is on and I can't straddle them, for that's where all the rest of the candidates are now.

June 28, 1931

★   ★   ★

Fellows would like to live in the White House, and in order to get there they will promise the voters anything from perpetual motion to eternal salvation.

November 4, 1928

CANNIBALISM

In a Sunday article I stated that the Donner Party was our only cannibalism. I was wrong, as usual, for I just learned of this case.

Crossing the divide from Utah to Colorado in 1872, a man named Packer evidently practiced it. He was convicted in Del Norte, Colorado and the judge passed sentence as follows:

"Packer, you have committed the world's most fiendish crime. You not only murdered your companions, but you ate up every Democrat in Hillsdale County. You are to hang by the neck till you are dead, and may God have mercy on your Republican soul."

They lived off the Democrats but this was the only one we could ever convict.

October 12, 1930

CAPITAL PUNISHMENT

I see that all the papers have been commenting on the novel

way of asphyxiation, by which the State of Nevada "executed a man for committing murder."

Well, the novelty of that was that a prisoner was executed in ANY way for committing murder!

June 5, 1930

★   ★   ★

I'm in Kansas City this morning, where the girl was kidnapped. If I live a thousand years, I will never know what would keep any state from making that punishable by death.

May 29, 1933

★   ★   ★

If we are going to do away with Capital Punishment and sell guns to everybody, let's fix it so the party behind the gun will be at least a clear-headed marksman, instead of a drunken, drugged amateur.

Think of the humiliation of being shot by one of the present-day bandits.

September 20, 1925

★   ★   ★

Anybody whose pleasure it is watching somebody else die, is about as little use to humanity as the person being electrocuted. There is some excuse for the man being electrocuted. He may be innocent, he may have killed in a wild rage of passion; or not in his right mind, or self-defense. But the people who asked to come there just for the outing—there is no excuse in the world for them.

I believe I could stand to be the victim, rather than to see one.

June 7, 1925

CAPONE, AL

I interviewed Al Capone for two hours, but I never did write the story. There was no way I could write it and not make a hero out of him.

What is the matter with us when our biggest gangster is our greatest national interest?

March 11, 1932

★   ★   ★

Al Capone was arrested in Philadelphia, that is, he arranged for his arrest. An opposition gang was just two machine gun lengths behind him, and he was looking for a refuge, so he had himself put where the industry couldn't get at him.

March 30, 1930

CATTLEMEN

There will never be any class of people in our country that can replace the old western cowman for common sense, shrewdness, humor and fine citizenship.

December 12, 1934

CAVIAR

Russia's big importation is caviar—that's a kind a gooey mess of fish eggs that I suppose is without doubt the poorest fodder in the world, but it costs a lot and the rich just lap it up.

I was surprised, I didn't think a fish in Russia would lay anything but hard-boiled eggs.

December 3, 1933

CENSUS

Say, have you had your census taken? That's just about the last thing we've got left to take from us.

December 2, 1923

★   ★   ★

This is the year of the census. We take a tally—that's what we used to call it when I was on a ranch and we counted cattle. In other words, we run 'em by us and see how many we got.

Well, Uncle Sam takes a tally every ten years and it's a good thing. Not that it means much to anybody to know how many other people there are, but it does give work to the ones that do the counting.

April 13, 1930

★   ★   ★

Just reading these late census reports and it shows that the small town is passing. We not only ought to regret it, we ought to do something to remedy it. It was the incubator that hatched all our big men, and that's why we haven't got as many big men as we used to have. Take every small-town-raised big man out of business and you would have nobody left running it but vice-presidents.

April 16, 1930

We spend millions of dollars every 10 years, trying to collect the census of this commonwealth of America, when all we would have to do is wait until a presidential election year and then count the candidates.

December 2, 1923

If at times you feel that your government is not interested in you, you are all wrong. Why, every ten years they send around to see if you are still living, and why. They take your name and address and if anything shows up during the next ten years, they will notify you.

April 17, 1930

Knowing how many of us there is don't mean a thing. Censuses are just for Chamber of Commerce oratorical purposes. The new census will give California six new Congressmen. Now if you can call that adding to human welfare, you are an optimist.

April 17, 1930

Say, did you read the latest census figures? Talk about putting a quota on immigration. Why, the Yankees are swarming into the South like locusts. Get some of these gains: Houston, Texas, showed a gain of 110 per cent. Atlanta, 73 per cent gain and Miami 273 per cent. There is only one drawback—these rascals bring their Republican politics with 'em. They ought to be met at the Mason-Dixon line and deloused.

June 1, 1930

★ ★ ★

Every city kicked on its Census returns, claiming they didn't count the suburbs. Well, the whole United States just published their count—122 million.

Now I guess we will claim America was short changed. We should have taken in Mexico and Canada.

July 8, 1930

CHAMBER OF COMMERCE

The minute a fellow gets into the Chamber of Commerce, he quits mowing his own lawn.

May 20, 1923

★ ★ ★

The Chamber of Commerce of the United States that is in session in Washington now is running true to form. They have a maximum of objections with all the minimum of remedies for all national ills.

May 2, 1930

CHANGE

Conditions and events change so fast that what is passable today, is ridiculous tomorrow.

January 20, 1935

I don't know, the older we get the more "standpat" we get. The only change we want as we grow older is a change back to the things of our early life. We don't want a lot of new ones. Just because a things is new, don't mean that it's better.

September 11, 1932

CHAPLIN, CHARLIE

I consider Charlie Chaplin not only the funniest man in the world, I consider him to be (and this comes not from hearsay but from personal observation and contact with him) to be one of the smartest minds in America. Any man that can stand at the absolute head of his profession as long as he has can't do it on a pin head. It's an education to be associated with Charlie Chaplin. He is a student of every form of government, and well informed on every national and international question.

He is the only man, actor, statesman, writer, painter that has ever been able to please the entire world.

December 14, 1924

★　★　★

Big headline is: "CHARLIE CHAPLIN'S WIFE ONLY 16 YEARS OLD!" Now Los Angeles has said she would be compelled to go to school.

This girl don't need to go to school. Any girl smart enough to marry Charlie Chaplin should be lecturing at Vassar on "Taking Advantage of your Opportunities."

December 14, 1924

CHARACTER

England never looks good, till it looks bad, then she comes through. A nation is built on character, the same as a person is and no matter what their financial difficulties are, that old character shows up.

September 20, 1931

CHARITY

That's one trouble with our charities: we are always saving somebody away off, when the fellow next to us ain't eating.

March 22, 1932

★　★　★

There ain't anything that will dampen a man's public spirit any more than to cut off his salary. He just kind of loses his taste for doing something for his fellow man after that.

May 19, 1935

★　★　★

We shouldn't be giving people money and them not do anything for it. No matter what you had to hand out for necessities, the receiver should give some kind of work in return—say, four hours a day. Instead of money being handed out as charity, you work for it at some state, or national public work.

It wouldn't cheapen labor, it would cheapen public works, the thing that belongs to all the people, and the thing we would like to have cheapened.

It may not be a great plan, but it sure beats the one we got now.

January 18, 1931

CHEWING GUM

Chewing gum is the only ingredient in our national life of which no one knows how, or of what it is made. We know that sawdust makes our breakfast food. We know that tomato cans constitute Ford bodies. We know that old, second-hand newspapers make our 15 dollar shoes. We know that cotton makes our all wool suits. But no one knows yet what constitutes a mouth full of chewing gum.

December 9, 1923

CHICAGO, ILLINOIS

The snow was so deep today, the crooks could only shoot a tall man.

January 9, 1930

★　★　★

Headline says: "Chicago electrocuted four gangsters!"
Their limousine must have crossed a live wire.

October 16, 1931

★　★　★

Chicago is like the stock market. It has been away off par lately, but it got back to normalcy yesterday. They machine-gunned seven.

June 2, 1930

★　★　★

Here is something Chicago ought to put on billboards about its gangsters, and announce to the world: rival gangs do not murder each other! They are killed by members of their own gang for "holding out" and double-crossing. A "square" gangster can die in this town of old age.

I tell you, this system has a lot of merit to it. Wouldn't it be great if bankers "bumped off" the crooked ones?

June 26, 1930

Five bandits were acquitted here in Chicago yesterday, but I guess that wouldn't come under the heading of news.

December 18, 1926

There is only one way to avoid being robbed of anything in Chicago, Illinois, and that is not to have anything.

July 29, 1923

Chicago, there is just an awful lot of fine things about the old town besides bullet holes. It's one of the most progressive cities in the world. Shooting is only a sideline.

June 29, 1930

★   ★   ★

Box score for today: Died of gunshot and other natural Chicago causes: 13; wounded 23.

Bad weather kept outdoor shooting down to a minimum.

November 23, 1926

★   ★   ★

Just passed through Chicago. It's not a boast, it's an achievement.

January 9, 1930

★   ★   ★

I was in Chicago. There was a few murders while I was there but not enough to keep up the town's reputation.

May 6, 1928

★   ★   ★

It's a great old city and they are doing the best they can, and time has proven that they haven't got the sole and exclusive right to organized crime.

May 28, 1933

The Census report that knocked the country cuckoo showed that you here in Chicago had now almost four million people. Of course, you shoot a lot of people here, but you breed a lot, too.

Your breeding so overshadows your shooting that you have no cause for worry at all. It's only when your marksmanship excels your propagation that you want to start to worry.

June 22, 1930

CHILD LABOR LAW

I have been asked how I stand on this Child Labor Amendment. If Congress or the States would just pass one law, as follows, they wouldn't need any Amendment: "EVERY CHILD, REGARDLESS OF AGE, SHALL RECEIVE THE SAME WAGE AS A GROWN PERSON." That will stop your child labor.

December 28, 1924

They are trying to pass an Amendment to keep children from working. Now children didn't want to work, but they got tired waiting for somebody else to do it.

Notes

CHILE

Chile and Peru are arguing over a boundary line. We sent General Pershing down and he saw the piece of land that is in dispute and he has suggested that if Peru can't get Chile to take it, and if Chile can't get Peru to take it, that they both try and get Argentina to take it, as Argentina has never seen it.

August 16, 1925

★   ★   ★

The idea in one of these elections is to be able to vote before being shot. Any ballot without a bullet hole in it is counted.

August 16, 1925

★   ★   ★

They have had elections before down there, but no one has ever lived long enough to count the votes. You see, one side would always claim they had run out of ammunition and didn't have a fair vote.

August 16, 1925

CHINA

China is in a mess, not only again, but still.

October 16, 1930

In the old days in China, the rulers promised 'em nothing, and made good. But now they get promises, so you see yourself just how much better off they are. No comparison to the old days.

Sounds like our 100 percent American campaign pledges, don't it? Their pledges are fulfilled, too, just like ours.

April 2, 1932

The Chinese are the most fortunate nation in the world, for they know that nothing that's going to happen to 'em can possibly be worse than something that's already happened to 'em.

April 2, 1932

There is China, a Republic, yet China is so big that nine-tenth of her people never find out that all these wonderful benefits that they are enjoying, are called "Liberty."

April 30, 1932

Here is another thing that handicaps the Chinese: take one separate and he is smart, alert, able, clever, and can get things done. But let him be joined by another Chinese and their efficiency usually drops 50 percent.

April 2, 1932

Always dodge the "expert" who lived in China and "knows" China. The last man that "knew" China was Confucius, and he died feeling that he was becoming a little confused about 'em.

December 30, 1931

When American diplomacy gets through messing us around over in China, I will tell them what has caused this hate of us over there. It's our missionaries who have been trying to introduce "Chop Suey" into China.

China didn't mind them eating it there, but when they tried to call it a Chinese dish, that's what made them start shooting at us.

Yours, for corn bread, chitlins and turnip greens.

May 15, 1927

★   ★   ★

A Japanese wants to die for his country, but the Chinese, he ain't going to let patriotism run away with his life; he wants to live. Life ain't serious with him like it is with the Japanese.

The Japanese feel they were put on earth for a purpose, but the Chinese, he feels he was put here by mistake.

March 12, 1932

★   ★   ★

I came up to Peking here and I been looking at Walls and old Palaces till I am groggy. The Forbidden City—that's the way to attract attention to anything; call it "Forbidden" and you couldn't keep an American out of there with a meat ax.

Well, this wasn't forbidden any more than Palm Beach, but by calling it "Forbidden" they grabbed off the yokels, me included.

March 19, 1932

Not much news over the weekend, as we look at news today. The flood in China drowned a million. We take that with as little concern as a New York gang war killing, or the fifty people killed in motor cars over the weekend.

August 31, 1931

Every nation in the world have their own land, and every other nation recognizes it. But China, everybody looks on theirs as public domain.

England holds one of their towns. Now what right has England to hold one of their towns, any more than China has to make a laundry out of Buckingham Palace.

February 6, 1927

The Chinese, as a race, have forgotten more honesty and gentlemanliness than we will ever know if we live another century.

February 6, 1927

Let's get down to Eats. Lot of folks have had Chinese dinners, but this orgy of Bamboo Shoots started about 9:30 P.M.

Then along in the middle of dinner, they had lunch, and other things kept coming and we settled down to steady eating about 11:30. Up to then we had just been practically fooling.

At 1:30 in the A.M. when we shoved away from the table, there was at least ten Chinese still bringing in arms loaded with more unnameable provender.

April 30, 1932

You know, those chop sticks are really not so difficult; with just a little practice you can get so you can do quite a bit of gastronomic damage with 'em. They are great if you are on a diet, or have a tendency to eat too fast.

I got so that, finally, I could catch flies with mine.

March 5, 1932

★   ★   ★

No wonder the Chinese all come to 'Frisco and New York to carry on their Tong Wars. It's the only place where they can shoot each other in a friendly way without having some nation join in to protect their interests.

July 5, 1925

An Irish history in some round about way must have fallen into the hands of the Chinese, and as they read it they started loading their guns; and as they finished it, they started shooting.

You might ask: "Who did they shoot?" Well, if you get your schooling from an Irish History, you shoot anybody. The motto is: "When in doubt, Shoot."

July 5, 1925

CHRISTMAS

Merry Christmas to the Senate and the House of Representatives, and all my friends in there; may the literacy test never be applied to your constituents.

December 24, 1928

This was a very happy Xmas for me, in fact the best I have enjoyed in years. The shirts my wife gave me were the right size for the first time since wedlock. Of course they were the wrong color, but one, if married, must not be too particular. For a while it looked like I would spend a perfect Xmas.

Then, about noon, a necktie arrived.

January 4, 1925

Christmas was to give happiness to the young and it used to be a great day; the presents were inexpensive and received with much joy. It was a pleasure to see the innocent little souls as they rushed down to the big room with the fire place on Christmas morning and no matter what they found, it was great.

January 5, 1930

Now Santa Claus has been pretty thoroughly discredited by even our babes in arms. Why, I was a big old chuckle-headed nester, maybe 10 years old, before I even suspicioned that our friend of the long whiskers wasn't the one delivering things into my stockings. But nowadays we just ain't fooling nobody. They talk about civilization advancing. But boy, there ain't no civilization where there ain't no satisfaction, and that's what's the trouble now, nobody is satisfied.

January 5, 1930

CHRISTMAS CARDS

Xmas cards was invented by somebody that wanted to sell stamps and wanted to break the backs of mail carriers.

You pay a lot of money to get what is supposed to be an exclusive design and the first mail brings you twelve cards just like the ones you're mailing out.

January 6, 1929

★ ★ ★

Just on first thought a Xmas card don't mean much, but the older you get, the more you like to open 'em and know that somebody has remembered you.

January 15, 1933

CHURCHES

If they are going to argue religion in the church, instead of preaching it, no wonder you can see more people at a circus than a church.

January 20, 1924

★ ★ ★

I read statistics and it shows how church attendance is sorter falling off on Sunday mornings. But it's not lack of religious inclination. A preacher can have the best sermon in the world, but he just has to deliver it to folks without gas. Folks are just as good as they ever were and they mean well, but no minister can move 'em like a second-hand car.

May 20, 1934

★ ★ ★

If some of these birds would follow His example instead of trying to figure out His mode of arrival and departure, they would come nearer getting confidence in their church.

January 20, 1924

CIGARETTES

The minute they get Prohibition, they will hop on to something else; it will be Cigarettes, or room and bath, or something.

1919

★ ★ ★

Woman died in Savannah, Georgia, age 123. She had smoked a pipe for 112 years, while cigarette smokers figure they are passing out daily at the ripe old age of 30 and 40.

I think it is the fatigue from tapping 'em on the cigarette case that wears 'em down early.

April 16, 1934

★ ★ ★

Everywhere I go down here in Mexico, somebody invariably asks me for a cigarette, so, if you ask me, what that country needs, it's more cigarettes.

June 9, 1928

CIGARS

I tell you, the day has passed in America when the successful candidate can go about bragging on the fact that he "was elected on $22.45 worth of 5-cent cigars."

May 20, 1926

CITIES

There's just three cities in the whole of America that are different and distinct, New Orleans, Frisco and San Antonio. They each got something that even the most persistent Chamber of Commerce can't standardize.

November 4, 1931

Cities are full of country folks, and all the city folks are trying to get little places in the country.

August 5, 1934

CIVILIZATION

The more so-called civilized we get, the more we kill and take.

March 16, 1930

Anywhere you go, some bird will get up and tell "How our civilization is advancing, and how primitive it all was a few years back!"

Honestly, there is times when it looks like we haven't got over two ideas above a flea. Just give anything enough publicity and we would pay admission to see folks guillotined.

March 30, 1930

Any man that thinks civilization has advanced is an egotist.

July 5, 1931

CLAREMORE, OKLAHOMA

Claremore, Oklahoma, the best town between Foyil and Catoosa, in Oklahoma.

July 13, 1924

Claremore, Oklahoma, a town in physique but a city at heart.

June 5, 1927

CLEVELAND, OHIO

Can you imagine this town of Cleveland wants the Republican and Democratic conventions, both, next time?

The Republican Convention will be held further west and as for the Democratic one, a sanity test will follow any town purposely asking for it.

April 15, 1927

COAL MINING

There is only one form of employment in our country that I can think of that has no bright spots, and that is coal mining. There is generally an over-production and they are out of work; if not that, it's a strike. Then, when they do go to work, the mine blows up.

Then if none of these three things happen, they still have the worst job in the world.

December 19, 1929

★   ★   ★

The old coal miner packs a lot of sympathy on account of his work. That "going down into the very bowels of the earth" has stirred us all up more than any phrase about our anatomy.

And then, those accidents make it so they ought to be mighty well paid.

September 17, 1933

★   ★   ★

If I was a coal mine owner and couldn't understand my help any better than they do, I would resign and announce to the world that as an industrial leader I was a "bust," and I would devote my life to seeing that the world burned cow chips.

February 28, 1928

COFFEE

England has the best statesmen and the rottenest coffee of any country in the world. I just hate to see morning come, because I have to get up and drink this coffee.

Notes

★   ★   ★

England is taking the tax off tea. It's been on 300 years. Now why don't they take the quinine or assafidity (or whatever it is) out of their coffee? It tastes like something that has been in there 300 years, too.

April 16, 1929

COFFEYVILLE, KANSAS

It used to be our Post Office from our old home down in the Indian Nation. It was forty miles away, but then we didn't get much mail, anyhow.

In fact I have known some of us make the whole trip and never even get an oil circular.

April 14, 1929

COLLEGE, UNIVERSITY

College, I think, is better for the parents than it is for the students. You see, what you do is to send the kid out of the home just as he reaches the arguing stage of life.

Notes

A College President's work nowadays consists of thinking up new things for the students to play with that looks like studying.

All this stuff would have been a kick to Abe Lincoln, wouldn't it?

February 15, 1929

It's funny how quick a college boy can find out that the world is wrong. He may go out into the world from High School and live in it, and make a living in it for years and think it wasn't such a bad place. But let him go to College and he will be the first one down on the square on May Day to shout "Down with the Government!"

March 29, 1931

★   ★   ★

Right in the midst of this depression, why, one old boy hasn't had it so bad. He has been measuring 6,000 College girls. He compares 'em with co-eds fifty years ago.

I didn't know anyone ever thought of measuring one fifty years ago—and from what our elderly women led us to believe, we didn't think they would have allowed it.

Well, this fellow finds that the present ones are higher, wider and thicker (he don't say whether it's head or body) and these, he says, have more lung capacity.

Well, we knew that.

March 18, 1931

★   ★   ★

This "College Spirit" things is kinder over-estimated. Men will do every day for money what all the spirit in the world don't make 'em do. If you have something extra dangerous that requires nerve and skill, you don't try to go out and rig up a lot of cheering and spirit to get somebody to do it. You put a price of the old dollar sign on it and you get it done, even if you can't detect any spirit within a mile.

December 6, 1925

★   ★   ★

Do you think Colleges are becoming commercialized?
No, no more than the Steel Industry.

Notes

College Credits

All these Colleges, they got another gag, they call "credits." If you do anything 30 minutes, twice a week, why, you get some "credits;" maybe it's lamp shade tinting, maybe it's singing. If a thing is particularly useless, why, they give you more "credits."

July 31, 1932

★   ★   ★

If you tell where a Latin word was originally located and how it's been manhandled and orphanized down to the present day, they will claim that you have the nucleus of a "Thesis" and you are liable to get a hord of "credits." 'Course, you can't go out and get a job on it, but these old professors value it mighty highly.

And us poor old parents, we just string along and do the best we can, and send 'em as long as we are able, because we want them to have the same handicaps the others have.

July 31, 1932

College Degrees

In our days, the young folks that were fortunate enough to go to College didn't have this national havoc to look at like the young ones nowadays do. They looked forward to graduation with a great expectancy; they felt they would step out into a world and that there was a definitive notch awaiting them. It meant something to be a College graduate, there was jobs, there was positions, and all things being equal, you were given a little edge. That was, what might be called the "golden period" of the young College graduate.

Of course he knew that he knew more than his elders, but that goes, and always has, with a College degree.

December 9, 1934

★   ★   ★

I received a nice letter from a College president. He wanted to give me a degree and he said that they had given them to the Cabinet, the Supreme Court and leading industrialists.

I have had this same play come up a time or two and I think these guys are kidding. If they are not, they ought to be. Degrees have lost prestige enough as it is, without handing 'em around promiscuously. Don't give 'em to anyone just because he happens to hold a good job in Washington, or manufactures more monkey wrenches than anybody else, or because he might be fool enough to make people laugh. Keep degrees just for those kids that have worked hard for 'em; they step into a world not of their making, so let's at least not belittle their badge.

May 19, 1935

College Graduation Address

Every year I've been reading some of the addresses delivered to the graduating classes. Any man that's made mistakes is been asked to address the boys and girls somewhere, and tell 'em how to go through life. And they tell 'em that they are living in a time of great changes, and that they must prepare themselves for the new civilization that's coming.

I bet you there hasn't been a class graduated in the last hundred years that hasn't been told the same old gag.

June 10, 1934

I know you boys are in a hurry to graduate and nothing can slow up a graduation like advice. If you have waited four years for a street car to come along, you don't want anybody stopping you to give you advice, just when it does come.

Notes

If anybody hasn't had an offer to deliver one of these baccalaureate addresses to some college graduating class, they must be pretty low down.

June 15, 1930

College Sports

College athletes are always coming up to me and asking "When should I turn Pro?"

And I tell 'em "Not until you have earned all you can in College."

September 29, 1929

Does College pay?

It does if you are a good open-field runner.

Notes

★　★　★

I think you can learn the same at all schools, outside of football.

May 16, 1926

★　★　★

In the old days boys wanted an education. They even had reading, writing and arithmetic, instead of football. Up to then boys had gone there for their heads and not their shoulders.

August 26, 1928

★　★　★

There is only one fair way to ever arrange amateur athletics in any line in this country and that's let the athletes work on commission of what they draw at the gate, then make them pay their own schooling expenses.

May 27, 1929

★　★　★

The trouble with College football is, you can't carry your cheerleaders with you through life.

Notes

★　★　★

College is a great thing. I've got two boys and people ask me, they say: "Will, are you going to send your boys to college?" And I says: "Yes, I'm going to send 'em one year and if the football coach don't offer to pay their tuition, I'll bring them home."

April 16, 1928

★　★　★

I am just starting over to the big football game in Pasadena. This game don't decide anything, but it winds up the most successful financial season higher education has experienced since they took professors out of universities and replaced them with coaches.

January 1, 1930

★　★　★

It's open field running that gets your old College somewhere, not a pack of spectacled orators, or a mess of civil engineers. It's better to turn out one good football coach than ten College presidents.

September 29, 1929

★　★　★

Well, it's just as well to get baseball over with, for the boys that are working their way through football are all ready to break a leg for big gate receipts.

October 7, 1927

The football season is closing and College life is about over for the year. A few students will stay on the season for the dances, and some of the players may take up a couple of pipe courses and hang around till Spring practice starts.

The College president will be looking over the gate receipts to see if he stays on another year; alumni will start arguing over a new coach.

November 25, 1928

COLORADO SPRINGS, COLORADO

Colorado Springs is the Osage Indians' summer resort. They being the richest people in the world, are naturally able to pick out the best resort there is.

When the Osages come, the smaller fry have to move out and give way to wealth. I had heard all my life of the beauty of Colorado Springs, and believe me it had not been over estimated any.

Fine hotels there, the swimming pools, 4 polo fields, golf courses and private fishing lake; all for the guests.

There is a tepee in every room to make the Osages feel at home.

March 28, 1926

COLUMBUS, CHRISTOPHER

Old Eric, the Red, from Greta Garboland already had a home in America where he spent his summers, but this Columbus was quite a fellow. He is the only man, then or since, who ever had a queen pawning jewels. Columbus was Italian, but he made Spain pay his fare over.

October 12, 1933

I have always had quite an admiration for him. He was about the first of the foreigners to start coming over; he beat the immigration law. But somebody would have found America, even if Columbus hadn't, for you couldn't hardly get around without running into it. Why they didn't find it any sooner is more than I will ever know. If they couldn't find as big a place as North and South America, what would they do if they lost some little nation like Switzerland, or Latvia, or Rhode Island?

August 1, 1926

Christopher Columbus landed on some islands, but they always stretched a point and give him the best of it and said he landed in America. Spain and Italy are always having an argument over which country he really come from. Spain claims that he might have been born in Italy, but it was without his consent. Then Italy claims that when he died and Spain buried him in their country, that too, was without his consent.

August 1, 1926

Being an Indian, I don't mind telling you that personally I am sorry he ever found us. The discovery of America has been of no material benefit to us, outside of losing all our land. I am proud to say that I have never yet seen a statue to him in Oklahoma.

August 1, 1926

★ ★ ★

The Columbus Day celebration has rather an added significance to Los Angeles, as they want to celebrate the good fortune of his landing on the Atlantic instead of the Pacific side, because if he had landed in California, he never would have gone back to tell the Queen.

He would have stayed there and nobody would have ever known about America but him.

July 1, 1923

COMEDIANS

I certainly know that a comedian can only last till he either takes himself serious or his audience takes him serious, and I don't want either one of those to happen to me till I am dead (if then).

June 28, 1931

COMMANDMENTS, THE TEN

The moment a thing is long and complicated, it confuses. Whoever wrote the Ten Commandments made 'em short. They may not always be kept, but they can be understood.

They are the same for all men. No industry come looking for Moses saying: "Ours is a special business."

March 17, 1935

★ ★ ★

Moses just went up on the mountain with a letter of credit and some instructions from the Lord, and He just wrote out the Ten Commandments, and they applied to the steel men, the oil men, the bankers, the farmers, and even the United States Chamber of Commerce. And he said: "Here they are, Brothers, you take 'em and live by 'em, or else."

March 17, 1935

COMMON MAN

There is nothing that impresses the "common folk" like somebody that ain't common.

July 12, 1928

★   ★   ★

This bird kept talking about being for the common people. You are not going to get people's votes nowadays by calling them common. Lincoln might have said it, but I bet you it was not until after he was elected.

July 6, 1924

★   ★   ★

Nobody wants to be called "Common People," especially common people.

June 21, 1925

COMMUNISM, COMMUNISTS

You remember Communism? It's a disease that used to be prevalent in Russia, but it's almost starved out.

September 27, 1925

★   ★   ★

Communism is like Prohibition. It's a good idea, but it won't work.

November 6, 1927

★   ★   ★

Communism to me is one-third practice and two-thirds explanation.

November 6, 1926

★   ★   ★

It just looks to me like Communism is such a happy family affair that not a Communist wants to stay where it is practiced.

November 6, 1926

★   ★   ★

I guess you know, but the Communism that they started out with in Russia, the idea that the fellow that was managing the bank was to get no more than the man that swept it out, well, that talked well to a crowd, but they got no more of that than we have.

November 6, 1926

★   ★   ★

When I visited Russia, the whole system of Communism might have openly appeared to me to be cock-eyed and disastrous, but if I thought of an alleged wisecrack, it was immediately stifled before reaching even the thorax.

November 6, 1926

It seems the whole idea of Communism, or whatever they want to call it, is based on propaganda and blood. Now the country is run by the Communist Party, which has less than 600,000 members and they rule all those millions of Russians and instead of having one Czar, why, there is at least a thousand now and any of the big men in the Party hold practically Czarist powers. And the only way you can tell a member of the Party from an ordinary Russian is that the Party man will be in a car.

December 4, 1926

Outside of Russia, a Communist's whole life's work is based on complaint of how everything is being done. So you see, when they run everything themselves, why, that takes away their chief industry. They have nobody to blame it on.

December 4, 1926

That is why I don't believe they will ever be satisfied just to run their own country, especially if everything is running smooth. You make one Russian satisfied and he is no longer a Communist. If they ever get their country running good, they will defeat their own cause.

December 4, 1926

★   ★   ★

Communism will never get anywhere till they get that basic idea of propaganda out of their head and replace it with some work.

If they plowed as much as they propagandered, they would be richer than the Principality of Monaco. The trouble is they got all their theories out of a book, instead of any of them ever going to work and practicing them.

I read the same books these birds learned from, and that's the books of that guy Marx. Why, he was like one of those efficiency experts. He could explain how you could save a million dollars, and he couldn't save enough himself to eat on.

1926

CONFERENCES

Congress ought to pass a law prohibiting us conferring with anybody on anything, till we learn how.

February 1, 1927

I originated a remark many years ago that I think has been copied more than any little thing I ever said—and I used it in the Ziegfeld Follies of 1922. I said that America has a unique record:

We never lost a war and we never won a Conference in our lives.

I believe we could, without any degree of egotism, single-handedly lick any nation in the world. But we can't confer with Costa Rica and come home with our shirts on.

January 27, 1935

As I sit down to chase a herd of news into one corral and get it all rounded up and cut out on the typewriter, there ain't a whole lot of things going on that's really vital to us. Now, of course, there is a mess of Conferences going on, but they are just like the Poor and the Democrats, they will always be with us.

January 14, 1923

The Allied Debt Conference broke up last week in London. They called that an Economic Conference, and as we didn't attend, it was.

December 24, 1922

A Conference is just an admission that you want somebody to join you in your troubles.

July 20, 1932

A Conference is a place where countries meet and find out each others' shortcomings, and form new dislikes for the next Conference.

Sometimes it takes two or three conferences to scare up a war, but generally one will do. I'll bet there was never a war between two nations that had never conferred first.

July 5, 1933

Conferences started after the war. When the nations quit fighting they had nothing to do, so they started in to confer and it has always been a matter of doubt as to whether fighting wasn't better than the conferring is, because we had more friends when we was fighting than we have now since we started into conferring.

April 6, 1930

You know, at most of these Conferences we get nothing but the trip. It looks as if this depression would have hurt the Conference business, but it don't. They can always dig up enough to go, and get in wrong.

June 9, 1931

You will hear a lot of 'em say that the Conference didn't accomplish anything, but it did. They stayed in session till every nation got thoroughly disgusted with each other. There is no place in the world like a Conference to find out the shortcomings of each other. Now every delegation goes home and tells tales on the others. Of course, we left as the principal villain. We were supposed to bring the pie that they were to cut. When we didn't bring it, the banquet was a total loss.

July 27, 1933

At the Pan-American Conference, they have done nothing but form Committees and then those Committees would form Sub-Committees, and the Sub-Committees would form Advisory Committees and they have just committeed their self to death.

In years to come, the question will be asked by some fond child of its father, who was a delegate to this Conference: "What did you do father, at the big Conference?"

"Why, I was the fellow who thought of all the different names for all the different committees. If it hadn't been for me, the Conference would have been a failure, for forming Committees was the sole accomplishment of the Conference."

February 26, 1928

You see, it's a funny thing about us. We never was very good in a Conference—Americans are great talkers, but we are mighty poor conferrers. Individually we are not bad, but as a delegation we are terrible.

I bet you right now that they could have an egg-laying Conference in Czechoslovakia, and if America could find out where it was, we could send more delegates and lay more eggs than any nation in the whole hen house.

April 6, 1930

Nobody can ever get in wrong by not attending a conference. But every time you go, you take a chance either of getting in wrong, or being misunderstood.

The only time we ever attract any attention at a conference, is when we don't go.

October 23, 1926

★   ★   ★

That is where these other nations have got it on us. They can play a half dozen Conferences at once, while with us, if we can find a man to send to one, why, we are lucky and we feel uneasy till he gets home again.

January 14, 1926

At this conference, in any accord, I bet you it'll say: There is to be no more wars, and there will be a paragraph a little further down that tells you where to get your ammunition in case there was one.

1919

★   ★   ★

We get all excited over each of these conferences we read of as though it would settle everything. Then two weeks after it's over, we can't for the life of us remember what happened.

I tell you, we are plodding along just as though we were in our right minds.

November 8, 1931

CONFIDENCE

I have just joined the great movement of "Restoring Confidence." There is a lot of people got "Confidence" but they are careful who they have it in.

We have plenty of "Confidence" in this country, but we are a little short of good men to place "Confidence" in.

Notes

CONSERVATIVES

A Conservative is a man who has plenty of money and doesn't see any reason why he shouldn't always have plenty of money.

March 26, 1933

COOLIDGE, CALVIN J.

There come Coolidge and did nothing and retired a hero, not only because he hadn't done anything, but because he had done it better than anybody.

March 24, 1929

Our President knows he come into the Presidency from the Vice-Presidency, where nothing is expected; he knows that he didn't look like much when he arrived; he knows that even the Atheists, after looking him over, prayed for the salvation of the country.

June, 1929

This big Catholic Society thought that Mr. Coolidge in his address to them would perhaps name the Ku Klux Klan. It seemed like an opportune moment to do so, but he didn't. He named the Democrats.

I guess he figured of the two evils, as far as he was concerned, the Democrats were the worst.

October 5, 1924

★   ★   ★

It wasn't a "third-term-bugaboo" that kept Coolidge from running again, it was horse sense. He knew just to an inch how much American wind the financial balloon would hold and he got out just two days before it busted.

Poor Mr. Hoover didn't see the thing any more than poor Rin Tin Tin, or for that matter, the rest of us.

October 23, 1932

★   ★   ★

Do you think Coolidge will run again?
Only in case they have an election.

January 31, 1926

★   ★   ★

Calvin Coolidge said: "I don't want the government to go into business."

If I was him, I wouldn't worry over that. The Government has never been accused of being a businessman.

December 20, 1925

★   ★   ★

Why did Mr. Coolidge think we were trusted in South America?
He had never been there.

January 31, 1926

★   ★   ★

When he first become President there seemed to be quite a sentiment to nominate him again for Vice-President.

September 16, 1923

★   ★   ★

You see, that was one great thing about Coolidge. Coolidge never thought half the things that are wrong needed fixing. He knew that over half the things just needed leaving alone. It's like writing a letter to everybody you hear from. He knew that if you leave nine-tenths alone, it didn't need answering.

April 17, 1932

CORRESPONDENCE

Once a month I answer telegrams marked "Urgent." Once a year I answer letters marked "Important."

Notes

CORRUPTION

Corruption and Golf is two things we just as well make our minds to take up, for they are both going to be with us.
September 25, 1928

We have talked more corruption and got less of it than any known denomination. Americans are funny people; they never get het up over anything unless they are participating in it.

The fellow that ain't getting any corruption, he don't think that it can possibly be so common, or it would have reached him. And the ones that are getting some of it don't want it brought up.
March 30, 1929

CORSETS

If it wasn't for the corset ads in magazines, men would never look at a magazine.
March 4, 1923

I was called on to speak to the Corset Manufacturers. They told me they had a "Front Lace" model that could be operated without a confederate.

Judiciously holding your breath with a conservative intake on the diaphragm, you arrange yourself inside this model. Then you tie the strings to the door knob and slowly back away. When your speedometer says you have arrived at exactly 36, why, haul in your lines and tie off.
March 4, 1923

Now, of course, not as many women wear corsets as used to, but what they lost in women customers, they have made up with men.
March 4, 1923

COSMIC RAYS

Do you know what a "Cosmic Ray" is? Just what I thought! Well, "Cosmic Rays"—well, the fellow that explained 'em to me wasn't any too plain. It's sorter like the "Atom." They are a possible new source of energy.

Now I am all mixed up in this science racket. I had no idea there was so much to it.
October 28, 1934

COST OF LIVING

I see by this morning's papers where the cost of living has decreased since December. In figuring these statistics—and by the way, who is it that figures up all these fool things?—well, anyhow, you might be living cheaper, but that don't figure in the worry. If worry is worth anything, we never was living as expensive.

July 28, 1932

COUNTRY FOLKS

You can kid about the old rubes that sat around the cracker barrel, spit in the stove and fixed the nation, but they were all doing their own thinking; they didn't have their minds made up by some propagandist speaker at a luncheon club.

April 16, 1930

COURAGE

Ain't it funny how many hundreds of thousands of soldiers we can recruit with nerve. But we just can't find one politician in a million with backbone.

February 18, 1929

COWARDICE

I just wonder if it ain't cowardice instead of generosity that makes us give waiters most of our tips.

November 25, 1923

CREDIT

There is no other country in the history of the world that ever lived in the high class manner we do—radio, bath tubs, almost antique furniture, pianos, rugs—'course, other countries could have had all those things but they can't buy 'em on credit.

August 8, 1928

★   ★   ★

This country is not prosperous. It's just got good credit.

Notes

★   ★   ★

All you got to do in America to enjoy life is to "Don't let your next payment worry you."

August 8, 1928

We live better and owe more than anybody in the world.

August 8, 1928

★   ★   ★

In the old days there were mighty few things bought on credit. Your taste had to be in harmony with your income, for it had never been any other way.

I think buying on credit has driven more folks to seek the revolver as a regular means of livelihood than any other one contributing cause. All you need nowadays to make a deferred payment on anything is an old rusty gun.

January 4, 1931

CRICKET

England had an earthquake yesterday. There is a cricket match going on here that has been for three months—one game!

The earthquake didn't even wake up the spectators.

August 16, 1926

★   ★   ★

That same cricket match I told you about before, is still going on. One man has been batting three days. Come over and see it. If the tea holds out, it will be running till winter.

I have been thrown out of the grounds twice for applauding. They contend I was a boisterous element.

August 17, 1926

CRIME

Well, all I know is just what I read in the papers. In fact, all I know is just what I read about Criminals and Congress.

May 13, 1934

★   ★   ★

Of course, the surest way out of this crime wave would be to punish the criminals, but of course, that is out of the question, that's barbarous and takes us back, as the hysterics say, to the days before civilization.

September 20, 1925

★   ★   ★

Crime today, say robbery, or some minor event, we fine them; and if it's confessed murder, why, they plead insanity. We go on the theory that if you confess you must be insane.

September 20, 1925

★   ★   ★

We don't seem to be able to even check crime, so why not

legalize it and put a heavy tax on it? Make the tax for robbery so high that a bandit couldn't afford to rob anyone unless they knew they had a lot of dough.

We have taxed other industries out of business—it might work here.

March 20, 1931

There is a thousand policemen to see that you don't park your car too long, where there is not one to see that your child is not kidnapped. Every man on the street can have an automatic pistol in every pocket, yet he will never be searched. But you let your tail light be out, and you are in for life.

May 31, 1925

As for Crime and Robberies, they are carrying just as heavy a burden as they possibly can. It looks like they was making a lot of money, but they don't. The business is overcrowded.

August 28, 1926

Some like pictures of their favorite murderers in the tabloids, just like some others like movie stars. It's getting so a murderer to draw well in the papers must be good-looking. There is no use in an ugly man committing a crime, no one will look at him. He just can't get in the papers.

May 10, 1931

Crime looks like it's making money, but it isn't. When you pay your lawyer and have to retain him by the year, whether you are robbing, or not, and then pay the bondsmen, and hand out hundreds among the various police forces—I tell you, you don't have much left in the end.

Then the late hours and with the present price of ammunition and the inconvenience of getting a pistol—why, sometimes you have to walk a block—it just in the end figures out to a fair living.

August 28, 1926

There is two types of Larceny, Petty and Grand, and the courts will really give you a longer sentence for Petty than they do for Grand. They are supposed to be the same in the eyes of the law, but the Judges always put a little extra on you for Petty, which is a kind of a fine for stupidness. "If that's all you got, you ought to go to jail longer."

April 22, 1929

CRIMINALS

We don't give our criminals much punishment, but we sure give 'em plenty of publicity.

February 2, 1934

Here, in New York nowadays, the so-called bad man is either an escaped lunatic or a thick-headed drug user, or somebody full of terrible liquor. He shoots people just to get his picture in the papers. Some of our newspapers, if you take the murders out of them, would have nothing left but the title of the paper.

September 20, 1925

Los Angeles come through with something yesterday that looks like one of the best measures to help offset this crime racket.

Los Angeles makes every visiting ex-criminal register. Course, you will say, "Yes, but he won't register." Well, that's the catch. If he don't he is liable to six months' imprisonment for not complying with the law.

September 13, 1933

Lots of people think that racketeering and corruption are just a fly-by-night business, run in a slipshod haphazard way. Well, you were never more wrong in your life. Why, meanness has always been better organized than righteousness.

July 6, 1930

★ ★ ★

Of all the cockeyed things we got in this country at the present time, it's some of our judges, and courts and justices.

We got more criminals out on bail than we have people for 'em to rob.

December 19, 1930

★ ★ ★

Oh, we're living in progress! All our boasted inventions, like the auto and the automatic, and our increased dope output, lost confidence in our justice, graft—top to bottom, all these have made it possible to commit anything you can think of and in about 80 per cent of the cases get away with it.

June 7, 1931

CRITICS

There is nothing as easy as denouncing. It don't take much to see that something is wrong, but it does take some eyesight to see what will put it right again.

July 28, 1935

A drama critic's contribution to the success of most theaters is in about the same ratio as a fire would be.

February 4, 1923

CROONER

I've got a voice, it's what you call a fresh voice. I'm kinda like a crooner, I've got an ideal voice for everything—outside a satisfied listener.

January 28, 1934

CULTURE

They live in Rome amongst what used to be called Culture, but that don't mean a thing. Men in Washington, D.C., live where Washington and Jefferson and Hamilton lived, but as far as the good it does them, they just as well have the Capitol down at Claremore, Oklahoma—and, by the way, I doubt if Claremore would take it; there is a town that has never had a setback.

June 5, 1926

★   ★   ★

Association has nothing to do with Culture. I know English-men that have had the same well-bred butler all their lives and they are just as rude as they ever were.

Why, do you know, one of the most cultured men I ever saw come from Texas, and where he learned it, the Lord only knows.

August 21, 1926

D

DAYLIGHT SAVINGS TIME

We're here an hour earlier today. It seems kind of funny, with everybody advised to spend, and the Government spending everything, well, it seems kind of funny for somebody to save a little daylight nowadays.

April 28, 1935

DEATH

Deaths get twice the notice that births do in newspapers. Nobody wants to know who was born, but everybody is anxious to know who dies, and the better known they are, the more anxious they are to read about their deaths.

January 30, 1927

DEATH VALLEY

Los Angeles and Death Valley is two places Frisco folks seldom ever go. To them one is just about as desolate as the other.

October 9, 1932

DEBATES, POLITICAL

I will meet the Republican and Democratic candidate in joint debate. It just looks like the only way we can get the issues of the day straightened out, is in a joint debate. You know the American custom is that when you can't beat a man at anything—why, the last straw is to debate him.

August 9, 1928

★　★　★

The rules of political debates are as follows: the first half of the debate is to settle on what the issues are, and the last half is just to debate on 'em. In case there is no issue, why, then of course there would be no use holding the second half.

August 9, 1928

DEBTS

A debt is just as hard for a Government to pay as it is for an individual. No debt ever comes due at a good time. Borrowing is the only thing that seems handy all the time.

March 1, 1931

DECORATION DAY

Well, another Decoration Day passed, and Mr. Abraham Lincoln's 300 word Gettysburg address was not dethroned. I would try and imitate its brevity, if nothing else.

Of course, Lincoln had the advantage—he had no foreign policy message to put over. He didn't even have a foreign policy. That's why he is still Lincoln.

May 31, 1927

DEFICIT SPENDING

A Senator named Tydings, the other day, introduced a bill where the Government couldn't appropriate more money than was coming in. That is, if you didn't have any money, you couldn't dole out any.

Well, the Senate like to have mobbed him. They called his idea treason, sacreligious, inhuman and taking the last vestige of power from a politician, that is, the right to appropriate your money which you don't have.

January 29, 1933

We are three billion in the hole and will be three billion more next year, and not a Congressman has got the nerve to ask voters to pay part of it in taxes.

March 17, 1932

I tell you another argument a fellow wants to keep out of, and that's this printing money thing—this deficit spending. It's a subject where nobody knows exactly what it would do. And yet, every person thinks he knows exactly what it would do. Well, all I know is that it's easier to print money than to make it by work.

But please, don't write or wire, explaining it. If you know all about money, you're awful lucky, and it's a secret you should cherish and not let even your grandchildren know about.

March 22, 1935

DEMOCRACY

On account of us being a Democracy, and run by the people, we are the only nation in the world that has to keep a government four years, no matter what it does.

February 21, 1930

One of the evils of democracy is that you have to put up with the man you elect whether you want him or not.

November 7, 1932

DEMOCRATS

Denouncing is not only an art with the Democrats, but it's a profession.

July 28, 1935

That's one peculiar thing about a Democrat, he would rather have applause than salary.

September 22, 1929

The trouble with the Democrats up to now has been that they have been giving the people "what they thought the people ought to have," instead of "what the people wanted."

March 30, 1929

You can't train a man to be a Democrat. He acts like he is trained, but he ain't. Most of that devilment he just comes by naturally.

March 30, 1929

Dissatisfaction is what makes a Democrat; it's not environment or training or education.

March 30, 1929

I don't know why it is, but Democrats just seem to have an uncanny premonition of seizing up a question and guessing wrong on it. It almost makes you think sometimes it is done purposely. You can't make outsiders believe it's not done purposely. For they don't think people could purposely make that many mistakes accidentally.

And what makes it funny is that the Democrats usually have

the first pick of either side of a question.
January 19, 1929
★ ★ ★

The Democrats already have started arguing over "Who will be the speaker at the next Convention?"

What they better be worrying about is "Who is going to listen?"
May 11, 1932
★ ★ ★

Remember when the Democrats ran on the slogan "Honesty?" Why, if the Democrats had brought back Thomas Jefferson, he couldn't have carried his own precinct on that platform.
May 1, 1926
★ ★ ★

Democrats start on a campaign with pretty good prospects, but manage to talk themselves out of enough votes by November to finish second.

Nothing in the world exposes how little you have to say as making a speech, so as manager of the Democratic Party I am in the market for a speechless Democrat.
March 30, 1929

Democratic National Convention

Well, the next 'American Follies' is about to be held. We have our amusements so arranged that we have two every four years, and they draft various cities where they are to be held. This year Houston, Texas was one of the convicted. You see, the Republicans watch the comedy in the Democrat one, and then they improve on it.
June 1928
★ ★ ★

What a day to conjure with! This will go down in Democratic political history as one of the memorable days of their Party. Now they have adjourned and can't do anything. If you can keep a Democrat from doing anything, you can save him from making a mistake.
June 29, 1924
★ ★ ★

Tomorrow the Democrats will spend the day fighting over who will be permanent ticket taker. The Democrats are the only known race of people that give a dinner and won't decide who will be toastmaster till they all get to the dinner and fight over it. No job is ever too small for them to split over.
June 29, 1932
★ ★ ★

When the nomination finished, all hell broke loose, noise

accompanied by Bedlam. The parade brought no votes, but like all these half-witted Convention parades, it kept anybody else from getting votes, until every marcher had become thoroughly disgusted with himself.

I am glad Chicago's children didn't come by on their way to school, to see how this wonderful system of choosing our country's leaders was conducted.

June 30, 1932

★   ★   ★

That seems to be the penalty of a man being governor during a Presidential year. Some yap will humiliate him by naming him as their favorite son for President.

June 26, 1924

★   ★   ★

Illinois has forty delegates and they are all for different candidates and all have to make either nominating or seconding speeches.

According to the speeches, a candidate is harder to second than he is to nominate.

June 27, 1924

★   ★   ★

A state that didn't send at least two bands has their badges taken away from them. Why, even Arizona—they are allowed one delegate, one-half a delegate-at-large, and one alternate (not to weigh over ninety-five pounds, stripped), why, they arrived behind their band.

June 24, 1924

★   ★   ★

A man handed around the press stands some thick, paper-backed books. I asked: "Is this the life story of Old Hickory?"

He said: "No, this is the keynote speech."

June 24, 1924

★   ★   ★

Alben Barkley delivered the keynote. What do you mean "keynote?" This was no "note," this was in three volumes. Barkley leaves from here to go to the Olympics to run in the Marathon and he will win, too, for that race only lasts about two or three hours.

June 27, 1932

★   ★   ★

The keynote speaker told things on the Republicans that would have made anybody else but Republicans ashamed of themselves.

June 24, 1924

A man read the Platform last night. He was perhaps the last man that will ever read it.

June 29, 1928

They just read the Platform. It was forty-five pages long. If they had come out in the open on every question, and told just where they stood, they could have saved themselves forty-two pages of paper.

When you straddle an issue, it takes a long time explaining it.

June 28, 1924

I asked: "What about a Platform?" They told me: "Oh, we don't need much of a one. All we do is point with pride and let the Republicans view with alarm.

June 29, 1920

At the Democratic Conventions I tried to get the Platform Committee to just send in the first plank of the Platform. That would have kept them fighting for the rest of the day.

June 29, 1932

They are stalling with the Platform, and when it's ready, there is not a wire walker in America that can stand on it.

June 28, 1928

Talk about civilization! Why, if they ever took a sanity test at a political Convention, 98 per cent would be removed to an asylum.

June 26, 1924

The Democratic National Convention opens on Monday at Madison Square Garden—that's where Ringling Brothers' Circus always plays.

June 23, 1924

The Convention Hall was full. It looked kinder like a church— everybody was sleeping.

July 8, 1924

I could never understand the exact connection between the flag and a bunch of politicians. It's beyond me why a political speaker's platform should be draped in flags, any more than a factory where honest men work.

June 23, 1924

Had a private chat today with every candidate here. Garner's men feel that if the nomination should ever accidentally get to a question of ability, they have a splendid chance.

June 27, 1932

★   ★   ★

Some fellow talked for two hours, nobody knew who he was. You couldn't tell who he was for—or against. And when he finally finished and mentioned his man, we were more in the dark than before.

June 28, 1928

★   ★   ★

No candidate will accept the Vice-Presidency. By Saturday all of 'em will be grabbing at it.

June 28, 1932

★   ★   ★

If you don't think the Democratic Party is not a large Party, you just sit and count the men in it that are nominated. There was candidates' names presented that the newspapermen had to go back to old United States census reports to find any mention of them. Most of the speeches were not nominations, they were letters of introduction.

June 28, 1928

★   ★   ★

At this Democratic Convention, this past Saturday will always remain buried in my memory as long as I live as being the day when I heard the most religion preached, and the least practiced of any day in the world's history.

June 29, 1924

★   ★   ★

If they don't hurry up and start voting on a President, why, some of these delegates will become so hungry, they will vote for the first man with a ham sandwich.

June 29, 1932

★   ★   ★

Here is a tip to prospective delegates who are coming to New York: "Leave your watches and jewelry at home. Bring nothing but your Alternates. It's a cinch you can't lose them."

June 12, 1924

★   ★   ★

They have been balloting all day at the Democratic side show at Madison Square Garden, for that is what some misguided people think is the nominating place. The real nomination is taking place in a room at some hotel, with less than six men present.

July 1, 1924

What the Democratic Convention lacks in class, in comparison to the Republican one, why, they will make up in noise.

June 12, 1924

Some man prayed. I didn't get his name or political faith. But from his earnestness I should say he was a Democrat. He not only asked for guidance, but he wisely insinuated for votes in November.

June 26, 1928

I read about Al Smith's fine acceptance speech. What did he say? Well, what do they all say? Did he come out on the leading issues of the day? He did! Did he solve them? He sure did! How did he solve them? By promising anything that was wanted!

September 2, 1928

Being with the loser at a Convention may get you credit for being a game guy, but it don't bring you any federal pork chops.

July 4, 1924

I said to a senator: "There is somebody praying."

He said: "Yes, even a Democrat needs a little religion every four years."

July 1920

★　★　★

Our National Conventions are nothing but glorified Mickey Mouse cartoons, and are solely for amusement purposes.

May 29, 1932

★　★　★

I found a book of rules on Conventions. Did you know that an uninstructed Delegate is one whom his district sent with a free rein to use his own judgement? When he comes back he is supposed to give up 50 per cent of whatever his vote brought.

An Alternate is a man sent along to watch the Delegate and see that he turns in the right amount.

July 1, 1924

★　★　★

This Convention is a good spot for a delegate to be in. Never was a delegate so much in demand. I am sure sorry I didn't decide to 'del.' I had a chance in California. They wanted to make me one, only, I think, they discovered I had none of the qualifications of one.

June 29, 1920

★　★　★

They know this Convention thing is just an ordinary routine.

Somebody is going to be President. It don't make any difference who is in. None of them, from any Party, are going to purposely ruin the country. They will all do the best they can and if weather and crops, and no wars, and a fair share of prosperity is with them, they will go out of office having had a good administration.

July 8, 1928

★   ★   ★

At a Convention a noisy vote don't count any more than a quiet one does.

July 1, 1920

★   ★   ★

A little fellow was asking his daddy: "Is that man praying for the Convention?"

And his daddy told him: "No! He took one look at the Convention and he's praying for the country."

Notes

★   ★   ★

Yesterday a priest offered the prayer. Today it was offered by a rabbi. They both prayed for guidance for the Republican Party, but not guidance to be elected.

June 1928

★   ★   ★

At a Democratic National Convention there is always something that will stir up an argument, even if they all agree.

June 24, 1928

★   ★   ★

I tell you, if we got just one-tenth of what was promised to us in either the Democratic or the Republican acceptance speech, there wouldn't be any inducement to want to go to heaven.

August 20, 1928

★   ★   ★

During the nominating speeches, when you heard all this unnecessary spouting about each man, I wondered what their wives must have thought of all these new men that they had been married to all these years and were just finding out how wonderful they were.

June 27, 1924

★   ★   ★

Talk about presidential timber. Why, man, they has a whole lumber yard of it here.

There were so many being nominated that some of the men making the nominating speeches had never even met the men they were nominating. I know they had not from the way they talked about them.

July 6, 1924

Maybe in the old days nominating speeches were just as idea-less. But then they were only being listened to by delegates, and the man making the speech only had to appeal to intelligence as high as his own, but people are now getting wise to the type of man that is supposed to be saving the country.

So let's don't hold another convention till someone can think of a new speech.

July 15, 1928

DEMOCRATS AND REPUBLICANS

I could never see much difference between the two gangs.

November 27, 1932

Both Parties have their good and bad times, only they have them at different times. They are each good when they are out of office, and each bad when they are in.

May 1, 1926

It takes nerve to be a Democrat, but it takes money to be a Republican.

February 10, 1929

The difference between a Republican and a Democrat is that the Democrat is a cannibal, they live off each other, while the Republicans live off the Democrats.

Notes

Democrats come nearer getting what they want when they have a Republican President than they do with one of their own.

March 18, 1923

Andy Jackson was the first one to think up the idea to promise everybody that if they will vote for you, you will give them an office when you get in, and the more times they will vote for you, the bigger the office you will give them. That was the real start of the Democratic Party.

Then the Republicans come along and improved on Jackson's idea by giving them money instead of promises. Nobody with any business sense wants to wait till after election to see if they get something. They liked the idea of "Paying as you go."

February 5, 1928

The Republicans have always been the Party of big business, and the Democrats of small business. The Democrats have their eye on a dime, and the Republicans on a dollar.

So you just take your pick.

April 22, 1928

★   ★   ★

There ain't any finer folks living than a Republican that votes the Democratic ticket.

November 8, 1934

★   ★   ★

The only way in the world to make either one of those old Parties look even half way decent is to keep them out of office.

November 11, 1923

★   ★   ★

When a Republican turns Democrat, that is just like a horse thief joining the church. I mean, you can't depend on it, you know?

The reformation is not permanent. I mean they will stay that way just as long as they are being fed or something, but the minute they see another horse, they are liable to go back to the original trade.

June 4, 1933

★   ★   ★

A flock of Democrats will replace a mess of Republicans in quite a few districts. It won't mean a thing; they will go in like all the rest of 'em, go in on promises and come out on alibis.

September 14, 1930

★   ★   ★

There is something about a Republican that you can only stand him so long; and on the other hand, there is something about a Democrat that you can't stand him quite that long.

November 9, 1932

★   ★   ★

So many Republicans have promised things and then didn't make good, that it's getting so that a Republican promise isn't much more to be depended on than a Democratic one. And that has always been the lowest form of collateral in the world.

July 22, 1923

★   ★   ★

The Democrat just loves politics. He just wants to be known as a politician.

Now a Republican don't. He wants politics to be known as a side line. He's sorter ashamed of it. He wants to work at it, but he wants people to believe he don't have to.

December 2, 1928

The Republican and the Democratic Parties both split. The Republicans have their split right after elections, and Democrats have theirs just before an election.

December 28, 1930

There is something about a Democrat that makes 'em awful inquisitive, especially if it's on a Republican, and there is an awful lot to find out about most Republicans.

March 11, 1934

I will admit that it has rained more under Republican administrations but that was partially because they've had more than the Democrats. There is no less sickness, no less earthquakes, no less progress, no less inventions, no less Christianity under one than another. They are all the same.

December 2, 1924

Personally I am glad that they did unearth members of both Parties in this scandal in Washington, for if this thing had gone through showing no one but Republicans, it would have cast a reflection on the shrewdness of the Democratic Party.

In other words, they would have looked rather dumb to be standing around with shekels falling all around them, and they not opening their pockets to catch a few.

February 24, 1924

Some say the President will run again and some say he won't. The Republicans want him to run on account of him being known.

The Democrats have the best idea. They are trying to find somebody that ain't known.

1921

The Democrats and the Republicans are equally corrupt; it's only in the amount where the Republicans excel.

Notes

★   ★   ★

I guess you know that either political Party is not entirely composed of the brains of our commonwealth. They don't know that, as a matter of fact, the President never gets what he wants. Every President has wanted something he didn't get, but only Mr. Coolidge was smart enough not to let anybody know what it was he wanted, so Congress would never know what he had been disappointed over.

October 29, 1927

DENTISTS

There are two things that seem like got started wrong in life. One was the Constitution of the United States.

And the other thing was teeth. It seems the Lord when He layed out our original teeth, didn't know much about teeth, so He put those we have in temporarily till the doctors could come along and get 'em out, or get 'em remodeled so they amount to something.

June 6, 1926

★　★　★

No dentist pulls your teeth any more. That's a separate branch all together. All he requires is a strong arm, two nurses, no conscience, some gas, or a hammer.

This is a side line to the medical highwaymen's profession.

June 6, 1926

DETROIT, MICHIGAN

Headline says: "13 Bankers in Detroit Indicted!"
You would think Detroit was a bigger town than that.

June 29, 1934

★　★　★

When you think of Detroit, it's of Henry Ford's Incubator and a stuck customer.

January 30, 1927

★　★　★

This is the first game of the 1934 World Series. A German town on Hitler Day couldn't be any nuttier than Detroit.

October 2, 1934

★　★　★

Take Detroit, for instance. Chicago has been receiving tremendous amounts of advertising on their crime waves, while Detroit was having as many casualties and not getting one tenth the publicity out of it. They were becoming discouraged: "What's the use of having all these robberies and killings? Nobody ever reads about them. Chicago gets more national recognition out of one retail shooting, than we can out of the same thing done wholesale."

January 30, 1927

DICTIONARIES

I got me a dictionary one time, but goodness, it didn't last long. It was like looking in a telephone book. I never called up anybody in my life if I had to look up their number. Nobody is worth looking through all those numbers for, and that's the way it was with my dictionary.

I could write the article while I was trying to see what the word meant, and that's one good thing about language, there is always a shorter word for it. Course, the Greeks have a word for it, and the dictionary has a word for it, but I believe using your own for it.

October 29, 1933

DIETS

People were just about getting over this crazy epidemic of dieting when along come this depression and the stock market and drove 'em all back on it again.

November 9, 1929

★   ★   ★

When the old diet comes back, you don't want to be mixed up with a kitchen where there's one of those "dieticians." They know what's good for your health, but they don't know what's good for your appetite. They figure out calories, but I like to figure out aroma.

July 17, 1927

DILLINGER, JOHN

A bank robber like Dillinger don't take it until after you get it, but Congress is making us sign I.O.U.s for all we will ever get during our lifetime.

May 13, 1934

DIPLOMACY

There's one thing no nation can accuse us of, and that is secret diplomacy. Our foreign dealings are an open book, generally a check book.

October 21, 1923

★   ★   ★

Diplomacy was invented by a man named Webster, to use up all the words in his dictionary that didn't mean anything.

June 9, 1928

★   ★   ★

A diplomat is a man that tells you what he don't believe himself, and the man he is telling it to, don't believe it any more than he does.

June 9, 1928

Diplomats write notes because they wouldn't have the nerve to tell the same thing to each other's face.
June 9, 1928

★   ★   ★

Diplomacy is a great thing, if it wasn't so transparent.
June 6, 1929

★   ★   ★

Diplomats are just as essential to starting a war as soldiers are for finishing it.
June 9, 1928

★   ★   ★

That's called diplomacy, doing just what you said you wouldn't.
June 30, 1929

★   ★   ★

Nations don't do things the easy way—if they did, there would be no diplomats, and diplomats are nothing but high-class lawyers—and some ain't even high-class.
January 14, 1923

★   ★   ★

Stay out of that Europe, that's a tough game to enter into. Their diplomats are trained, it's their life's business. Ours make a campaign contribution and wake up in Belgium and don't know which ocean they crossed to get there.

These old diplomats you see sitting around, they don't look much but they out-deal foreigners all their life. What they had to contribute was from their head, and not their purse.
January 19, 1935

★   ★   ★

A diplomat has a hundred ways of saying nothing.
July 5, 1933

DISARMAMENT

No nation can tell another nation what they need to defend themselves. That's a personal affair.

If I sleep with a gun under my pillow, I don't want somebody from across the street to "advise me that I don't need it."
September 21, 1932

★   ★   ★

Now here's one thing you got to keep in mind on all this Disarmament thing. It takes years to get even plans scrapped. What I'm getting at, by the time all these marvelous plans are about to be in effect, none of these men might be in power. And most of this is their idea, but who knows what the next man's ideas are?

October 20, 1929

We just had a Disarmament Meeting but both our nations are still building and still arguing. If both nations was absolutely on the level with this disarmament, they would agree on a grand total of armament each one could have, whether it was in battleships or battle axes, cruisers or cuspidors, pistols or paper wads, shotguns or slingshots, submarines or subways, airplanes or airedales. But when it was all added up, it should weigh the same.

September 9, 1929

Disarmament Conferences have been going on for so long that by now I figured that everybody's navy would be scrapped, poison gas would be turned into fertilizing nitrates and all airplanes would be beaten into windmills.

October 23, 1926

It's all right to go to these Disarmament conferences. But it's always well to come home and reload your gun after one is over.

December 14, 1930

DISCONTENT

Discontent comes in proportion to knowledge.

May 11, 1930

DIVORCE

An awful lot of divorcing going on now in the movies—getting ready for next season's marriages.

February 25, 1923

I get a bundle of invitations every day to attend Hollywood weddings, but I would always rather wait a few weeks and take in the divorce. Weddings are always the same, but no two divorces are alike.

February 27, 1932

I read where one of the most honest divorce reasons I ever heard was given the other day by some fellow: "She suits me fine, your Honor, but I just can't afford her."

December 16, 1934

Divorce is a great industry, and I guess the only way to stop it, is to stop marriage.

September 21, 1930

As for divorce, I think people put too much dependence in it. You don't see many cases where the Parties did any better the second time than they did the first, or the third and fourth or the fifth and so on marriages.

It just looks like the people are grabbing at straws.

January 30, 1928

There is nothing that denotes prosperity quicker than to hear that "so-and-so and his wife ain't getting along."

May 15, 1928

DOCTORS

This is the day of specializing, especially with the doctors. Say, for instance, there is something the matter with your right eye. You go to a doctor and he tells you: "I am sorry, but I am a left eye doctor. I make a specialty of left eyes."

Or take the throat business. A doctor that doctors on the upper part of your throat, he doesn't even know where the lower part goes to.

November 5, 1927

We kid about our doctors and we hate to pay 'em after it's all over and we have quit hurting. But I expect a lot of us have got to thank 'em for being here.

November 5, 1927

DOGS

I love a dog. He does nothing for political reasons.

December 3, 1933

In London five years ago, old Lord Dewar, the greatest whiskey maker in the world, gave the children a little white dog, a Sealyham terrier, saying: "If this dog knew how well he was bred, he wouldn't speak to any of us."

We have petted him, complained on him, called him a nuisance. But when we buried him yesterday we couldn't think of a wrong thing he had ever done.

His bravery was his undoing. He lost to a rattlesnake, but his face was towards it.

March 24, 1931

DOLLAR

Everybody likes to make a dollar his way, but if he finds he is not allowed to make it his way, why, he is not going to overlook the chance of making it your way.

December 15, 1933

The American dollar is down to 75 cents abroad. Be a good time to go over and buy some, for they are still worth $1.00 over here.

June 21, 1933

The dollar may have been cheap in London, but there certainly wasn't any laying around for nothing in our country. And after all, it is a home talent commodity.

November 10, 1933

Our problem is not what is the dollar worth in London, Rome, or Paris, or what even it is worth at home. It's how to get hold of it, whatever it is worth.

July 23, 1933

★ ★ ★

This thing of "we can't go ahead till we know exactly what our dollar is worth," is hooey.

Your bankers and your financiers marry with no gold clause. The preacher just guarantees you she is a wife. How long you can keep her, and what she is worth to you, is all up to you.

December 10, 1933

DOMESTIC SCIENCE

They call Domestic Science a course now. In the old days you learned that at home. You had to be good at it for you had to eat it.

Notes

DRUGS

We have a delegation in Geneva at a Conference on dope. We want to limit output. We don't manufacture it and the other nations do, so you know where this Conference will end.

June 9, 1931

Been reading in the papers today about the big drug combine that they said they had captured in the East. Do you know what will happen when the whole thing goes through the courts? Why, the delivery boys will be sent to jail and the leaders will open bigger and better than ever.

October 17, 1929

DULUTH, MINNESOTA

My experience in the frozen North consists of playing one week in Duluth, Minnesota in the month of September. The audience had on light mittens and two suits each of woolen underwear. They hadn't really dressed for the winter yet.

January 27, 1924

E

EARTHQUAKES

I wouldn't trade California with its earthquakes for any other state. Why, there is more people eaten up by alligators in a month in Florida than earthquakes kill here in a generation.

July 12, 1925

★ ★ ★

In this earthquake, nine lives were lost out in California. Why, there's that many innocent bystanders shot in one day in New York—to say nothing of the guilty bystanders.

July 12, 1925

★ ★ ★

Us and Mexico had a joint earthquake. That's the only thing I ever heard we split 50-50 with Mexico. Lucky for Mexico that she didn't grab off more of the earthquake than we did, or she would have got a note from our Secretary of State.

Yours for reciprocity in earthquakes.

January 2, 1927

★ ★ ★

Last night we had the whole house trembling and shimmying. My typewriter fell off the table. Now don't get me wrong, it was no earthquake—just a disturbance, they call 'em.

Don't say much about it. We keep these things quiet so Frisco won't hear anything about it. They always make a lot out of nothing. We don't want anything said about it.

That's why I don't mention it.

August 5, 1923

★ ★ ★

Here is a suggestion that will help you out of a lot of anxiety and anguish in case your town or district should be hit by some disaster. Run quick and turn off the radio! Otherwise you will hear

109

where your own home has been swept away by floods and you have been lost in a fire.

We in California had an earthquake out here. That's all we had—which was plenty, but that wasn't enough news for the radio. They added "oil wells overflowing and on fire!" and as a P.S., "a tidal wave coming in from the ocean!"

So in case of disaster, run, don't walk to the nearest radio and turn it off, for they take delight in killing you, whether you have been killed or not.

March 22, 1933

EASTER

I bet any Sunday could be made as popular at church as Easter is, if you made 'em fashion shows too. The audience is so busy looking at each other that the preacher might just as well recite Gunga Din.

We will do anything, if you just in some way turn it into a show.

April 22, 1935

ECLIPSE

The big event last week for people who go in for outdoor amusements was the eclipse. It was also the only thing that ever went off on schedule. I wish these scientists would run the railroads.

February 1, 1925

★   ★   ★

The eclipse is scheduled to happen here in New York at 9 A.M. Can you imagine somebody putting on a show for New Yorkers to take place at 9 A.M.?

New Yorkers are so used to traffic stops that they cannot realize how any two objects could pass peacefully by each other without hitting.

February 1, 1925

★   ★   ★

Well, the eclipse come and went away and the scientists had a picnic. It wasn't as dark as it was at that eclipse five or six years ago. That was a dandy. We are not putting on as good eclipses as we did under the Coolidge administration. This President is falling down on our eclipses. What we want is bigger and darker eclipses.

May 11, 1930

ECOLOGY

We're just now learning that we can rob from nature the same way as we can rob from an individual. The Pioneer thought it was nature he was living off, but it was really future generations that he was living off of.

April 14, 1935

★   ★   ★

I got a wire from a very influential club in New Orleans, saying: "The government has cut our levees so that sewage from Chicago, Kansas City, St. Louis and Memphis can get past Canal Street here in New Orleans."

I wonder if there ain't a bit of truth in that statement. Even a town where people live on top of a hill, they are not allowed to just throw everything out of their doors and let it roll down the hill on to the people that live at the bottom.

May 15, 1927

ECONOMISTS

One way to detect a feeble-minded man is to get one arguing on Economics.

October 6, 1933

★   ★   ★

Speaking of taxes, I don't know what it's all about; I don't know any more about this thing than an economist does, and God knows he don't know anything.

April 7, 1935

★   ★   ★

All this "nut" thinking is not my business. It's for some economist—all that stuff is his racket. You see, we all got a racket and I am not going to try and muscle in on some thinker's racket.

October 2, 1932

★   ★   ★

That's one drawback with these economists in Washington; his work is entirely with a pencil on paper, but the moment that pencil is traded for coin of the realm, why, life takes on an entirely different outlook.

It's like driving a car. If you are the only one on the street, you are like the economist with his pencil—you have things pretty much your own way. But when they commence to coming from every way, all making for the same corner, no man living can tell just exactly what will happen.

And it's the same way with our economy.

May 20, 1934

★ ★ ★

An economist is a man who can tell you what can happen under any given conditions, and his guess is liable to be just as good as anybody else's.

May 26, 1935

ECONOMY

This would be a great world to dance in if we didn't have to pay the fiddler.

June 27, 1930

★ ★ ★

There is nothing that will upset a state's economic condition like a legislature. It's better to have termites in your house than the legislature.

March 31, 1935

★ ★ ★

Everybody is saying that the trouble with the country is that people are saving instead of spending. Well, if that's a vice, then I am Einstein. Since when did saving become a national calamity?

It was spending when we didn't have it that put us where we are today. Saving when we have got it will get us back to where we were before we went cuckoo.

November 24, 1930

The Economic Conference

There is just about to be wound up in Europe what is called an 'Economic' Conference, which at this early day and date looks like we will be lucky if it don't wind up costing us an awful lot of money.

January 14, 1923

★ ★ ★

Our Secretary of State and our Secretary of the Treasury went over to London to this Economic Conference. America said that it would not shell out any more money. Now we could have written and told 'em that, but no, we like to get in wrong personally.

June 9, 1931

The Great Depression

We will just about have to save ourselves accidentally. That's the way we stumbled on prosperity.

August 19, 1931

Do you think the world leaders can get us out of this?

They might; ignorance got us in.

January 3, 1933

★   ★   ★

Do you think we will get out of this Depression just because we got out of all the others?

Lots of folks drown that's been in the water before.

January 3, 1933

★   ★   ★

It isn't what we need that is hurting us, it is what we are paying for that we have already used up.

January 4, 1931

★   ★   ★

Why don't everybody try to make a living out of the conditions we got, instead of waiting to make it under the conditions that are supposed to come? Suppose "Good Times" don't ever come?

Last year we said: "Things can't go on like this!" and they didn't. They got worse.

January 11, 1930

★   ★   ★

Things are in a poor state right now. I know a hitch-hiker out here in California that is having such poor luck getting a ride, he is standing in the middle of the road, offering to go either way.

November 21, 1932

★   ★   ★

It wasn't you, Mr. President, the people just wanted to buy something new and they could go out and vote free and get something new for nothing. So cheer up, you don't know how lucky you are.

November 9, 1932

★   ★   ★

On January 7, the Senate passed a bill appropriating 15 million for food, but the House of Representatives had not approved it. They said NO! They seem to think that's a bad precedent, to appropriate money for food. They must think it would encourage hunger.

January 15, 1931

★   ★   ★

All I know is just what I read in the papers or what I gather from pamphlets that people send me, solving the depression.

Somebody is sure doing good and that is the printing line.

November 19, 1933

★   ★   ★

This depression was deep, and you don't climb out of anything as quick as you fall in.

December 31, 1933

★　★　★

We ought to have plans ready in case of a depression, or recession—just like we do in case of fire: Walk, don't run, to the nearest exit.

November 16, 1931

★　★　★

Our tastes were acquired on credit and we want to keep on enjoying 'em on credit but now a guy is knocking on the back door and says: "Here, pay for the old radio or we will haul down your aerial!"

January 4, 1931

★　★　★

I don't know any more about it than a prominent man knows about relieving Depression. But it looks like the financial giants of the world have bungled as much as the diplomats and politicians.

This would be a great time in the world for some man to come along that knew something.

September 21, 1931

★　★　★

We used to call depression a "state of mind," but it's just about to reach a state of health. It really is with us, in spite of all the after-dinner speakers.

But we are learning to handle this depression now. In fact, it really ain't depression at all; it is just old man normalcy in disguise.

October 25, 1931

★　★　★

The one way to detect a feeble-minded man is to get one arguing on economics.

October 6, 1933

★　★　★

This depression has offered every man, woman and child in America 100 guesses as to how to end it. One of those fellows running for office used up one of his guesses yesterday when he said we would "have good times if everybody disarmed."

Why, the people who are drawing a salary now is the army and navy. What does he want to do, put them among the unemployed?

May 5, 1931

EDITORIALS

Do you know there is four pages of funny pictures to two columns of editorials?

That shows what the people read.

May 2, 1926

★   ★   ★

I don't think I can rightly be criticized for not settling controversies between Mexico and us, controversies that have been problems for a hundred years. Those things should always be left to Editorial writers at home, who have never been there.

They always seem to settle them to their own satisfaction.

May 19, 1928

★   ★   ★

I would like to state to the readers of *The New York Times* that I'm in no way responsible for the editorial or political policy of this paper.

I allow them free reign as to their opinions as long as it is within the bounds of good subscription gathering, but I want it distinctly understood that their policy may be in direct contrast to mine. Their editorials may be put in purely for humor, or just to fill space. Every paper must have its various entertaining features and their editorials are not always to be taken seriously and never to be construed as my policy.

December 7, 1930

EDUCATION

That's one thing about a little education, it spoils you for actual work. The more you know, the more you think somebody owes you a living.

September 4, 1931

★   ★   ★

If I were a rich man, I wouldn't give any money to Learning. I would amend the Constitution and Congress will do it if you suggest it to 'em. Have 'em pass a Constitutional Amendment, prohibiting anybody from learning anything! And if it works as good as the Prohibition one did, why, in five years we would have the smartest race of people on earth.

1925

★   ★   ★

Did you ever see or hear of a thing so nutty in your life as those chain letters?

I tell you, when a country falls for a thing like that, it just makes you doubly sure that our school system is a failure.

May 5, 1935

★   ★   ★

Some of these days they are going to remove so much of the

"punk" and "hooey" and the thousand of things the schools have become clogged up with, and we will find that we can educate our broods for about one-tenth the price and learn 'em something they might accidentally use after they escape.

July 31, 1932

Education is just like everything else. You got to judge it by results. Here we are better educated—according to educational methods—than we ever were. It's costing us more than it's worth, yet the smarter a nation gets, the more wars it has.

The dumb ones are too smart to fight.

July 31, 1932

The smarter the guy, the bigger the rascal.

January 6, 1929

There is nothing as stupid as an educated man if you get him off the thing he was educated on.

July 5, 1931

Kemper Military Academy, one of the finest military schools anywhere. I was two years there, one year in the guard house and the other in the Fourth Reader. One was about as bad as the other.

January 1, 1933

ELECTIONS

In this country people don't vote for, they vote against.

June 9, 1935

Conditions win elections and not speeches.

June 9, 1935

★   ★   ★

Every man looks good until he is elected.

October 18, 1925

★   ★   ★

If I was running for office, I would rather have two friends in the counting room, than a Republican slush fund behind me.

November 9, 1924

★   ★   ★

The locusts I saw swarming in the Argentine are houseflies compared to the destruction caused by a Presidential election.

November 13, 1932

It takes a great country to stand a thing like that hitting it every four years.

November 13, 1932

★ ★ ★

So much money is being spent on the campaign that I doubt if either man, as good as they are, are worth what it will cost to elect him.

October 8, 1928

★ ★ ★

I was born on November 4th, 1879, that was election day. Women couldn't vote in those days, so my mother thought she would do something, so she stayed home and gave birth to me.

That's why I have always had it in for the Government.

Notes

★ ★ ★

I want to bring elections back to where they occupy almost as much importance as the World Series.

May 1, 1926

In some competitive events it is still an honor to finish second in a race—but a national election is not listed among those games.

May 1, 1926

History has proven that there is really nothing in the world as alike as two candidates. They look different till they get in, but then they all act the same.

November 6, 1934

★ ★ ★

We have various pestilences every once in a while, but the only advertised and known calamity, is our elections. We got one coming on and we might as well start steeling our systems to it.

It's just like an operation, the anesthetic (or whatever you call the gas they give you), why, that is the worst part of it. An election without all these preliminary gasses wouldn't be so bad, but it's these weeks of slowly putting you under, that is the trying part of an election.

February 26, 1928

★ ★ ★

Elections are a good deal like marriages, there is no accounting for taste. Every time we see a bride groom, we wonder why she ever picked him—and it's the same with public officials.

May 10, 1925

★ ★ ★

Now as far as this late election is concerned, this is no disparagement on the losers. And as for the third party fellow, he is sitting as pretty as ever—you just wait; this guy will dig him up a gang before another month. You could put him up in Heaven with everything going fine, and he would get himself up an organized minority, and have Saint Peter compromising with him.

November 16, 1924

I've been reading about the Primary Elections back home. Looks like everybody that remains honest is getting beat.

September 20, 1926

The candidates were "high-type gentlemen" till the contest got close, then the brutes came out in 'em. What started out to be a nice fight, wound up in a street brawl. But it all comes under the heading of Democracy, and as bad as it is, it's the best scheme we can think of.

November 13, 1932

I honestly believe there is people so excited over this election that they must think that the President has something to do with running this country.

October 30, 1932

Who cares nowadays who is elected to anything? They are not in office three days till we realize our mistake and wish the other man had got in. We are a nation that runs in spite, and not on account of our government.

May 20, 1926

As for the third-party candidate, he ran on the dissatisfied vote, but the trouble was that they were so dissatisfied that they didn't even vote.

November 16, 1924

What is the greatest sporting event we have in America? Why, our national election, of course—that is, it used to be. But the thing has been deteriorating, and so one-sided, that you haven't even got an audience to watch it. At the last election they didn't even count the votes, they just used the old tally from the time before.

May 1, 1926

★   ★   ★

Before you know it, there will be another election along to pester us. What they have those things for, nobody has ever been able to tell. I guess it's just to distribute the jobs around.

But the whole thing will mean nothing in our lives. All we do is just dig up their salary—and they all get the same price, Republicans or Democrats, so you see, there is no way we can win.

October 12, 1930

★   ★   ★

In the old days elections used to be so close that people would bet on them. One time, I have heard, it got as close as even money. But the last few elections people haven't even taken interest enough to vote once, much less all day.

May 1, 1926

★   ★   ★

Well, the election is finally over. The result was just as big a surprise as the announcement that Christmas was coming in December.

November 16, 1924

★   ★   ★

Take this election. Both sides just spent the whole summer hunting things to cuss the other side on. That the other side might be right in a lot of things never entered their heads—they wouldn't let it enter it.

October 30, 1932

★   ★   ★

Voters go to the polls and if their stomachs are full, they keep the guy in that's already in, and if the old stomach is empty, they vote to chuck him out. So along about June or July of an election year put America to a tape-measure test and if the center section is not protruding, you will see a real race in November. But, if the public's stomach sounds like a watermelon, just crawl back in with the ground hog and don't come out as long as their middle makes a shadow.

March 30, 1929

★   ★   ★

You can't beat a party when the people are reducing purposely. But you let 'em start getting thin through lack of nourishment and you can defeat the party in power with nothing but a Congressman.

March 30, 1929

ENDORSEMENTS

If I wanted to put an object on the market today, I would say: "It will last until it is paid for!"

Nothing could be better than that.

July 1, 1930

★   ★   ★

Nothing can get you in wrong quicker than an endorsement.

July 22, 1934

ENGLAND

If I were England, I would give Ireland Home Rule, and reserve the motion picture rights.

1920

★ ★ ★

We dislike their tea, we kid their poor English dialect and we think they are snobbish, but by golly, we know that their honor all over the world is recognized.

October 9, 1933

★ ★ ★

Winston Churchill's party is running on "No Tea Tax and No Betting Tax!" Lloyd George's gang is running on "More Employment!"

Churchill will win. If an Englishman has got tea and can bet on a horse race, what does he want with employment?

April 16, 1929

★ ★ ★

England without her navy would be another Czechoslovakia.

May 19, 1930

★ ★ ★

There is one thing about an Englishman, they won't fix anything till it's just about totally ruined. They like to sit and watch it grow worse.

August 15, 1926

★ ★ ★

It's cost us more to fight with England than it did against her.

May 12, 1928

★ ★ ★

Poor coffee and no bathtubs have drove more Americans out of England than unfamiliarity with their language has.

April 16, 1929

★ ★ ★

That's one thing about an Englishman, he can insult you, but he can do it so slick and polite that he will have you guessing till way after he leaves you, whether he was a friend or foe.

September 8, 1929

ENGLISH CHANNEL

All cross-Channel swimming was called off today on account of rain and a wet track.

September 12, 1927

EQUALITY OF SEXES

You have heard of equality of sexes in Russia? That's not so! The women are doing the work.

August 28, 1934

Another American woman just swam the English Channel from France. Her husband was carried from the boat, suffering from cold and exposure.

Yours, for a revised edition of the dictionary explaining which is the weaker sex.

August 28, 1926

★   ★   ★

You can't pass a park without seeing a statue of some old codger on a horse. It must be his bravery, you can tell it isn't his horsemanship.

Women are twice as brave as men, yet they never seem to have reached the statue stage.

April 2, 1934

★   ★   ★

If women must insist on having men's privileges, they have to take men's chances.

November 1, 1925

ETHICS

The first thing they do if they are taking up crime as a profession—even before they buy the gun—is to engage their lawyer. Now the California Bar Association is to rid its ranks of any attorney found to have connections with the underworld.

Bar Associations invented the word "Ethics," then forgot about it.

December 30, 1934

EUROPE

There ought to be a law against anybody going to Europe till they had seen the things we have in this country.

August 14, 1930

★   ★   ★

That's one good thing about European nations: They can't hate you so much they wouldn't use you.

March 31, 1935

★   ★   ★

There is only one way we could be in worse with Europeans

and that is to help 'em out in another war.

July 10, 1926

★   ★   ★

Europe is supposed to be artistic, but if I had to judge I should place their financial ahead of their artistic ability.

So in offering prayers for the downtrodden races, I would advise you not to overlook the "downtrodden tourist."

June 27, 1926

★   ★   ★

In Europe public men DO resign. But here it's a lost art. You have to impeach 'em.

June 7, 1928

★   ★   ★

I see where they are forming in Europe a new organization called "The United States of Europe," or something. Nobody knows what it is or what its aims are, but we ought to be for it if only for one reason and that is, it's the first thing been formed since the war that we haven't been asked to go over and join.

September 12, 1929

★   ★   ★

I would like to stay in Europe long enough to find some country that don't blame America for everything in the world that's happened to 'em in the last fifteen years whether it's disease, fog, famine or frostbite. If the dog had two pups and they were expecting more, they will show in some way that we are directly responsible for the canine delinquency. The other day they had a prison mutiny and so every paper said it was American movies and American influence that give their prisoners this unusual idea.

Now the birth rate is falling off, so I am going to get out of here before we get blamed.

January 26, 1932

★   ★   ★

Tourists here in Europe go in great for ruins. Now a ruin don't just exactly spellbind me. I don't care how long it has been in process of ruination. I kept trying to get them to show me something that hadn't started to ruin yet.

June 5, 1926

★   ★   ★

I had been over to Europe two or three times, years ago, but I thought, well, I will go and see if the boys have scared up anything new. They hadn't anything new, except the prices.

June 27, 1926

Some Americans in Europe are traveling incognito. They are not bragging on where they come from and nobody knows they are Americans.

September 23, 1926

In Europe, I have been in all kinds of countries—about all that they have over here now, if somebody don't come along with self-determination for small nations and carve out a dozen more.

August 26, 1926

I have just arrived home from Europe with 850,000 other half-wits who think that a summer not spent among the decay and mortification of the Old World is a summer squandered.

January 8, 1927

Our poorly paid but highly costing politicians are talking about lending some European countries a billion and a half more.

Of course, the interest ain't going to get paid—but perhaps the Government could charge it off on their income tax to publicity.

December 24, 1922

★   ★   ★

France and England think just as much of each other as two rival bands of Chicago bootleggers. A Frenchman and an Italian love each other just about like Minneapolis and St. Paul. Spain and France have the same regard for each other as Fort Worth and Dallas; Norway, Sweden and Denmark are apparently getting on pretty good, but you call a Swede a Dane and you better reach for your hat.

August 26, 1926

They say all European nations are sore at us. Unfortunately for us, they didn't get sore at us quick enough. If they had, we would have saved money.

We are the ones that should be sore at them for not getting sore at us quicker.

December 29, 1926

★   ★   ★

I am not one of those guys that think we ought to hide by ourselves—I think we ought to be sympathetic to Europe and join in with them on a lot of things—you know, help 'em out, but I don't believe everybody you want to help, you got to go in and marry them. You can't get married to Europe and run off to Reno and get a divorce by noon from those birds. That's a hard gang to break lose from. Besides, if there was going to be a divorce, they're liable to sue us for non-support.

January 27, 1935

There ain't a nation over in Europe that got any use for another one, and you can't blame 'em for looking out after themselves. Say, if I didn't have any more friends around me than some of these nations have around them—the way they are setting—why, say, I not only would sleep with a pistol in each hand, but I wouldn't go to sleep at all.

August 28, 1926

★   ★   ★

When I was over in Europe, they said to me: Rogers, why is it that nobody seems to like America? I had to admit that we was in kinda bad. We wasn't hardly what you would call the world's sweetheart.

But after they kept this up for quite a while, I used to ask them—be it Englishman or Frenchman or Italian, or whatever: Well, we are in bad, but will you just kinda offhand, just casually, name me a list of your bosom friends among other nations?

I tell you, they can't hate us as bad as they hate each other.

April 6, 1930

★   ★   ★

I see where they captured an American spy in France. He must have been working on his own, for we already know all we want to know about 'em.

December 21, 1933

EVANGELIST

Am here at Winona Lake. It's to the Presbyterians what the River Jordan was to those foreigners over there in the old days. Billy Sunday, the great evangelist, lives here and I am pinch-hitting for him. I am not only preaching on the evils of liquor, but the evils of the stuff they sell for liquor.

July 26, 1928

EVOLUTION

William Jennings Bryan tried to prove that we did not descend from the monkey, but unfortunately picked a time in our history when the actions of our people proved that we did.

September 16, 1923

There is a terrible lot of us who don't think that we come from a monkey, but if there are some people who think that they do, why, it's not our business to rob them of what little pleasure they may get out of imagining it.

July 19, 1925

As far as Scopes teaching children evolution, nobody is going to change the belief of Tennessee children as to their ancestry. It is from the action of their parents that they will form their opinion.

July 19, 1925

I don't know why some of these states want to have their ancestry established by law. There must be a suspicion of doubt somewhere.

February 21, 1927

Nobody knows where they come from. Everybody looks at their enemies and hopes and prays that they didn't come from the same place.

August 9, 1925

★   ★   ★

These fellows who honestly believe that their great, great, grandfathers were as proficient with their toes as with their fingers, have that right. Most people are proud of their ancestry and it is a touchy thing to cast reflections on any man's forefathers, even if they did arrive here on all fours.

July 19, 1925

EXPLANATIONS

We are living in an age of explanations, and plenty of 'em, too. No two things that's been done to us has been explained twice the same way by even the same man.

January 28, 1934

EXPORTS

No wonder our exports to the rest of the world fell off. We started wrapping everything in cellophane and nobody knows how to open anything.

Notes

★   ★   ★

Every nation has something they could make a good living on if given an exclusive world market at a reasonable price.

Among the commodities which we could prove we excelled in is officeholders and politicians. We could send 'em all the politicians they needed. For instance, send Russia some Senators for some of their Vodka; send little Nicaragua some Congressmen for some bananas.

I tell you, the whole fool scheme is worth trying, just for the sake of this last part. If we can furnish the world with our politicians, we can compete with 'em!

January 9, 1933

F

FANATICS

A fanatic is always the fellow that is on the opposite side.
June 8, 1930

FARMERS

Farmers have had more advice and less relief than a wayward son.
1926

★ ★ ★

Somebody once had a plan to teach hogs birth control, and now it's a habit with them.

Somebody else had a plan to plow under every third acre of wheat, and the wind came along and blew out the other two.
April 21, 1935

★ ★ ★

A man in the country does his own thinking, but you get him into town and he soon will be thinking second-handed.
May 1, 1926

★ ★ ★

If the farmer could harvest the political promises made him, he would be sitting pretty.
September 14, 1930

★ ★ ★

Good news in the papers, it rained in the Middle West. Farmers are learning that the relief they get from the sky beats what they get from Washington.
June 4, 1934

★ ★ ★

I find newspapers all over the United States devoted yards of space to what some rich men think of the prospects for the coming year.

It's the same old thing every year: "Head of Steel Trust says: I am at heart an optimist!"

Why in the name of common sense don't they ask somebody else what they think of the coming year? Why don't they ask a farmer? There is ten million farmers and only one head of the steel trust! See what the farmer is paid every year for his optimism? And he has to be an optimist, or he wouldn't still be a farmer.

January 13, 1924

Jim Wadsworth of Texas, owns a farm in the panhandle of Texas and he really makes it pay and any man that can make a farm pay in these times deserves not only to be Senator, but to be sainted.

October 17, 1926

What has the poor farmer done against the Almighty and the Republican administration that he should deserve all this? If it's not the heat, it's the deep snow. If it's not the drought, it's a flood. If it's not boll weevil, it's the tariff. If it's not relief he needs, why it's rain.

But there is one pest that he is always free from—that's the income tax.

August 6, 1930

★   ★   ★

The Middle West got rain. Even the Lord couldn't stand to wait on the Republicans forever.

August 19, 1930

Farm Machinery

Do any of you radiator folks know what a "Combine" is? Well, here is all it does—just one machine and in one trip over the ground. On the front end of it is an arrangement that makes a deal over the ground from the bank that is holding the present mortgage. Then, just a few feet behind that, are the plows that plow the ground and right in the furrow is the seeder, then another plow that plows the furrow back where it was in the first place. Then come the fertilizer, and the sickle that cuts the grain. Then into the threshing machine and out into sacks.

Then near the back end is a stock market board, where a bunch of men that don't own the farm, the wheat, or the combine, buy it back and forth from each other and then announce to the farmer that on account of supply and demand, the wheat is only worth two bits.

That's what you call a combine.
December 27, 1931

Farm Prices

When a steer starts from the feed pen to the table, there is about 10 to take a bite out of him before he reaches the family that pays for him.

FASHIONS

Let women leave off something; they do it so much better than men. Every time a woman leaves off something, she looks better, but every time a man leaves off something, he looks worse.
December 20, 1928

With longer dresses, you watch the marriages pick up again. Concealment will beat exposure anytime.
April 20, 1930

According to law, fashions must change every year and in order to change dress styles, you have to either go up or down, the crossways change don't count. Well, skirts had just gone so high, there wasn't anything to 'em, and the material people put up a howl. It was just legs, legs, legs. Every imaginable shape, size, contour was on free exhibition.
April 20, 1930

Women's fashions sure have changed. They first showed us their calves. Well, that looked fairly promising and we seemed enough shocked to add spice to our views. But then, they just practically overnight yanked another foot off their apparel and we woke up one morning with thousands of knees staring us in the face.

Now most knees are practical knots, they are pliable but not what you would call gorgeous.

So some genius conceived the idea to cover up the whole thing again.

So long skirts mean Democracy, there is no privileged class. Society is not rated on its curves, as it has been. You got to get by with your head now instead of underpinnings.
April 20, 1930

You see, short dresses was made for certain figures, but fashion decrees that everybody be fashionable, so that means there is going to be folks try and keep up with fashions that while they might be financially able, are physically unfit—their purse is good but their build is bad. Now with long skirts, that will all be remedied. Every girl gets an even break—till she hits the beach.

April 20, 1930

FATHERS

There is a lot of hooey about Father being imposed on. Dear old father gets away with quite a bit of murder just because he is father. If he was some outsider and pulled the junk he does, they would chuck him in the alley. There is nothing outside an economist that's been any more overestimated than a father. He is a necessity and that about lets him out.

June 18, 1933

FEDERAL RESERVE BANK

The whole financial structure of Wall Street seems to rise or fall on the mere fact that the Federal Reserve Bank raises or lowers the amount of interest. Any business that can't survive a one per cent change must be skating on thin ice.

Why, even the poor farmer took a raise of another ten per cent just to get a loan from the bank, and nobody from the government paid any attention. But you let Wall Street have a nightmare and the whole country has to help to get them back into bed again.

August 12, 1929

★ ★ ★

All our financial papers are talking about how cheap money is now, with the Federal Reserve Banks charging around 3 and 3½ per cent.

I don't see why they don't say the rate is half-of-one per cent, for there is no way of getting any of it, anyway.

June 22, 1930

FERTILIZER

Everybody wants land irrigated by the Government. For, as anyone knows, new land with plenty of water will raise quite a bit. But so will *old* land if it's fertilized. So why should the whole of American tax payers pay for water for newly irrigated land any more than they should for fertilizer for old land?

May 13, 1928

FILIBUSTER

The Senate filibustered all last night. We pay for wisdom and get wind.

May 29, 1928

★   ★   ★

The Senate is having what is called a filibuster. The name is just as silly as the thing itself. It means that a man can get up and talk for 15 or 20 hours at a time, then be relieved by another, just to keep some bill from coming to a vote, no matter about the merit of this particular bill.

To imagine how bad this thing is, did you ever attend a dinner and hear a Senator speak for 50 minutes or an hour? If you have, you remember what that did to you! Well, just imagine the same thing only 12 times worse.

March 4, 1923

★   ★   ★

If a distinguished foreigner was to be taken into the Senate and not told what the institution was, and he heard a man rambling on, talking for hours, he would probably say: "You have lovely quarters here for your insane, but have you no warden to see they don't talk themselves to death?"

March 4, 1923

★   ★   ★

One Senator threatened to read the Bible into the Congressional Record and I guess he would have done it if somebody in the Capitol had had a Bible.

March 4, 1923

★   ★   ★

When a bill is introduced in Congress, let it be voted on and either approved or rejected by a majority. It was never meant by the original founders that by political manoeuvering any bill could be prevented from being voted on. In other words, you don't find out if the prisoner is innocent or guilty—you just keep him in jail till he dies.

May 21, 1928

FILLING STATIONS

And then, of course, it's a question what we can convert these four billion filling stations into in years to come. But it ain't my business to do you folks' worrying for you. I am only tipping you off and you-all are supposed to act on it.

June 2, 1928

FINGERPRINTS

I tell you one thing they sure got down pat, and that is that fingerprint thing. As the President of the Police Chiefs' convention said, they had the fingerprints of every crook there is.

Now all they got to do is find the fingers.

May 13, 1923

★ ★ ★

In the old days police had to hunt till the found a crook. With modern methods they have his fingerprints. So what's the use getting him, if you know who he is.

Then, if he ever surrenders, you know if he is telling the truth or not.

June 17, 1923

FINLAND

This is Finland, integrity's last stand. This is Helsinki, it's a beautiful little city, and clean. When these Finns aren't running a twenty-five mile race, they are scrubbing on something.

September 4, 1934

★ ★ ★

Finland, in their government, have only one House, it's not like ours with a Senate and a House of Representatives. Now there is civilization for you, just one House!

Just think if we could get rid of one of ours. The trouble is we could never agree on which one.

November 4, 1934

FISHING

The Society for the Protection of Single and Unmatured Worms won't let President Coolidge load his hook with one.

Next they'll be requiring an anesthetic be given the fish.

June 23, 1927

★ ★ ★

Say, I've heard nothing but "fishing" since I got here to Alaska. All these boys do is brag about who caught the biggest salmon. Last night an oil man brought one weighing 50 pounds into my room and wanted to put it in bed with me.

I can't see the use of catching salmon when they crawl out of the water to meet you. The first handshake I got when I stepped ashore was from a big coho. A coho, they tell me, is a king salmon that's on relief.

August 8, 1935

FLOODS

If you have never seen a flood, you don't know what horror is.

June 19, 1927

★   ★   ★

I got more faith in high ground than any Senator I ever saw.

May 1927

★   ★   ★

I see where they are going to take these floods up in Congress so that means the sufferers will at least have the consolation that Congress is thinking and talking about 'em, anyway.

May 15, 1927

★   ★   ★

I got a wire from my ranch, or what I thought was my cattle ranch—it is now a fish hatchery.

May 15, 1927

★   ★   ★

These spring floods have been a great lesson to us. But the cry of those people in the south-west is: "We don't want relief and charity! We want protection!" And Congress will have to take it up. Course, I would just as soon try to swim upstream against the flood as to be in the hands of Congress. For if you want to get some comedy, wait till they start in suggesting what to do.

One fellow seriously wanted to bore holes in the bottom of the rivers and let the water out. Another wants to dig a ditch alongside of the river and run the extra water back into the Great Lakes. He had it all figured out, with the possible exception of the water running uphill.

June 19, 1927

★   ★   ★

The people down there better not put too much dependence in Congress. They can grow web feet quicker than Congress will relieve 'em.

May 15, 1927

★   ★   ★

I would rather have one canoe than the entire Congress behind me. All Congress did was to pass a resolution against floods.

April 15, 1928

★   ★   ★

Just speeding along the Hudson River the last three hours, I was thinking how many millions would be raised overnight if it was out of its banks and doing the same amount of damage that the old Mississippi is.

Makes a lot of difference where a thing happens.

May 3, 1927

★　★　★

We still have 600 thousand of our own whose homes are floating towards Nicaragua. I wish you would send some checks to the Red Cross. If 600 thousand people had lost their all and were being fed by charity somewhere in the East, America would raise fifty million dollars in a day.

Come on, let's help them even if they are not Armenians. They can't help their nationality.

May 27, 1927

★　★　★

If every man of every committee that has gone to the Mississippi to investigate had put in one hour's actual work raising the levee, why, it would be so high now you couldn't have got water over the edge even with a hydraulic pump.

June 2, 1928

FLORIDA

Florida has the longest seacoast of any state, I am told. They have 1,145 miles and that is 100 miles more than California has.

But what has a long coast line to do with the quality of a state? According to the latest returns from Rand McNally, Siberia has quite a mess of seacoast but I have never heard of any emigration—that is, voluntarily—on account of their seacoast.

May 29, 1926

★　★　★

Florida claims their grapefruits sell for 10 million dollars a year, and they think they are the best in the world.

We in California use the juice of their grapefruit as a fly spray. We had no idea anyone ate them.

May 29, 1926

★　★　★

Florida claims they are known for their oranges. Why, I will admit there is a bootleg variety of orange that thrives up to the size of a green plum on the banks of Florida's swamps, but as far as being called an "orange," that is only done, of course, through a sense of humor.

We take Florida oranges to California, dry them and use them for golf balls.

May 29, 1926

Florida claims that this year alone, oranges brought them $15 million!

Well, in California that would just about pay for the labels on the ones we shipped.

May 29, 1926

The Everglades

Florida claims she has 3 million acres of Everglades and when they are drained, they will support 3 million people!

California says she has 20 million acres of mountains and when they are leveled out they will support the whole of India, with the Chinese nation invited as weekend guests.

I know you may ask "Who is going to flatten the mountains?" Why, the same fellow that drains the Everglades.

May 29, 1926

FLORISTS

This is Mother's Day. Florists are keeping open this evening to accommodate late consciences.

May 12, 1935

★　　★　　★

I doubt if this thing of Mother's Day would have gone through if it hadn't been for the florists. They grabbed it and started putting the idea over.

Of course, florists, they got mothers, too, but they have more flowers than they have mothers.

May 12, 1935

FOOLS

A fool that knows he is a fool is one that knows he don't know all about anything, but the fool that don't know he is a fool is the one that thinks he knows all about anything. Then he is a damn fool.

August 7, 1927

FOOTBALL

Is education necessary to football?

No, a good coach and good interference is all that's necessary.

Notes

★　　★　　★

Jim Thorpe is a Sac and Fox Indian. When he played football, he is more Fox than Sac.

June 23, 1935

★   ★   ★

When I played football, you either played, or you didn't play. You wasn't allowed to run in and out like a bell hop.

December 30, 1934

★   ★   ★

Football is getting all the play now and it behooves us old alumni to get out with the cash and do our bit for—I forgot the name. I don't mean spend the money now; I mean get ready to spend it later on when you see whether they need Ends, or Backs, or Tackles.

In school, I looked like a promising End. I could run pretty fast; in fact, my nickname was "Rabbit." I could never figure out if that referred to my speed, or my heart.

September 29, 1929

★   ★   ★

Went to see one of the modern football games and the thing that struck an old timer was that on every play, there would be twenty-two different men facing each other. They could go in and come out, go in and come out—in fact, that's what tired 'em out, was going in and out so much.

Football don't need referees, they need United States census takers.

November 5, 1929

★   ★   ★

I used to play me a pretty good "End," what you might call a "Wide End." I would play out so far that the other 21 would be pretty well piled up before I could possibly reach 'em—I would arrive a little late for most of the festivities.

That's why to this very day I don't carry any football scars or bruises.

December 30, 1934

FORD (AUTOMOBILE)

A Ford car and a marriage license are two of the cheapest things known, and both lead to an ambition for something better.

December, 1929

★   ★   ★

You see, "Sir" is about the lowest form of title there is. It's the Ford of titles.

July 17, 1926

FOREIGN POLICY

Our gunboats are all in the Chinese war, our Marines have all landed in Nicaragua, Secretary of State is sending daily ultimatums to Mexico and President Coolidge is dedicating memorials to peace.

Who is the next country wants their affairs settled?

December 4, 1926

Foreign Aid

You see, that's the trouble; you just can't do a nation a favor, or they will want it continued.

May 8, 1932

★　★　★

If we are out upholding downtrodden nations, it will take a bookkeeper to keep track of our wars.

February 18, 1931

Foreign Relations

I see where the President says we are "in accord" with France. That is one awful good time to watch those babies, and that is when they are "in accord."

April 25, 1933

★　★　★

England takes their Foreign Relations serious; it's a business with them.

It's a hobby with us.

March 5, 1932

FRANCE

The Frenchmen, individually, have plenty of humor, but as a Government they take everything mighty serious.

September 3, 1930

★　★　★

A bunch of American tourists were hissed and stoned yesterday in France, but not until they had finished buying.

August 2, 1926

★　★　★

The French don't even in their hearts appreciate, or even like us.

I would say to France: You don't seem to think you owe us anything. What we did for you, if it wasn't worth anything, why, let it go. But if it wasn't worth anything in the last war, why, don't expect us in the next.

February 1, 1925

If France ever paid their taxes once, they would be the richest nation in the world.

August 1926

★   ★   ★

France says that the harvest crop of tourists has not reached the expected yield. The number has been beyond expectation but the shake-down per person has been very low.

Americans are going there nowadays to look, and France can't find any way to keep 'em from looking without paying.

September 13, 1925

French Language

I am here in Nice, France. It's pronounced neece, not nice. They have no word for "nice" in French.

August 28, 1926

FRANCHISE, THE

Now Congress says the women can vote. They used to could drink and not vote, now they can vote and not drink.

1919

FREEDOM

Ammunition beats persuasion when you are looking for Freedom!

September 15, 1931

FRIENDS

The best friends anyone can have is their neighbors.

January 21, 1934

G

GANDHI, MOHANDAS K. (MAHATMA)

They got Gandhi in jail. He preached "Liberty without Violence." He swore all his followers to "Truth and constant Poverty." He wanted nothing for himself, not even the ordinary comforts.

The whole thing gives you an idea of what would happen to our Savior if He would come to earth today. Why, say, He wouldn't last near as long as He did then.

May 5, 1930

GANGSTERS

You are not going to get me coming out here telling jokes about these racketeers and gangsters, or any of that. I arrived in Chicago intact, and I am going to try and leave likewise, that is all.

June 22, 1930

★ ★ ★

Racketeering is America's biggest industry, and their funerals is "big business."

March 26, 1931

★ ★ ★

I think some of these crooks are just getting killed to show that they can have a bigger and finer funeral than their rival had.

September 14, 1928

★ ★ ★

It's hard to tell whether there is more guns or flowers at a gangster's funeral. I would rather have the undertaker's privilege with some high-class gang, than to have a seat on the Stock Exchange.

September 14, 1928

139

GASOLINE

You could put a dollar a gallon tax on gasoline, and still a pedestrian couldn't cross the street in safety without armor.

March 17, 1932

★ ★ ★

In 1918, Motorless Sundays were invented, not to save gasoline, but to save lives.

Undertakers made strenuous objections.

January 25, 1925

GENERATION GAP

The trouble with this generation is they are getting too wise. That is, they are getting too wise about things which they ought not to get wise about, and learning none of the things that might be any good to 'em afterwards.

January 6, 1929

★ ★ ★

Us old folks, we raise up on what was, until a few generations ago, our hind legs, and we say: "What are these young coming to? They didn't do that when I was young."

But all a young man or woman has got to do today is to look over the mess that us old-timers have made of everything, and if we are fair with the young "upstarts," there is no reason why they should look on us with any great "huzzas."

December 9, 1934

★ ★ ★

Your mother gets mighty shocked at you girls nowadays, but in her day, her mother was just on the verge of sending her to a reformatory.

August 24, 1930

GENTLEMAN

I often wonder how they distinguished a gentleman in the old days, when there was no golf?

January 21, 1923

★ ★ ★

What is a Gentleman? It's easy to define: a Gentleman is, to my way of thinking, a man that can play Golf and don't say so.

But as there are so few in fact, it has been discussed whether there is any at all.

August 10, 1930

GEOGRAPHY

Geography has more to do with Brotherly Love than civilization and Christianity combined.

July 7, 1935

GERMANY

England promised to protect France against Germany. What is the consequence? As soon as Germany gets strong enough so she thinks she can lick both of them, there will be another war.

June 28, 1925

Germany has banned that splendid film "All Quiet on the Western Front," on account of it showing Germany losing the war.

I guess they are going to take it back and make it with a different finish.

December 12, 1930

They are talking about bringing our soldiers back from Germany. They would have brought them back sooner but we didn't have anybody in Washington who knew where they were.

February 18, 1923

We had to leave our soldiers over there so they could get the mail that was sent to them during the war. Had to leave 'em over there anyway, two of them hadn't married yet.

February 18, 1923

Germany, the winner of the last war, why, when the Allies took their army and navy away from them, shortsighted statesmen didn't know it, but they did them the greatest favor that was ever done a nation. They didn't have any army and navy to support, so it didn't leave them a thing to do but go to work.

August 26, 1926

GOD

God is a lot more broad-minded than we think He is.

Notes

Which way you serve your God will never get a word of argument or condemnation out of me.

January 8, 1933

GOLD

Papers every day in big headlines tell us what gold sells for. Just as well tell us what radium sells for. Who has any of either?

October 27, 1933

★   ★   ★

I've been up in the gold mining district here in California. Ah, for the good old days, when the boys used to dig the gold out of the hills, and the girls used to dig it out of the boys. You know, in the old days, if you wanted any money, you got yourself a pick and went out and got it—not out of the government, like you do now.

You see, it used to be harder to get money out of the government than it used to be to get it out of the ground, but nowadays, why, the government just gives it away.

October 28, 1934

GOLF

Golf is the only game where practicing it and playing it is the same thing.

January 24, 1926

You let the poor all get to playing golf, and you watch the rich give it up. Americans don't like common things.

January 6, 1929

★   ★   ★

Golf is a wonderful exercise. You stand on your feet for hours, watching somebody else putt. It's just the old-fashioned pool hall moved outdoors, but with no chairs around the walls.

July 20, 1930

★   ★   ★

Golf is the only game, outside of solitaire, where you play alone. What you do with your ball has nothing to do with what the other fellow does with his. I can play you a game and I can play in the morning, and you can play a month from then.

It's solitaire, only much quieter.

January 24, 1926

I guess there is nothing that will get your mind off everything like golf will. I have never been depressed enough to take up the game, but they say you can get so sore at yourself that you forget to hate your enemies.

December 2, 1928

Golf! Why, half of America is bent over. In two more generations our children will grow upwards as far as the hips, then they will turn off at right angles with their arms hanging down. We will be right back where we started from.

Darwin was right!

August 5, 1930

★　★　★

Golf is played for conversational purposes.

April 17, 1934

★　★　★

There are men belonging to swell Golf Clubs today, who, if their wives ever wanted a cook, would faint. Their dues are paid before the grocery bill.

February 25, 1923

GOODWILL, INTERNATIONAL

There just ain't any such animal as international "good-will." It just lasts till the loan runs out.

December 20, 1931

★　★　★

It's great to be friendly with a foreign nation, but it's terribly expensive. If the worst comes to the worst, and we do have to be friends with any of 'em, why, pick out little ones that haven't got the nerve to ask for much.

February 27, 1932

GOVERNORS

The governors of all the states are gathered together in Connecticut to show how far apart they are.

July 19, 1929

★　★　★

An awful lot of new Governors going to be sworn in this week and next. Now, if we can just keep 'em from wanting to go to the Senate, they are liable to make good men.

January 8, 1931

★　★　★

It's a funny thing about the job of a District Attorney. They try and attract enough attention to become Governors.

There should be a clause in every District Attorney's contract, "This office does not necessarily entitle you to Governorship ambitions. Keep your mind on your own job."

December 18, 1929

We are having a Governors' convention here in California and I met them at the state line. We fired a nineteen gun salute which took quite a while as we only had one cannon.

Today they all planted state trees, so we at least got 'em working for the first time since they been in office.

This herding Governors ain't near as bad as I thought it would be. Just give 'em plenty to eat and let 'em speak, and they don't give you any bother.

July 1933

★   ★   ★

The President gave a luncheon for the visiting Governors, where they discussed but didn't try Prohibition.

It was the consensus of opinion of all their speeches that there was a lot of drinking going on and that if it wasn't stopped by January, that they would hold another meeting and try and get rid of some of the stuff.

December 31, 1922

★   ★   ★

If a man don't need the money, and he don't just want the glory, I don't know why he should go into the Governorship. You see, "Good Intentions, a Business Administration, and Throw the Rascals Out!" that's been tried by better men than you. There is graveyards in every state capitol where the headstones say: "Here lies Governor Meantwell. Here lies Governor Honesty. Here lies Governor Reform."

Yet the barnacles of connivance, political graft, lobbyists, and party leeches are still hanging onto every one of our states.

June 17, 1934

★   ★   ★

We overestimate this Governor job anyhow. States have good ones, bad ones and every kind, and yet they drag along about the same.

Things in our country run in spite of government. Not by the aid of it.

July 28, 1930

★   ★   ★

Being Governor is sort of a thankless job, after the applause is over.

June 17, 1934

★   ★   ★

They say no state is better than its Governor's secretary.

August 13, 1933

★   ★   ★

At the Democratic Convention, the two or three states that did not nominate their Governors as favorite sons for President must have done away with the Governor system and put in the commission form of government.

June 27, 1924

All these Governors being nominated as favorite sons for the Presidency, why, the only purpose I can see that the whole thing has answered is that it has educated the Convention up on who the Governors of the Democratic states are.

If I was a Governor I would have it in my contract that I was not to be nominated at a Presidential convention.

June 28, 1924

At this Democratic National Convention the favorite son Governors who have been holding their states to the last, finally told them: "Boys, leave me and get out and do the best you can, but remember one thing: don't ever let it be said that our glorious state is cheap!"

July 1, 1924

GRAFT

Course, the way we do things, always have done things, and always will do things, there just has to be so much graft. We wouldn't feel good if there wasn't.

November 25, 1934

We just have to get used to charging so much off to graft, just like you have to charge off so much for insurance, taxes, or depreciation. It's part of our national existence that we just have become accustomed to.

November 25, 1934

Mayor Jimmy Walker called a committee of one-hundred and told 'em something should be done about small graft in New York City.

Small graft, he said, was getting the city a bad name and it would eventually lose its reputation for doing things on a big scale.

September 4, 1930

These U.S. Senators look to be about the best graft, as there is no one watching them. Guess the people figure that the class of men they send to the Senate would get caught if they took anything, whether they had any one watching them, or not.

December 2, 1923

I certainly am not going to make the usual mistake that the Democrats make every time an election comes up. We have talked more Graft and Corruption and got less of it than any known denomination. Americans are funny people they never get het up over anything unless they are participating in it. The fellow that ain't getting any Corruption, he don't think that it can possiobly be so common, or it would have reached him; and the ones that are getting some of it, don't want it brought up.

Jimmy Cox, the Democratic candidate for President in 1920, run claiming Corruption in the Republican Party, and there were seven million more people in favor of it than there was of abolishing it.

Mr. Davis resurrected the same platform in 1924, and this time eight million were in favor of it—a clear gain of a million in four years that were living in hopes of getting their clutches on some of it.

March 30, 1929

GUN CONTROL

I see by the papers that during this kidnapping epidemic a well-known machine gun company has patriotically agreed to not sell any to gangsters till they have used up the ones they have.

August 13, 1933

★   ★   ★

I was born and raised in the Indian Territory, at Claremore to be exact. Well, even in those days it was against the law to carry a gun and every once in a while, the Sheriff would search a fellow to see if he was overdressed, and they fined 'em heavy.

But today, these addle brains can go and buy a gun any place they want to.

September 20, 1925

★   ★   ★

That automatic pistol, it's all right to have it invented, but it should never have been allowed outside the army, and then only in war time.

September 20, 1925

★   ★   ★

Let the government confiscate and forbid the entire sale of automatics, because they kill 10 innocent people to 1 guilty one with those sprinkling guns, and then prohibit the six shooters to anybody but police officers and when you catch a guy with a gun, send him to jail and don't just fine him!

September 20, 1925

★   ★   ★

I see where a lot of men are advocating letting everybody

carry guns with the idea that they will be able to protect themselves. In other words, just make civil war out of this crime wave.

If you think that being armed protects you, why, how about the amount of policemen that are shot down here in New York? They are all armed!

September 20, 1925

★   ★   ★

The biggest question that is agitating the public is: Are all lunatics to be furnished with guns and ammunition? This gun thing is getting pretty serious here around New York. Everybody that hasn't got a gun is getting shot by somebody.

They pinch a thousand people a day for parking 5 minutes too long, but I have yet to read where a policeman ever searched a bunch of tough guys hanging around a place, to see if any of them carried concealed weapons. They could start searching everybody and in one day here in New York, they would get enough pistols to dam up the Hudson River.

September 20, 1925

★   ★   ★

Can you imagine arresting a man in America for carrying a gun nowadays?

Why, in Chicago there is a pistol pocket put in your pajamas. There is thousands there that are faultlessly dressed in artillery that haven't got underwear on.

March 30, 1930

★   ★   ★

It is funny, what respect and National Honor a few guns will get you, ain't it? Now we gather to disarm, when a gun has put every nation in the world where it is today. It all depended on which end of it you were—on the sending or receiving end.

March 12, 1932

Automatic Weapons

The automatic pistol is as much more dangerous and destrutive than the old six-shooter, as poison gas is over perfume.

September 20, 1925

This gun thing is getting pretty serious. There has never been a case where the attempted killer missed everybody with an automatic pistol; there has been very few cases where only the one originally shot at has been hit. They always get somebody, because they don't have the presence of mind to stop the thing from shooting.

September 20, 1925

The automatic pistol has made no practice necessary to be a criminal.

Give any young egotist two shots of dope and an automatic, and he will hold up the Government Mint. He goes in and gets the money quicker than you can get it with a bona fide check.

June 7, 1931

★   ★   ★

Do you know what has been the cause of the big increase in murders? It's been the manufacture of the automatic pistol.

There is no skill or nerve required in using an automatic pistol. They should advertise those guns 'Killing Made Easy! Just Hold the Trigger Down and We Guarantee You Somebody!'

And the more drunk or drugged a man is, the more he will hit.

September 20, 1925

H

HAMBURGERS

This is Labor Day. A good stiff sales tax on hamburgers today would have paid our national debt.

September 4, 1933

HAMILTON, ALEXANDER

Alexander Hamilton started the U.S. Treasury with nothing—and that was the closest our country has ever been to being even. It's the only consecutively losing big business in the world that keeps on losing, and still keeps going.

Notes

★　★　★

Alexander Hamilton was the man that originated the "put and take" system into our National Treasury: the taxpayers put it in, the politicians take it out.

HATS

There has been an awful lot of fashion shows and all their byproducts held here in New York. So, on behalf of New York City, I had to help welcome them at their various banquets. There was the retail milliners' big fashion show at the Astor Ball Room, where they showed 500 hats and me.

Some of the hats were just as funny looking as I was.

March 4, 1923

HAWAII

We are going to get into a war some day either over Honolulu or the Philippines.

May 1, 1932

You don't have to be warlike to get a real kick out of our greatest Army Post, Schofield Barracks, and the Navy at Pearl Harbor. If war was declared with some Pacific nation we would lose the Philippines before lunch, but if we lost these here, it would be our own fault.

August 1, 1934

HEAD NURSE

There is nothing outside of a motor cycle cop with more authority than a head nurse.

May 26, 1935

HEALTH

In the old days, when we wasn't sanitary, why, we were strong enough to withstand germs. But nowadays, we have to be careful of the microbes, for if they get a hold on us, we are goners.

The old-fashioned gourd that the whole family drank out of, from birth till death, would today kill more of the modern population than a war would.

Notes

HEAVEN

Old New York, the so-called heartless city, houses some great people in every denomination in the world, and I can't see any difference in any of them. I haven't been able to see where one has the monopoly on the right course to Heaven.

May 24, 1925

★   ★   ★

Don't have an ideal to work for. That's like riding towards a mirage of a lake. When you get there it ain't there.

Believe in something for another world, but don't be too set on what it is, and then you won't start out that life with a disappointment.

Live your life so that whenever you lose, you are ahead.

July 15, 1931

HEROES

This thing of being a hero, about the main thing to it is to know when to die.

Prolonged life has ruined more men than it ever made.

July 17, 1928

We can't all be heroes, because someone has to sit on the curb and clap as they go by.

Notes

HIGHBROWS

There is a great tendency all over the country now to be High Brow. Everybody is four-flushing and pretending they are not what they really are.

More people should work for their dinner, instead of dressing for it. Half the stiff bosom shirts worn nowadays, the laundry is due on them yet.

February 25, 1923

HIGHER EDUCATION

The higher the education, the higher priced drinks they become accustomed to.

February 3, 1929

HIGHWAYS

Iowa has been trying for seven straight years to get an election held to vote bonds for roads.

The election requires half the voters to vote. Well, the roads are so bad they have never been able to get the voters to town.

February 22, 1928

HISTORY

Statesmen really thought they were going to "make History." Well, History makes itself and the statesmen just drag along.

July 14, 1933

There is an awful lot of difference between reading something and actually seeing it, for you can never tell, till you see it, just how big a liar History is.

1926

I doubt if there is a thing in the world as wrong and unreliable as History. History ain't what it is; it's what some writer wanted it to be, and I just happened to think I bet ours is as crooked as the rest. I bet we have started just as much devilment as was ever started against us—maybe more.

March 12, 1932

Don't be misled by History, or any other unreliable source.
April 14, 1935

HITLER, ADOLF

A guy named Hitler has Germany like Capone has Chicago.
October 16, 1930

★   ★   ★

Been reading a lot about that guy Hitler, in Germany, that's getting quite a following. He advocates forgetting everything connected with the Peace Treaty and starting all over new.

And that is about what will happen in a few years.
September 29, 1930

★   ★   ★

Papers all state Hitler is trying to copy Mussolini. Looks to me like it's the Ku Klux that he is copying. He don't want to be Emperor, he wants to be Kleagle.
March 27, 1933

★   ★   ★

Hitler ain't got no sales tax, but he ain't selling anything.
April 7, 1935

★   ★   ★

That fellow Hitler kinder prides himself on his oratory. Say, if he could have heard Rabbi Wise of New York at a great Jewish convention here today, Hitler would have been speechless. Wise had everything.
May 21, 1933

HOCKEY

I saw a hockey game put on here Saturday night, and war is kinder effeminate after it.
December 18, 1928

HOG-CALLING

Got a wire from an old boy in Parsons, Kansas, and he wanted me to enter a hog-calling contest.

You know, I used to be an awful good hog-caller when hogs were cheap. But the way hogs have gone up in price, it's changed the whole system of calling 'em. It would take Henry Ford hollering with his check book to get one to come to you nowadays.

I hollered all morning just for three slices of bacon and it didn't come. So there ain't much use of me hollering my head off to try and get a whole hog to come.

April 16, 1935

HOLDING COMPANIES

A Holding Company is a thing where you hand an accomplice the goods while the policeman searches you.

March 13, 1935

HOLIDAYS

Why don't they have all Holidays on a Sunday?

If this plan is adopted, look at the attractions on a Sunday: watch a parade (any kind desired), hear a speech (on anything or in any tongue), and if it rained and all these attractions fell down, why, then you could go to church.

November 20, 1927

I see where Mussolini says there is going to be no more celebrations, demonstrations, inaugurations, centenaries, either large or small, or speeches of any caliber given on any week day. That's an inspiration.

How many hours have you stood on one side of an avenue in a car, waiting for a parade to pass? It looks like parades are just formed to keep people that are in a hurry from getting from one side of town across to the other.

November 20, 1927

HOLLAND

Holland's highest point is eight feet six and a third inches above sea level. That is called the mountainous region of Holland. That's where they do their skiing and winter sports.

October 23, 1926

Look at Holland, great country, big as England, but do you ever hear of them when they talk of what the big powers want? No, you would think they were Rhode Island. Why? No navy!

March 16, 1930

HOLLYWOOD, CALIFORNIA

That is unusual in Hollywood, for anybody to get married the first time.

June 15, 1930

It's kinder the off season; Spring marrying is about over, and Summer divorces haven't quite got going good.

June 10, 1928

★ ★ ★

Hollywood is just like a desert water hole in Africa. Hang around long enough and every kind of animal in the world will drift in for refreshments.

November 11, 1931

★ ★ ★

It seems that old Hollywood has reconciled itself to conditions of this depression perhaps better than any other place. They have charged off 50 per cent of their husbands as a total loss, voluntarily cut alimony, reorganized with less overhead and going back to pre-war mates and conditions.

May 1, 1931

★ ★ ★

You know, on this earthquake we had out in California, Hollywood tried to claim that it felt the shock. It was purely an advertising scheme with them. They hated to hear of something visiting California and not calling on them.

If a plague struck Scranton, Pennsylvania, Hollywood would claim they had a touch of it. If the Devil should appear at Chicago, Illinois, Hollywood would immediately claim: "He is coming here on his way home!"

July 12, 1925

★ ★ ★

There is no more interesting place in the world to meet characters than a movie set. If you have lost anybody anywhere and don't know where they are, they are in Hollywood trying to get in the movies.

September 20, 1931

HONESTY

I would rather be the man who bought the Brooklyn Bridge than the man who sold it.

Notes

★ ★ ★

I would rather tell 'em what I think and retire with satisfaction, than be President and be hampered.

March 4, 1934

★ ★ ★

They gave Walter Johnson a big demonstration the other day

in Washington, D.C. You know, he's that great pitcher for the Washington Senators—the baseball team, not the politicians. The President, himself, made the speech. After a diligent search for 150 years, Washington, D.C. finally found an honest man. Johnson is the first man in public life in Washington to be publicly commended for his honesty.

In no other city would an honest man be more of a novelty.

October 12, 1924

HONOR

In wars the slogan is "Honor" but the object is Land.

March 19, 1932

HOOVER, HERBERT C.

Hoover is formally into the race now. He is the only candidate in either Party by acclamation. The others are candidates by personal desire.

It will be interesting to see what kind of race a known qualified man can make, This election will decide whether qualifications are an asset, or a liability.

February 13, 1928

★   ★   ★

I always wanted to see him elected. I wanted to see how far a competent man could get in politics. It has never been tried before.

April 20, 1930

★   ★   ★

I attribute Hoover's victory to the fact that we have never seen his picture on a golf course. Nothing outside of a Senatorial investigation can ruin a man so completely with the general public as golf pictures can.

November 20, 1928

★   ★   ★

Hoover gets rid of something useless every day.

Wait till he sees Congress.

March 26, 1929

★   ★   ★

I see where Mr. Hoover has invited Mr. Coolidge down to Washington. That's what I would call the last word in hospitality, to invite somebody to Washington in July.

You watch Calvin get out of it.

July 21, 1929

One thing we have always heard of our President is that while he may not be a political spellbinder and able to sway a vast audience, that he could take a small bunch of men, talk to 'em and explain what he was after, and he could have them coming out of the conference promising to give up golf, cut off a leg or quit smoking.

November 28, 1929

HOOVER DAM

Hoover Dam is entirely between Nevada and Arizona. All California gets out of it is the water.

September 6, 1932

The Democrats are going to change the name of Hoover Dam. That is the silliest thing I ever heard of in politics. They are going to take the name of Hoover away from that dam.

Lord, if they feel that way about it, I don't see why they don't just reverse the two words.

May 14, 1933

It's the biggest thing that's ever been done with water since Noah made the flood look foolish. They have been bothered with only two things. One is silt and the other is a Senatorial investigation; they both clog everything up.

September 6, 1932

HORSES

Dopey had lived with us for nineteen years and now he left us. He was a little, round-bodied, coal-black pony with glass eyes, the gentlest, greatest pony. I don't know why we called him Dopey, we meant no disrespect.

When nineteen years of your and your children's lives is linked so closely with a horse, you can sorter imagine our feelings. He was one of the family, he raised our children and learned them to ride. He never hurt one in his life. He did everything right.

And that's a reputation that no human can die with.

December 16, 1934

A man that don't love a horse, there is something the matter with him.

August 17, 1924

Arabian Horses

The Arabian horses also have an American characteristic, they are long-winded. There is a Senator among every colt born.

An Arabian horse's nostrils are always extended. He seems to smell everything pretty good. Well, we Americans, don't. There is things about our affairs that you sometimes think we have no sense of smell at all, or we would certainly smell some of the things that are being put over on us every day.

June 5, 1932

They say that the Arabian horse has one less vertebra in his back and one less in his tail, and his shin bone from the knee down is shorter. Now our American shin bones are shorter, too, because we have worn it out kicking at everything so much. We have worn out an inch just kicking our poor last President, alone.

Now I think we ought to commence wearing out the heel bone by kicking ourselves a few times each day. Our kicks have always been aimed at somebody else for our own troubles. And a few good ones directed at the proper source would find us getting 'em right where they are deserved.

June 5, 1932

Horse Thieves

You know, of course, or perhaps you have had it hinted to you, that we stand in Europe about like a Horse Thief.

Now I want to report to you that that is not so. It is, what you'd call "erroneous." We don't stand like a Horse Thief abroad.

Whoever told you we did is flattering us.

August 26, 1926

I started to have my ancestors looked into one time and they got back one generation and I had one of my family up on a limb for horse stealing; so I asked them to discontinue.

April 29, 1928

HORSESHOE PITCHING

I am here in St. Petersburg, the only town in America where two World Series sporting events are held. The outdoor, under-a-shade checker championship and the horseshoe pitching finals are here.

The mule-slipper heavers can do more with a horseshoe than a manicurist can with a drunk.

February 7, 1927

HOSPITALS

The only way that we know that our civilization has advanced in this country is by our splendid hospitals.

May 11, 1930

HUMANITY

Humanity is not yet ready for either real truth, or real harmony.

July 15, 1923

HUMAN NATURE

Funny thing about human nature. When we ain't feeling so good ourselves, we always want to read about somebody that is worse off than we are.

December 9, 1930

HUMAN RACE

Take offsprings in the human race. A race horse is almost sure to breed another race horse. And dogs follow along the wake of their ancestors. You take a couple of well-bred Airedales and you can rest assured you are not going to get a Pot Hound.

But with the human race, you may just as well throw your register book in the creek; you're just as liable to have some fine old stock bring forth a family of human mutts, as to produce an amateur Lincoln.

August 4, 1929

HUMOR

My humor is not so hot, my philosophy don't philo, and my jokes are pre-war, but my feelings toward mankind is 100 per cent.

November 1, 1932

HUNGER

We are going through a unique experience. We are the first nation to starve to death in a storehouse that's overfilled with everything we want.

November 26, 1930

HUNTING

The deer season just opened. Any one driving an automobile on Beverly Boulevard or Mulholland Drive should wear red coats and carry an American flag.

August 2, 1927

★   ★   ★

A deer hunter in Ventura county brought in his first man yesterday.

August 4, 1927

★   ★   ★

Grouse in Scotland has been shot at so much, they know just about who can hit 'em, and who can't.

It's a racket, and the grouse and the Scotchmen work together and the Americans and the Englishmen pay the bill.

September 19, 1934

★   ★   ★

Deer season opened in Scotland for all those who can't hit grouse.

August 25, 1926

HURRY

We are in too big a hurry in this country to even save time. We would rather talk about how big a hurry we are in than do the hurrying.

November 25, 1928

HYDE PARK, LONDON

I went to Hyde Park, London, where, if you have anything against the Government, or King, or even as low as a Sir, why, you jump up on a box and get it all out of your system.

They sink the Navy, impeach the Crown, and cancel debts, and when they finish they are just as happy as if it had been done. It's real Democracy.

Over home, you have to be elected to the Senate before you can do it.

February 3, 1930

I

IDEALS

People love high ideals, but they got to be about 33 per cent plausible.

IDEAS

Everything worthwhile is a good idea, but did you ever notice there is more bad ideas that will work than there is good ones?

★　★　★

We have some great ideas, but most of 'em come too late to do us any good.

★　★　★

I have a lot of big ideas. They just don't seem to work out. There must be a bit of College professor in me somewhere.

IGNORANCE

Everybody is ignorant, only on different subjects.

★　★　★

When ignorance gets started, it knows no bounds.

★　★　★

America is becoming so educated that ignorance will be a novelty. I will belong to a select few.

Notes

All I know is just what I read in the papers and that's an alibi for my ignorance.

August 12, 1930

ILLITERACY

The state of Louisiana without any blare of trumpets is doing the biggest thing being done in our land today. They opened up "Moonlight Schools" and are teaching over a hundred thousand to read and write, mostly older people.

They are going to wipe out illiteracy in two years with both whites and blacks. That is like learning the crippled to walk and the blind to see. One hundred thousand happy citizens will bring your state more dividends than one hundred thousand miles of concrete roads will.

May 14, 1929

IMMIGRATION

We make drastic laws and stay with them. Didn't we pass an immigration law to even keep people out of our country? Well, that was all right. It was a good law. It's our country and we got a right to say who shall come in, but, of course, it was discrimination.

March 20, 1927

IMMORALITY

Imagine with all our crime and immorality in the papers, and our small attendance in our churches, a nation that no one person in it ever did any job a month that he was trying to get out of it and into something else, about as much contentment and repose as a fresh caged hyena, and then we go to tell some calm, contented people how to live.

April 10, 1927

INCOME

There is a tremendous movement on to get lower taxes on earned incomes. Then will come the real problem, "Who among us on salary are earning our income?"

December 8, 1929

INDEPENDENCE

We talk more independence than we practice.

May 19, 1935

In wars they are always fighting for "Independence," but at the finish they always seems to be able to use quite a bit of the defeated opponent's land to be "Independent" on.

March 19, 1932

INDEPENDENCE DAY

July 4th, 1776—that's when we tore ourselves loose from England and it's a question of who it was a better deal for. There was an awful lot of things before 1776 that we wasn't 'blessed' with when we were under England. Just mention any problem that's facing us today, and it wasn't with us before 1776! Do you realize there was no Senate and no House?

June 10, 1934

July 4th, 1776—the only thing like today was we had no money—but we had no debts! Course, we had a little Indian trouble—about one-tenth as much as you do today with our criminals. And the tax we fought to do away with, why, it must have been at least 5 per cent of what it is today.

June 10, 1934

That Liberty that we got all those years ago was a great thing, but they ought to pass a law that we could only celebrate it every 100 years, for at the rate of accidents yesterday, we won't have enough people to celebrate it every year.

And the speeches! Did you read them? Never was so much politics indulged in under the guise of 'Freedom and Liberty.' They was 5 per cent what George Washington did, and 95 per cent what the speaker intended to do.

July 5, 1935

INDIANA

Children in Indiana are born in voting booths and are weaned on ballots.

May 1, 1926

Indiana is noted for its great crop of humorists—George Ade, Kin Hubbard and a flock of others. Indianans, jealous of these men's reputation, used to say: "We have people in Indiana besides humorists."

And sure enough, they did have, but they were all in jail but the humorists. So why don't they elect some of them?

April 4, 1928

INDIANS

My ancestors didn't come over on the Mayflower—they met 'em at the boat.

Notes

★   ★   ★

You know I am an Indian. My folks are Cherokees and I am very proud of the fact.

April 27, 1930

★   ★   ★

At my old school, Drumgoole, it was all Indian kids went there and I being part Cherokee, had enough white in me to make my honesty questionable.

September 29, 1929

★   ★   ★

Indians used to be wards of the Government, but now we all are. Everybody is an Indian.

May 19, 1935

★   ★   ★

Our record with the Indians is going to go down in history. It is going to make us mighty proud of it in the future when our children of ten more generations read of what we did to them.

April 27, 1930

★   ★   ★

Every man in history that killed the most Indians has got a statue built for him.

April 27, 1930

★   ★   ★

The Government, by statistics, shows that they have got 456 treaties that they have broken with the Indians. That is why the Indians gets a kick out of reading the Government's usual remark when some big affair comes up: "Our honor is at stake!"

April 27, 1930

★   ★   ★

There ain't nothing to life but satisfaction. If you want to ship off fat beef cattle at the end of their existence, you got to have 'em satisfied on the range.

Indians and primitive races were the highest civilized, because they were more satisfied, and they depended less on each other, and took less from each other. We couldn't live a day without depending on everybody, so our civilization has given us no liberty or independence.

July 5, 1931

Do you know that Claremore, Oklahoma, is going to open the only Indian hospital in the United States? We have the only one, built by the Government entirely for Indians.

You know, Columbus discovered this country about 400 years ago or something, and it took 400 years for the Government to build a hospital for the Indians. Look what the Indians have got to look forward to in the next 400 years. They are liable to build us a cemetery.

April 27, 1930

★   ★   ★

The Indians say you must never disagree with a man while you are facing him. Go around behind him and look the same way they do, when you are facing him. Look over his shoulder and get his viewpoint, then go back and face him and you will have a different idea.

October 30, 1932

★   ★   ★

As you saw all those Indians, you couldn't help but think of the old days. Here was the old war-like Apaches that fought to hold all they had, and most of them wound up in jail; but there was Washington, that fought for his tribe and wound up with a flock of statues and a title of "Father" of his country.

And yet, I expect, if the truth were known, the old Apache Chiefs went through more and fought harder for their country than George did. But George won, that's the whole answer to history; it's not what did you do, but what did you get away with at the finish.

March 16, 1930

★   ★   ★

An Indian told me the reason a white man always got lost and an Indian didn't, was because an Indian always looked back after he passed anything so he got a view of it from both sides.

You see, the white man just figures that all sides of a thing are the same. That's like a dumb guy with an argument, he don't think there can be any other side, only his. That's what you call politicians.

October 30, 1932

Hopi Indians

You talk about learned scientists that know all about when things are going to happen, well, let me tell you, the Hopi Indians out in Arizona that put on that Snake Dance every year, they know as much about the moon and stars and what's going to happen as these college birds do.

These old Indians study the heavens for weeks ahead and they know about the time that rain is maybe leaving Honolulu and headed this way, well, then they say: "We will dance on the 6th of next month!"

These Indians say the rain come down so thick and the roads was so bad and slippery that the Indians had no more stopped praying for rain to come, than the whites started praying for it to stop.

May 11, 1930

★   ★   ★

I am up to the Hopi snake dance. This dance is an old Indian custom.

One snake was not notified that this dance was supposed to be religious and he bit an Indian. Intolerance is even an issue among the snakes.

August 22, 1928

Indian Affairs, Bureau of

I see by the papers this morning where the Department of Indian Affairs has promised that it will have its Indian agents do better this year, I mean, do better for the Indians, for a change.

March 30, 1931

Osage Indians

Lots of people think 'cause the Osages have oil, that all Indians are rich. Why, the Pine Ridge Agency Sioux have eaten so much horse meat, they are wearing bridles instead of hats.

March 30, 1931

★   ★   ★

The Government tried to prove that rich Osage wasn't in his right mind because one time, when his car stalled, he traded it for an old pony, got on him and rode off. And they call that crazy.

If everybody did that, they would be out of debt in a couple of years. Just think, no gas, no tires, no roads to pay for. Why, instead of prosecuting the old Indian, they ought to erect a monument to him for being that far ahead of his time.

February 20, 1933

Seminole Indians

I met a Seminole Indian who had starved in Florida all his life. He seemed like such a nice fellow, this Indian, and such a gentleman, that I asked him how is it that he was not selling lots in Florida, being native and knowing the country and its possibilities. He should be a star salesman.

He said: "I am an Indian—I have a conscience."
May 1, 1926

INDIAN TERRITORY

They sent the Indians to Oklahoma. They had a treaty that said: "You shall have this land as long as the grass grows and the water flows." It was not only a good rhyme but it looked like a good treaty—till they struck oil. Then the Government took it away from us again. They said that the treaty only refers to water and grass, it don't say anything about oil.

So the Indians lost another bet—the first one was to Andrew Jackson and the second was to the oil companies.
February 5, 1928

Pawhuska, Indian Territory, is near Tulsa and fifty-five miles from Claremore. People from Pawhuska used to come to Claremore. People did from Tulsa, too. Pawhuska and Tulsa people used to come over to Claremore for their mail and to find out what time it was.

We had a clock.
April 20, 1930

Every time the Indians moved, the Government give 'em a treaty. They say: "You can have this ground as long as the grass grows and the water flows."

Now they moved the Indians and they settled the whole thing by putting them on land where the grass won't grow and the water won't flow, so now they have it all settled.
April 27, 1930

It would be interesting if they would allow every country to do like they did with the Saar—you know, vote on whether they want to go back with who they come from, or go with somebody else, or go with the League of Nations, or go it alone.

I think you would see a lot of changes. In fact, you would see our own country given back to the Indians.
January 14, 1935

★   ★   ★

It does look like after flying over as much of these old United States as I have lately, and seen the millions of acres that we don't use anyway, as I say, it does look like America was big enough that they could have staked off, say, at least a fourth, or a fifth of it and given it to the Indians for all time to come.

They would have never bothered a soul if we had just split the country, even 80-20 with them.

April 17, 1927

★   ★   ★

We were out there on Indian land, dedicating a dam to get water for white people to come out and use and gradually take more Indian land away.

There is going to be nothing different. It started with Leif Ericsson in 996, then skipped over Columbus in 1492, for he couldn't find this country in four trips. Then come the Spanish settlers, and then the Mayflower, that was the last straw.

March 16, 1930

INFLATION

Now when Congress becomes ten per cent efficient, why, that is Inflation!

May 7, 1933

★   ★   ★

Inflation, there is one thing about it. It's made every man's intelligence equal.

May 2, 1933

★   ★   ★

As high-priced as it is to live in, I don't see anybody leaving the country.

April 13, 1934

★   ★   ★

I tell you, inflation is more important to every individual than the name of any man that will ever be in the White House.

November 2, 1924

★   ★   ★

I have been accused of being worried over this inflation. I wasn't worried. I was just confused. There is quite a difference. When you are worried, you know what you are worried about, but when you are confused you don't know enough about a thing to be worried.

April 24, 1933

★   ★   ★

The House of Representatives is going to limit debate on "Inflation" to five hours tomorrow.

I wish to goodness there was a way to limit individuals that try to explain it to you to five hours.

May 2, 1933

INGRATITUDE

It's the old gag; people that pay for things never complain. It's the guy you give something to that you can't please.

January 3, 1926

INSANITY

Headline in all the papers say: "Authorities Having Trouble Rounding Up Twelve Escaped Lunatics."

The main trouble is recognizing 'em. I bet they get a different twelve back in.

June 5, 1930

You see, medical science has developed two ways of actually determining insanity. One is if the patient cuts out paper dolls, and the other is if the patient says: "I will tell you what this economic business really means!"

April 24, 1933

There is only one county institution needs enlarging and that's the insane asylum, and put us all in there 'till we know enough to vote to cut at least 50 per cent of our governing expenses.

July 5, 1932

INSURANCE

In the midst of this Depression, we started sinking our Navy to save taxes. Saving taxes don't help the unemployed; they got nothing, are earning nothing, hence they pay nothing.

To reduce your Navy in these times is exactly like the man who is not doing so well financially, canceling all his life insurance, figuring it's a dead loss because he hasn't died yet.

October 27, 1930

Fire proofing and Insurance have caused more fires than going to bed with a lighted cigarette.

May 4, 1930

I was as agreeable to everybody as an Insurance Agent before he lands you.

November 6, 1926

Some people will bet on anything. Take Life Insurance Companies.

You, like a fool, will bet them that you will die, when they have every available information from doctors and everybody that you will live.

Why, if it looks like you will die, they won't bet you.

July 10, 1926

INTELLIGENCE

You can't legislate intelligence and common sense into people.

March 16, 1934

INTERNATIONAL DATE LINE

When you reach the 180th Meridian sailing west, you lose a whole day. Don't ask me why. If you come back this way, you get it back; if you don't, you just lose it.

The way days are now, it don't look like it's worth coming back for. We go to bed tomorrow night, Thursday, and wake up Saturday—maybe.

November 25, 1931

I was told we was going to lose a day for no other reason than to make somebody's calendar come out even.

Well, we lost a day. We gained a typhoon. We lost a life boat and I lost my whole internal possessions.

November 27, 1932

INTOLERANCE

Now which is the narrowest, religious intolerance or political intolerance? Politicians think an umpire's decision is based on "What will my decision do for the Party."

April 19, 1927

I have sometimes wondered if the preachers themselves have not something to do with intolerance. You hear or read a sermon nowadays, and the biggest part is taken up by knocking or trying to prove the falseness of some other denomination. They say that the Catholics are damned, that the Jews' religion is all wrong, or that the Christian Scientists are a fake, or that the Protestants are all out of step.

Now, just suppose, for a change they preach to you about the Lord and not about the other fellows' church, for every man's religion is good. We are all trying to arrive at the same place according to our own conscience and teachings. It don't matter which road you take.

March 11, 1923

Let's don't get down in intolerance as far down as the Indians. Because if you monkey around, I'm Cherokee, and a few of us will get together and run you all out of this country and take it back again.

June 2, 1935

INVENTORS

It's inventors that put us where we are today. There ain't enough jobs to go around. Why? Because every lazy man in the world has invented something to knock others out of work, and fix himself financially so he wouldn't have to.

November 9, 1930

INVESTIGATIONS

The more people study about you, nowadays, the less they think of you.

June 3, 1923

★   ★   ★

All we got to do in this country to find out something is wrong, is just to investigate it.

August 12, 1931

★   ★   ★

Our investigations have always contributed more to amusement than they have to knowledge.

August 11, 1932

★   ★   ★

The United States Senate investigates everything—usually after it's dead.

April 11, 1932

★   ★   ★

There is two places where what a person says should not be held against 'em in a court of law. One is at a dinner, and the other is on the witness stand of a Washington investigation.

Both affairs are purely social and should be covered only by the society editor.

April 18, 1934

★   ★   ★

Taxpayers don't mind paying for work, but it's investigations and reports that keep us broke.

June 2, 1928

★   ★   ★

Investigations are held just for photographers.

April 4, 1934

The American people would trade 10 investigations for one conviction.

June 25, 1924

Some think that this investigation will not do much good. But any time one half learns how the other half lives, why, it does us all good.

You see, there is lots of things these old boys have done that are within the law. But it's so near the edge that you couldn't slip a safety razor blade between their acts and prosecution.

May 24, 1933

Investigating Commissions draw people's attention to our ills. Now we know there is an awful lot of things wrong with us, that if we hadn't picked up a paper and seen where a commission had been appointed to investigate it, why, we wouldn't have known we had it.

February 27, 1932

You see, the trouble with these hearings is that it just looks like nobody can emerge with their noses entirely clean. I don't care who you are, you just can't reach middle life without having done and said a whole lot of foolish things.

I tell you, if I saw an investigating committee headed my way, I would just plead guilty and throw myself on the mercy of the court.

December 29, 1934

These Boys in Washington have had a lot of fun investigating. You see, a Senator is never as happy as when he is asking somebody a question, without the party being able to ask him one back.

November 24, 1929

★　★　★

I can't help but believe that all these Washington hearings must be sponsored by the railroad and hotels. There can't possibly be any other reason for holding them.

March 6, 1930

IOWA

I am just entering Iowa. I haven't been here in years, not since it moved to Long Beach, California. I am looking forward with great anxiety to seeing the birthplace of 90 per cent of Southern California's native sons.

California really just uses Iowa as a sort of hatchery.

November 8, 1925

IRELAND

Ireland welcomes you, even if you don't buy something every minute.

September 26, 1926

Ireland treats you more like a friend than a tourist.

September 8, 1926

I like Ireland and Mexico better than any other foreign country. They both got humor, and while they both think they take life serious, they don't. They will joke with you, sing with you, drink with you, and, if you want, fight with you—or against you, whichever you want—and I think, if they like you enough, they would die with you.

May 19, 1928

Well, how about the seventeenth of Ireland?

Of all the nationalities that have helped root us Indians out over here, the Irish are the only ones that have made enough impression on everybody till we celebrate their holiday.

March 17, 1931

He said: "The trouble with Ireland is the English landlords own all the land."

"Well," I said, "the best way to settle that is to make every English landlord go to Ireland and collect the rent personally. That would not only solve the problem but eliminate the landlords."

July 1920

I have been in twenty countries and the only one where American tourists are welcomed wholeheartedly by everyone, is in Ireland. And the funny part is there is more to see there than in all others put together. They don't owe us and they don't hate us.

Americans go where you are welcome!

August 1, 1926

ITALY

Being an Italian is a very serious business in itself.

July 4, 1926

We had heard of all kinds of likely wars between nations, but this one that Mussolini dug up is a new one. Italy versus Ethiopia.

That's going a long way for an enemy.

December 18, 1934

★   ★   ★

As I came in to see Mussolini, he gave us the Fascisti salute—you look out straight and point your arm kinder up and out. They say it's a salute that originally come from the old Romans, but personally I think they copped it from traffic policemen over home, who have been giving it for years, but nobody ever paid any attention to them.

June 1, 1926

J

JACKSON, ANDREW

The Indians wanted old Andy Jackson in the White House? It was so he would let us alone for a while. Andy stayed two terms— he had to get back to his regular business which was shooting at the Indians; they were for a third term for Andy.
February 5, 1928

★　★　★

Got to give Old Andy credit. He fought duels when duels were duels, and not just the inconvenience of getting up before sunrise.
February 5, 1928

★　★　★

Andrew Jackson was the one who said: "If you don't get out and work for the Party, you don't get in on the gravy after election."
July 15, 1928

Jacksonian Democracy

President Andrew Jackson's Democracy consisted of inventing the plan of giving everybody jobs according to how many votes they delivered to the Democrats. He said: "If he ain't of our Party, give him nothing! Charity begins at the polls."

If Old Andy happened to be defeated at the polls, he would pounce on the Indians and take it out on them. According to Democrat Andy Jackson, an Indian had no more right to live than a Republican had the right to hold a job during a Democratic administration.
March 30, 1929

JAPAN

Japan. You got to admire 'em. They are so ambitious, and they just got everything all the other nations have, but a sense of humor.
April 26, 1934

174

Japan has picked China out an emperor for Manchuria. That's about like Al Capone picking out Prohibition Enforcement Officers for Mr. Hoover.

November 15, 1931

★   ★   ★

The Japanese are mighty polite and nice, and they want you to see and like their country. They got everything we got, and if they haven't, you show it to 'em and they will make it.

January 17, 1932

★   ★   ★

We never had a greater example of why there will always be wars. Twenty-one nations of the League of Nations denounced Japan's Chinese invasion, and the United States, while not a member, agreed with them. Now all in the world they got to do to stop it instantly, is to agree to not trade with an aggressor nation, meaning Japan.

But they won't sacrifice their trade to save bloodshed. The League has got the weapons to stop war, but try and get the nations to give up that trade. What's a few thousand dead Chinamen compared to Japan as a cash customer?

February 26, 1933

★   ★   ★

This Australian trip was planned with our Pacific fleet to impress Japan with the size of it. That was not necessary. Japan knows more about our war strength now than either of our Secretaries of War, or Navy.

August 16, 1925

★   ★   ★

As far as our trade is concerned, you can't force 'em to buy your goods. Japan has found out that any door is open to those that have the best product at the cheapest price. A manufacturer can sit in his office and if his car is cheaper and better that any other car, dealers will come clear there to buy 'em.

April 30, 1932

★   ★   ★

Did you know that Japan has got two Parties, too? I don't remember their names any more than they could remember ours. But they keep things in a turmoil, just like ours. You see, if we didn't have two Parties we would all settle on the best man in the country, and things would run fine. But as it is now, we settle on the worst ones and then fight over 'em.

January 17, 1932

Japan's Congress is called "Diet." Now ain't that a hot name for Congress? That's what our taxpayers are on, just on account of our "Diet."

March 5, 1932

Had dinner and long chat with President Roosevelt, who's vacationing here in Honolulu, and he gave me some advice. The President told me: "Will, don't jump on Japan! Just keep them from jumping on us."

August 12, 1934

The Japanese run their wars just like they do their trains—right on time. All their soldiers are trained between wars, not after one starts.

You see, we have been lucky that way; all of our wars have waited on us till we could get ready. But those Japanese figure that they may have one where the enemy won't wait. So, when it is booked, all the preliminaries have already been arranged. Each soldier knows not only where he is to go, but practically who he is to shoot.

March 12, 1932

JEALOUSY

You talk about actors being jealous. You haven't seen any jealousy till you watch diplomats work.

November 17, 1931

When we nearly lose the next war, as we probably will, we can lay in onto one thing and that will be the jealousy of the army and navy toward aviation.

March 11, 1927

JEFFERSON, THOMAS

Jefferson was the most far-sighted Democrat of his or any other time.

September 22, 1929

It seems that Jefferson was for the poor; well, that strikes me as being mighty good politics in those days, for that's about all there was. Nowadays, with everybody at least not wanting to be considered poor—it would be political suicide to take only the side of the poor.

March 30, 1929

Jefferson seemed to be the only Democrat in history with any kind of business ability.

February 13, 1927

Jeffersonian Principles

I have heard so much at this Democratic National Convention about "Getting back to the old Jeffersonian Principles" that, being an amateur, I am in doubt as to why they ever left them in the first place.

June 28, 1928

★ ★ ★

Nobody can remember what the old "Jeffersonian Principles," were, but they have furnished a topic for the poor Democrats to rave about for a couple of generations. He always wants to return to the Jeffersonian Principles and give the Government back to the people.

Well, the people wouldn't know any more what to do with it than they did back in those days. Nothing would please the rich more than to have the Government handed back to the people, for they would take it away from them so quick the people wouldn't know what it looked like while they had it.

October 28, 1928

JUSTICE

The Lord in his justice works everything on a handicap basis. California, having the best of everything else, must take a slice of the calamities. Even my native Oklahoma (The Garden of Eden of the West) has a cyclone; Kansas, while blessed with its grasshoppers, must endure its politicians; New York, with its splendor, has its Wall Street, and Washington, the world's most beautiful city, has its lobbyists.

So every human, and every place, is equal after all.

March 13, 1933

★ ★ ★

Here in London there was none of that habeas corpus and suspended sentence, or appealing it when you commit a crime. You just wake up surrounded by a small space. There was this case being tried where a fellow had swindled people through fake stock transactions, out of ten million dollars. They just give him fourteen years so fast it took all the Americans' breath away and all they have talked about today is English justice compared to ours.

It is the consensus of the Americans here that if it had been at home, this fellow would have gone into show business or the Senate.

January 24, 1930

K

KANSAS

Kansas, that state that is sometimes noted for its broad and narrow ideas.

May 25, 1924

★　★　★

When Kansas ain't kicking, things have got to be running about perfect.

January 24, 1934

★　★　★

The principal industry of Kansas was bootlegging.

1919

KILLERS

The fellow that kills you nowadays, why, he don't have it in for you, he don't even know you. You are not even pointed out to him till just before he bumps you off. That's all a business, done through an agency, just like any other agency. The fellow that's hiring the fellow to do the job has to pay so much and ammunition.

They can furnish killers for "Singles" or "Double Murders" or "Group." You get a rate if you want several put out of commission. It's cheaper to have it all done at once. It's very little more trouble to shoot down a group, than it is one.

June 7, 1931

L

LABOR

Coolidge solved his problem better than anybody when he said: "I am for Capital, but I am not against Labor."

In other words: "I love carrots, but I am equally fond of spinach."

March 30, 1929

★ ★ ★

Never did things look brighter for the working man, but none of us want to work. If we got to work for the money, we are just as bad off as if there was no prosperity.

December 22, 1929

Labor Leaders

Labor leaders don't do much laboring after they are able to lead.

January 21, 1928

Labor Unions

Unions are a fine thing, for they have them in every line of business. Bankers have their Association for mutual benefit, Governors have theirs, all big industries are banded together in some way.

August 6, 1933

LABOR DAY

This is Labor Day (I suppose by Act of Congress). Everything we do nowadays is either by, or against Acts of Congress.

How Congress knew anything about Labor is beyond us, but anyhow, this is Labor Day. It's a day in the big cities when men march all day and work harder than they have on any other of the 365. Even the ones that ain't working, labor on Labor Day.

September 1, 1929

179

Every holiday ought to be named 'Labor Day.' If we could ever get vacation down to where you wasn't any more tired on the day one was over than on a regular work day, it would be wonderful.

September 4, 1933

LAND

Land don't change hands by treaties. Land changes hands by arms.

October 3, 1932

We said: "Put it in land, and you can always walk on it."
We did, but no buyer would walk on it with us.

September 25, 1932

LAREDO, TEXAS

What do you think Laredo has? Hundreds of acres of onions! There was enough in one field there to change the breath of America!

Here was the great state of Texas, day-herding onions. You can never tell what a great state will come to.

May 12, 1928

LATIN AMERICA

The minute there is any trouble in any Latin-American country, that should be the tip right there for us to crawl in a hole and not even be allowed to poke our head out till it was all over—for as sure as we could see it, we would be in it, or offering advice.

We can't help it, it's just second nature with us. We mean well, but the better we mean, the worse we get in.

August 20, 1933

Here we are, a nation that is always hollering for disarmament and peace, and just because we are not smart enough to settle differences by diplomacy (because we have none), why, we are going to make it possible for somebody to exterminate the factions that we don't like.

Suppose they don't like our President and they would allow arms to be shipped into this country to arm a revolution against our Government that is in power. Boy, what a howl we would put up. But it's us doing it, so that's all right.

Here is the most humanitarian nation of the world fixing it so more people can get shot.

March 20, 1927

I was told not to drink water in these tropical countries. I had never tried their beer with ham and eggs in the morning, but I am managing to gulp it down.

However, I have heard of worse hardships.
April 16, 1931

LAW

I believe in strict observance of the Law, and as soon as I can get a policeman to tell me just what the law is, I'll observe it.
July 19, 1928

We are always saying: "Let the Law take its Course" but what we really mean is: "Let the Law take OUR Course."
February 19, 1935

Law is complications and complications are law. If everything was just plain, there wouldn't be any lawyers.
February 4, 1935

LAWYERS

Personally I don't think you can make a lawyer honest by an act of the Legislature. You got to work on his conscience. And his lack of conscience is what makes him a lawyer.
March 15, 1927

★ ★ ★

Thirty-five hundred lawyers of the American Bar Association are in California for their annual convention. They are here, they say, to save the Constitution and to preserve States' Rights.

What they ought to be here for, and what would make their convention immortal, is to kick the crooks out of their profession.
July 14, 1935

★ ★ ★

If it wasn't for Wills, lawyers would have to go to work at an essential employment.

There is only one way you can beat a lawyer in a death case—that is to die with nothing; then you can't get a lawyer within 10 miles of your house.
May 31, 1925

★ ★ ★

Thousands of students just graduated all over the country in Law. All trained to get a guilty man out on a technicality and an innocent one in on their opposing lawyer's mistake. This is the hey-

day of the shyster lawyer, and they defend each other for half rates.
June 15, 1931

★   ★   ★

Two lawyers can make a scandal out of anything they have anything to do with.
November 18, 1928

LEADERSHIP

Being leader of any country during the last two years was just like arriving at the railroad crossing as the stop signal was against you. There is nothing you can do but just stand and wait till somebody switches something over which you have no control.

I don't suppose there is a leader today, who, if he had known what was in store for him, wouldn't have thrown the job right back in your face when offered it. It's just an off-season for leaders.
September 6, 1931

Moral Leadership

There is one line of bunk that this country falls for, and always has: "We are looking to America for leadership during this Conference; she has a great moral responsibility!"

And we, like saps, just eat it up. Our delegates swell out their chests and really believe that the world is just hanging by a thread and the American delegates control that thread.
June 22, 1933

★   ★   ★

Europe has got a thing that America always falls for, and that's when they tell us they want our moral leadership!

It's almost like telling an old man he's got sex appeal.
January 27, 1935

★   ★   ★

Here we go again! America is running true to form, fixing some other country's business for 'em just as we always do. We mean well, but will wind up in wrong as usual.

When some nation wants us to help 'em out, they use the same old "gag," that we should exert our "Moral Leadership" and, like a yap, we believe it when as a matter of truth, no nation wants any other nation exerting "Moral Leadership" over 'em, even if they had one.

If we ever pass out as a great nation we ought to put on our tombstone: "America died from a delusion that she had Moral Leadership."
June 22, 1931

LEAGUE OF NATIONS

The League of Nations is just as clear as those income tax forms. Everybody is for something to prevent war, but they are afraid it is like Prohibition—it don't prohibit anything. If they ever have another war, let's have it understood before they start what each nation wants at the finish.

1919

★   ★   ★

France says they would have more confidence in this League if they would slip a couple of nations in between them and Germany.

1919

★   ★   ★

You thought the League of Nations was to prevent wars? Yes, and you thought the 18th Amendment was to prevent drinking, too? Oh, what's the use of arguing with a fellow like you?

January 31, 1926

★   ★   ★

All those member nations claim they were fighting for freedom, but of course, a little more land would make a little more freedom. America didn't know till they got over there that those nations have had a disease for years called "the Gim-mes."

1919

★   ★   ★

The League of Nations told Japan to get out of Manchuria and suggested that wet nursing of it be turned over to America or Russia. Neither one belongs to the League.

That's like a policeman turning a desperate criminal over to a couple of civilians and telling 'em: "Here. You watch this fellow. I am busy."

February 12, 1933

LEAGUE OF WOMEN VOTERS

The League of Women Voters are here in convention, demanding these planks in the next Platform: Democratic women want birth control for Republicans, and Republican women want equal corruption for both sexes.

April 23, 1928

LEGISLATION

All legislation is put through by the aid of swaps and trades. They are just a lot of horse traders: "You help me put over my new

Post Office and I will help you get your creek widened!"
July 1, 1928

LEXINGTON, KENTUCKY

I have seen today some of the most beautiful stock farms in America around Lexington, Kentucky. These old birds here sure know how to live. They know how to scramble a bran mash for a horse and a corn mash for a human that just about excels any hospitality in America.
January 15, 1927

LIBERAL

A Liberal is a man who wants to use his own ideas on things in preference to generations who, he knows, know more than he does.
February 4, 1923

I can remember way back when a Liberal was one who was generous with his own money.
Notes

LIBERALISM

Everything, even in religion, seems to have a trend to the liberal nowadays. Dr. Percy Grant, the Episcopalian minister, wants to go over the Bible and kinder brighten it up in spots where it appears to him to drag a little.
February 4, 1923

LIBERTY

Liberty don't work as good in practice as it does in speeches.
November 6, 1926

What might be one group's "Liberty" might be another group's poison. I guess absolute "Liberty" couldn't mean anything else but that anybody can do anything they want to do any time they want to. Well, any half-wit can tell that wouldn't work.

So the question rises: How much Liberty can you get and get away with? Well, you can get no more Liberty than you give! That's my definition, but you have perfect Liberty to work out your own.
September 30, 1934

LINCOLN, ABRAHAM

Papers today say: "What would Lincoln do today?"

Well, in the first place he wouldn't chop any wood. He would trade his axe in on a Ford. Being a Republican, he would vote the Democratic ticket. Being in sympathy with the underdog, he would be classed as a radical Progressive. Having a sense of humor, he would be called eccentric.

February 12, 1934

I was born at our old ranch; it was a two story log house, but on the back we had three rooms made of frame. Just before my birth, my mother had them remove her into the log part of the house. She wanted me to be born in a log house. She had read the life of Lincoln. So I got the log house end of it o.k. All I need now is the other qualifications.

Notes

If Abe Lincoln from Illinois was resurrected and was to fill an unexpired term, and he still insisted he was a Republican, there would be a Party vote against him.

December 26, 1926

LINDBERGH, CHARLES A.

Of all the things that Lindbergh's great feat demonstrated, the greatest was to show us that a person could still get the entire front pages without murdering anybody.

May 22, 1927

LIQUOR

You know, in the old days you had to be born courageous, but now they bottle courage. You take one dram of this White Mule and you go out and meet a street car head on purposely.

June 8, 1930

The minute a thing is high-priced, you immediately create a desire for it. You give away liquor tomorrow like water and the novelty of being drunk would be over in a week, and nobody would touch the stuff.

January 6, 1929

LOBBYISTS

A Lobbyist is a person that is supposed to help a politician to make up his mind, not only help him, but pay him.

August 25, 1929

Lobbyists have more offices in Washington than the President. You see, the President only tells Congress what they should do. Lobbyists tell 'em what they will do.

October 20, 1929

Can't Congress do anything that's not on a lobbyist's list?
They can, but they never have.

October 20, 1929

Well, why don't these lobbyists run for the Senate?
Would you get out of the driver's seat to go down and pull with the other horses?

October 20, 1929

Putting a lobbyist out of business is like a hired hand trying to fire his boss.

April 5, 1935

★ ★ ★

Any person that can't spot a propagandist or lobbyist a mile away, must be a person so blind that they still think toupees are deceptive, and can't tell a hotel detective from a guest.

September 29, 1929

LOS ANGELES, CALIFORNIA

Los Angeles, the city of the Lost Angels, the exclusive home of the Eighth Art, the ultimate home of the Performer and the Reformer.

January 21, 1928

★ ★ ★

The city of Los Angeles annexes more territory than Georgia and Cuba, combined. If that state line hadn't stopped us, we would have had Phoenix, Arizona.

May 29, 1926

★ ★ ★

It's a little foggy here in Los Angeles, but that's very unusual here in California. We seldom have fog—pardon me while I grin.

January 21, 1928

Headline in the papers says: "Crooks from Other Cities are Coming to Los Angeles."

The landlords there are going to have competition.

1920

★   ★   ★

You give a Los Angelician five more gallons of gas, two hot dogs, a bottle of red soda pop, and somebody to gab to, and you have just about covered his national diet.

July 17, 1927

LOUISIANA PURCHASE

There may be some doubt about the Louisiana Purchase being a mistake, but when Seward in '68 bought Alaska for $7,000,000 he even made up for what we overpaid the Indians for Manhattan Island.

August 13, 1935

M

MACHINES

Machinery is just doing fine. If it can't kill you, it will put you out of work.

December 27, 1932

MANKIND

No man is great if he thinks he is.

March 1, 1929

★   ★   ★

There is still a lot of monkey in us. Throw anything you want to into our cage and we will give it serious consideration.

June 25, 1935

★   ★   ★

It just looks like everything is doing fine but humans. Animals are having a great year, grass was never higher, flowers were never more in bloom, trees are throwing out an abundance of shade for us to loaf under.

Everything the Lord has had a hand in is doing great, but the minute you notice anything that is in any way under the supervision of man, why it's cockeyed.

April 17, 1932

MARRIAGE

It should cost as much to get married as it costs to get divorced. Make it look like marriage is worth as much as divorce, even if it ain't.

That would also make the preachers financially independent like it has the lawyers.

May 15, 1928

The other day they repealed a law here in California where you used to have to give three days notice when you wanted to get married. Well, they did away with that. It was longer than most marriages in California was lasting.

Now you don't have to file any intention of marriage at all. In fact, you don't even have to give your right name, according to this new law. You just pay a small amusement tax, is all.

May 19, 1935

MARX, KARL

Karl Marx wrote for the dissatisfied, and the dissatisfied is the fellow who don't want to do any manual labor. He always wants to figure out where he and his friends can get somebody dividing with them.

December 4, 1926

MASS PRODUCTION

If the other fellow sells cheaper than you, it is called "dumping." 'Course, if you sell cheaper than him, that's "Mass Production."

March 5, 1932

MEDICAL CARE

All doctors should make enough out of those who are well able to pay, to be able to do all work for the poor free. That is one thing that a poor person should never be even expected to pay for, is medical attention, and not from an organized charity, but from our best doctors. Your doctor bill should be paid like your income tax, according to what you have.

There is nothing that keeps poor people poor as much as paying doctors' bills. It always wipes out their savings, and it's that fear of not being able to pay, that makes it ten times worse on them.

It ought to be a law, not only a custom.

July 13, 1930

MEMOIRS

There ain't nothing that breaks up homes, country and nations, like somebody publishing their memoirs.

December 23, 1934

I never saw it fail—when a man starts selling his memoirs, he is about through.

November 23, 1922

"Memoirs," that's another Cherokee word, means when you put down the good things you ought to have done and leave out the bad ones you did do.

March 12, 1932

MEMORIAL DAY

One sure certainty about our Memorial Days is that as fast as the ranks from one war thin out, the ranks from another take their place.

Prominent men may run out of Decoration Day speeches, but the world never runs out of wars. People talk peace, but men give their life's work to war.

It won't stop till there is as much brain and scientific study put to aid peace, as there is to promote war.

May 31, 1929

Just been down to the old Soldiers' Home at Sawtelle, here in California. Flags flying, old men and young, marching. This is quite a day with them.

But free room and board and a day's speeches a year ain't hardly all we promised 'em at recruiting time, but they are good sports and keep on speaking to us.

They must just pity us. They know we will have the same bologna to hand out to the next bunch to keep our investments intact (although we won't call it "investments"—we will tell them it's "Democracy").

May 30, 1930

MERGERS

We are living in an age of "Mergers" and "Combines." When your business is not doing good, you combine with something else and sell more stock. The poor little fellow, he can't combine with anything but the sheriff in case he is going broke, which he generally is. But "big business" merges with another.

March 23, 1930

We are such bargain hunters that if two things are put together, we think they must be twice as good as they were singly.

March 30, 1929

We used to think that only things of the same nature could combine, but now it's liable to be the Pennsylvania Railroad and Mennen's Borated Talcum Powder.

Why, General Motor took over Fridgidaire Iceboxes. Now what's a Buick automobile got to do with keeping the smell of onions out of the butter?

I don't know, but Wall Street must know. The stock went up.

March 23, 1930

METHODISTS

I was raised predominantly a Methodist, but I have traveled so much, mixed with so many people in all parts of the world, I don't know just what I am. I know I have never been a non-believer. But I can honestly tell you that I don't think that any one religion is *the* religion.

January 8, 1933

★   ★   ★

I was a "South Methodist." You know there is two gangs of Methodists, the North and the South and our troops down home are the "South;" the difference is that one believed in Slavery and the other didn't. That is their only fundamental difference.

There is just as much reason for some of these denominations being separate as there is for the Blondes to belong to one church, and the Brunettes to another.

The Civil War has been over for 63 years, but the churches are the only ones that haven't found it out.

August 5, 1928

★   ★   ★

Southern Methodist Conference out here passed a resolution asking Congress to exempt them from war. I don't know what claim they have over other denominations, unless it's that they are always fighting so much among themselves that two wars at once would be a hardship on 'em.

June 30, 1931

MEXICO

Being President of the United States is child's play compared to pacifying Mexico.

March 30, 1928

★   ★   ★

Outside the oil interests and Americans who want to make money out of Mexico, the rest of the world's eyes don't even know

Mexico exists. I tell you, the difference in our exchange of people with Mexico is: they send workmen here to work, while we send Americans to work Mexico!

June 27, 1925

★   ★   ★

I paid my respects to Mr. Estrada, Mexico's Secretary of State, and he got out a wonderful bottle and gave me a swig of what he called Mexican Hospitality. It was Tequila.

Then he asked me how I liked Mexico. Why, with one more swig of that, a person would even have been fond of Siberia.

May 26, 1928

★   ★   ★

I brag on Mexico. I'm always blowin' about Mexico. I like Mexico. I like the Mexicans. Folks say: "Why, Will, you know that Mexico is run all wrong!" Well, that don't make any difference to me. It's their country. Let 'em run it like they want to.

Ireland is another pet of mine. If it's run cockeyed that don't make any difference to me. I like it. And they run it.

October 14, 1934

★   ★   ★

America has a great habit of always talking about protecting American interests in some foreign country. For instance if an American is killed in Mexico, we send them a note saying: "The murderer must be punished within 24 hours and $100,000 must be paid at once to his relatives!"

Now maybe this guy wasn't worth alive over 10 cents, but we "must protect American Rights." Now suppose a Californian is killed in New York City. Why, they will never in a hundred years find out even who killed him, much less punish him. But if he was killed in Mexico, oh how his value would rise. Getting killed in Mexico is better than having an insurance.

June 28, 1925

★   ★   ★

Now in Mexico they have their fairy tales, the same as we do here. Where we are told that every boy has a chance to be President, they are taught: If my ammunition holds out, and I can get them before they get me, I not only can be President, but will!

March 24, 1929

★   ★   ★

Nature so provided that the worst part of Mexico adjoins us. It's mostly level and nothing but mesquite brush. If it hadn't been, we would have taken any good part long ago.

May 12, 1928

★ ★ ★

In Mexico, we always speak of ourselves as being from America, as though they were in Asia. You know, Mexico feels—and with some slight justification—that they are in America too. They don't feel that America ends at the Rio Grande River.

Of course they may be wrong, but they are just childish enough to feel that way.

May 19, 1928

★ ★ ★

I have no humorous cracks about Mexico being lazy. If they are any lazier than us, which I doubt, but if they are and can make a living at it, why, then I give them the credit of being the smartest nation on earth.

May 19, 1928

★ ★ ★

We are trying to make up with Mexico now—they must have struck more oil lately.

August 5, 1923

MIDWEST

When a boy is born and brought up in the Mid-West, he decides on one of two things. If he is industrious and honest and wants to work for a living, he either stays home, or goes further west.

But, if he has a bit of the sharper or an underlying current of graft in his nature, he comes east—generally New York.

Notes

MILLIONAIRES

A man can make a million dollars overnight, and he is on every front page in the morning, but it never tells who gave up the million that he got. What you got tonight that you didn't have last night must have come from somebody.

We have dozens of magazines that print success articles, but you go broke and see what you can do to get your life story published. We love to talk and read in big figures. The old boy that didn't get the breaks and couldn't make the grade—him we don't care much for.

June 1, 1930

MINNEAPOLIS, MINNESOTA

I had froze both ears in a steam-heated hotel in Minneapolis.
May 17, 1925

★   ★   ★

Minneapolis and St. Paul were born the "Twin Cities" but since birth they have grown together. Now they are locked. One can't do anything without interfering with the other. If one dances, the other wants to sit down, and if one wants to sit down the other wants to dance. What one eats don't agree with the other one. The Mississippi River is between them, but Lord, that don't stop 'em from cussing each other—the Pacific Ocean should separate them.
November 8, 1925

MISSIONARIES

Missionaries are going to reform the world whether it wants it or not.
November 8, 1924

★   ★   ★

Between our Missionaries and our oil men we are just in wrong all over the world.
February 6, 1927

★   ★   ★

There is something wrong with the Missionaries. They will save anybody if he is far enough away and don't speak our language.
March 22, 1932

MISSISSIPPI RIVER

The Mississippi up here at Davenport, Iowa, is a beautiful river. There is just as much water in it here as in St. Louis, but not as much mud. Down there it don't flow; it just oozes along with just enough water in it to keep the mud moving.
November 8, 1925

MISSOURI

There is lots of politics in Missouri. Wherever you find poor soil, you will find politics. When you see you ain't going to raise anything, you sit down at the end of the row and cuss the party in power.
January 1, 1933

MONEY

This thing called "money" has got the whole mess of econo-mists buffaloed. Money, horse racing and women are three things the boys just can't figure out.

March 7, 1935

★　★　★

If a country is good enough to make money in, it's good enough for you to become a citizen of.

March 14, 1926

★　★　★

All you can learn about is "Money will be cheaper." Cheaper than what? If a dollar is worth only 10 cents, how are you going to get your clutches on it any easier than now?

Unless they give it away, I can't see where it's going to be any big help to everybody.

September 1, 1933

MONTANA

I flew over mountains today that make Switzerland look like a prairie dog town. If we could get our mountain farmers to wear feathers in their hats and yodel, we would be as picturesque as Switzerland.

March 31, 1927

MONTE CARLO, MONACO

This Monte Carlo is a queer layout. It's the only place in the world that has practically no rural population. You either live in the city, or you don't live in Monaco. If you are out of Monte Carlo, the town, you're in France or Italy. Or, if you get too far out in the country, you're in Spain or Switzerland.

July 25, 1926

★　★　★

I went to the Monte Carlo Casino. Well, to make a fair bank-roll short, it don't take me long to learn the game quick. When I bet without a system, why, they looked at me like I was crazy. I don't know why, because I was losing just as good as they were.

July 25, 1926

★　★　★

Monte Carlo has the right idea. Fix a game so you are going to get people's money, but the people don't know you are getting it. A fellow can always get over losing money in a game of chance, but he seems so constituted that he can never get over money thrown away to a government in taxes.

August 28, 1926

MORAL RIGHTS

I think nations talk too much about their "Moral Rights," when as a matter of fact, I don't think they have got any, any of them.

Nations are always yapping about "Honor" when, if you just read an unbiased history of all their carrying on, they just ain't got much honor.

Did you notice the fellow at a party who is always getting insulted the quickest and oftenest is really, if you know him, a guy that you would think it wouldn't be possible to insult at all.

May 26, 1928

MOTHERS

I doubt if a charging elephant, or a rhino, is as determined or hard to check as a socially ambitious mother.

May 10, 1932

My own mother died when I was ten years old. The mother I know the most about is the mother of our little group. She has been for twenty-two years trying to raise to maturity four children, three by birth and one by marriage.

While she hasn't done a good job, the poor soul has done all that a mortal human could do with the material she has had to work with.

May 11, 1930

★   ★   ★

Mothers are the only race of people that speak the same tongue. A mother in Manchuria could converse with a mother in Nebraska and never miss a word.

May 11, 1930

MOTHER'S DAY

As I write this, it is Mother's Day. You know, a mother is the only thing so constituted that they possess eternal love under any and all circumstances.

Now I was telling that to my wife and I said, you know, Betty, a mother and a dog is the only two things that has eternal love, no matter how you treat them—and my wife made me cut the dog out. So I can't use the dog, but my wife runs this outfit.

May 12, 1935

Mother's Day, it's a beautiful thought, but it's somebody's hurtin' conscience that thought of the idea. It was someone who had neglected their mother for years, and then they figured out: I got to do something about Momma. And knowing Momma that was easy, they figured, "We'll give her a day, and it will be all right with Momma."

Give her a day, and then in return Momma gives you the other 364. See?

May 12, 1935

MOTION PICTURES

The Motion Picture Code people say: "They got to be cleaner!"

The exhibitors say: "If you get them too clean, nobody is interested in them!"

September 1928

The novelists say: "What's the use of selling them a story? They don't make the story they buy."

The scenario staff says: "It reads good, but it won't photograph."

September 1928

★   ★   ★

The so-called intellectual says: "Give us something worthwhile in the movies that we can think about."

The regular movie fan says: "Give us something to see, never mind think about. If we wanted to think, we wouldn't go to the movies."

September 1928

★   ★   ★

We try to make moving pictures as good as we can. Bad pictures are not made with a premeditated design. It looks to you sometimes we must have purposely made 'em that way, but honest, we don't. A bad picture is an accident, and a good one is a miracle.

February 11, 1934

Academy of Motion Picture Arts and Sciences Awards

This is the day when the Academy of Motion Picture Arts and Sciences hands out those little statues. They are lovely things. They were originally designed for prizes at a nudist colony's bazaar—but they didn't take 'em. They must be terribly artistic for nobody has any idea what it is. It represents the triumph of nothingness over the stupendousness of zero.

March 18, 1934

You'll see great acting tonight, greater than you will see on the screen. We'll all cheer when somebody gets a prize that everyone of us in the house knows should be ours.

Yet we'll smile and take it—boy, that's acting!
March 18, 1934

Movie Producers

Producers decided to make fewer and worse pictures. They may make fewer, but they will never make worse ones.
Notes

Movie Stars

Lots of movie stars marry their leading lady, but the trouble is they marry every one they make a picture with.
April 19, 1925

A movie star is one person that can't be over-paid, that is, not for long. There is no other business in the world where the company you work for knows just to a penny just what you are worth to them.

Greta Garbo don't get that dough because she is a long tall Swede, she drags it into a box office and they know just how much she dragged in. So they are all worth what they can get. There comes a time soon enough in their lives when they don't get it.
March 19, 1933

The other night, at a benefit, back stage, I introduced a dozen screen friends to each other and then had them say, "Why, Will, we used to be married to each other!"

I just got discouraged and quit trying to be sociable and introduce anybody.
December 16, 1923

An actor is a fellow that just has a little more monkey in him than the fellow that can't act.
July 1, 1934

★   ★   ★

If the public judges the movie people by some of the interviews that appear in print, they must wonder how they have ever kept out of the asylum. If the President of the United States had as silly things written about him as appears in movie magazines and write-ups about movie people, he would be impeached in three months.
August 30, 1925

Movie Studios

The off-colored or risque pictures haven't been going so good as they used to. It isn't that tastes are improving, it is that there is nothing new they could shock folks with.

April 24, 1934

★　★　★

I been working in movies now for 15 years, off and on, and the pictures are about the same. Somebody will make a high-brow one that will play to about $1.80 and then some plain old country picture will come along and gross millions.

Maybe it will be just about what was made in the silent movies years ago, with the exception of having noise in it.

April 24, 1934

Movie Theater Owners

We got the moving picture theater owners out here on a big convention. Their convention informed the producers that about everything in the way of sex had been produced and that the audiences didn't care to see it over again. They suggested that for a change they thought the audiences would like to see just an old-fashioned movie.

April 11, 1934

Movie Titles

They will film the Lord's Supper, and when it's made figure that that is not a good release title and not catchy enough, so it will be released under the heading, "A Red Hot Meal" or "The Gastronomical Orgy."

October 13, 1929

★　★　★

They just can't think up enough suggestive titles to go around. They bring big writers out from New York just thinking all the time on titles that will lead you to expect you are going to see four of the most prominent Commandments broken, right before your eyes.

May 17, 1931

Movie Violence

Between "subtlety" and gangster films, we have run the old cowboy trying to save the sheriff's daughter right back to the dairy farm. No modern child would want to learn how to shoot a 45 Colt. He wants to know how to mow 'em down with the old Browning machine gun.

But we will live through it and come out with something worse. We always do.

May 17, 1931

MOUNTAINEERING

I never could see much percentage in that mountain climbing thing. Any time I want to do any cliff hopping, I'm going to let a goat do it for me. Any time I go up a mountainside, I'm not going to follow some guide. I'm going to go up after the surveyors have built a two way road.

February 18, 1934

MURDER

In the morning newspaper there will always be the fellow in the home town that has just killed his wife and then attempted to kill himself. That brings up another odd coincidence. Why is it that a person that is going to kill somebody else along with himself, why is it they never miss the other party but they are such poor shots on themselves.

You would think as close as they are to themselves that they couldn't miss. But they most generally do.

November 23, 1930

★ ★ ★

In this trial where a couple killed the woman's husband, both parties claim they were tempted by the other. Well, after looking at pictures of both of them, I have decided that neither one had much resisting power in the first place.

May 6, 1927

★ ★ ★

I just give up reading murders. You no more than get a few details of one murder, than the afternoon paper brings you news of another.

The best read man in the country couldn't tell you who killed who last week.

June 18, 1934

MUSIC CRITIC

Our country may be short of work, short of ready cash, but by golly we still breed real patriots. Right here in Beverly Hills (the heart of art) in the exclusive Beverly Wilshire Hotel, some friend of the common man sneaked in and stole six saxophones, four clarinets, a bull fiddle and a base drum.

Our town constable is looking for the thief to prosecute him. The people are looking for the thief to reward him.

March 28, 1933

★ ★ ★

A Jersey woman shot a man that wanted to organize a band. She claimed it made too much noise.

Don't sentence her, Judge! Give her more ammunition. She's not a culprit. She's a Joan of Arc.

May 7, 1930

MUSSOLINI, BENITO

With Mussolini, you don't have to pay a poll tax to vote in Italy, you know, but nobody votes.

April 7, 1935

Mussolini is raising five hundred thousand children every year and needs somewhere to stake 'em out. He will have to have some new land somewhere sometimes. So that means that Italy sooner or later has got to go out and fight for it.

They won't do it now because this guy is too wise, but he will when he thinks they are ready.

August 26, 1926

★ ★ ★

Mussolini just committed Italy to a 60 year plan!

Smart guy, that Mussolini. He laid out a plan where, if it proved at the end that it wouldn't work, they couldn't find him.

March 19, 1934

★ ★ ★

That Mussolini is a card! Yesterday he interviewed ninety-two mothers with a gross total of 1,288 children, which divides out to about fourteen head per each. While our great slogan for the perpetuation of civilization was "a car in every garage!" Mussolini's was "A baby in every arm!"

He knows no nation ever become great on garages. You can't win a war with a Ford sedan, or repel an invasion with a Chevrolet coup.

Those other dictators think they are doing some "dictating" when they announce a budget quota. But when you start laying out a maternity quota for the women, then you are really in the dictating business.

December 20, 1933

N

NATIONAL ANTHEM

It will take America two more wars to learn the words to our national anthem.

June 10, 1924

NATIONAL DEBT

Hold on to your seats: Interest on the Public Debt is $731 Million and we owe billions. That's where all the money goes we pay in taxes, most of it goes to pay Interest on money we owe.

Let's sell off enough of this country to somebody and pay off all National Debts, then the taxes wouldn't be nearly as much. The Democrats will agree to peddle Texas and Florida. And I am certain the Republicans will let Massachusetts and Rhode Island go.

December 16, 1928

NATIONAL SECURITY

Brothers, geography has been mighty good to us. It's wonderful to pay honor to Washington and Lincoln, but I want to tell you we ought to lay out one day a year for the old boy that laid out the location of this country. I don't know who he was, but boy, he was a sage, that bird was.

April 6, 1930

NATIONS

Nations are a lot like women with their babies. Each thinks that theirs is the best.

April 27, 1933

No nation can tell another nation how little it shall protect itself.

June 14, 1927

Nations are just like individuals. Loan them money and you lose their friendship.

January 11, 1925

You see, nations will give up their lives (even cheer about it). They will give up their money in order to give up their lives, but to ask one to give up their trade to prevent a war, well, that has never been done.

October 15, 1933

You know, nations have got a funny sense of humor, ain't they? English royalty waited till they had all married Germans, then they went to war with 'em. And Germans all married Russians and then they fought.

October 31, 1933

NATURAL RESOURCES

Americans have been getting away pretty soft up to now. Every time we needed anything, why, it was growing right under our nose. Every natural resource in the world, we had it.

But with them getting less and our national debt getting more, there will have to be some work going on in this country some day!

January 10, 1926

The Lord has sure been good to us. Now what are we doing to warrant that good luck any more than any other nation? Just how long is that going to last? Now the way we are acting, the Lord is liable to turn on us any minute; and even if He don't, our good fortune can't possible last any longer than our natural resources.

June 2, 1928

We are going at top speed and we are using up all our natural resources as fast as we can. If we want to build something out of wood, all we got to do is go and cut down a tree and build it. Suppose we couldn't build something out of wood till we found a tree that we had purposely planted. Say, we would never get it built. Suppose we didn't have any coal and had to ship it in. If we want any more oil we bore a well and get some.

But when our resources run out, if we can still be ahead of other nations, then will be the time to brag; then we can show whether we are really superior.

June 2, 1928

NEVADA

Nevada, that's a great state. When you feel that the people around you are taking too much care of your private business, why move to Nevada. It's freedom's last stand in America. Yet they don't do one thing that other states don't do. Only they leave the front door open.

You can get a divorce without lying, a drink without whispering, and a bet on a game of chance without breaking even a promise.

August 31, 1930

NEW ENGLAND

You can tell a New England delegate to the Republican Convention; he will be eating a box lunch in the lobby, which he brought from home.

June 10, 1924

★   ★   ★

New England is lovely and we all have a warm spot in our hearts for New England. Here is where all of our learning and culture and everything—whatever we got—comes from.

June 15, 1930

★   ★   ★

Every house in New England is where some old Revolutionary man slept, every one of them.

Some of them old generals must have done nothing but sleep. They must have slept in one house, then got up and moved over and slept in another.

June 15, 1930

NEW YEAR

Why don't they ask me what the New Year has in hiding for me? I want to tell you that it don't look too rosy from where I am sitting. With every public man we have elected doing comedy, I tell you, I don't see much of a chance for a comedian to make a living.

I'm just on the verge of going to work. They can do more funny things naturally than I can think of to do purposely.

January 13, 1924

★   ★   ★

Here it is, a New Year. We got to make some resolutions, as

well as interest and tax payments in this joyful season.

It's the start of a New Year of trials and tribulations, and if everybody that does anything gets caught, it will be mostly trials.

January 4, 1931

NEW YORK

I see where the Governor of New York wants some more public parks. There is no place to throw Sunday newspapers and egg shells. He claims that there are several million people in New York who have nowhere to get mosquitos or fleas on them.

July 5, 1925

New York City

There was a Moral Crusade on in New York City.

But it lasted only two days.

March 29, 1925

Never a day passes in New York City without some innocent bystander being shot. You just stand around this town long enough, and be innocent, and somebody is going to shoot you.

One day there was four innocent people shot here. That's the best shooting ever done in this town. Hard to find four innocent people in New York.

May 31, 1923

I see where the Mayor called a committee of one hundred to stop small graft. He said it had grown to such proportion that it was interfering with large graft, and that couldn't be allowed in New York.

Notes

We had quite a panic here the other day in New York, in the subway. Several people were trampled on and crushed. The cause of the trouble was that someone hollered out: "Here is a vacant seat!"

May 31, 1925

New York shows you that 25 years ago they still had a few street cars pulled by horses, but they were up on the level of the ground and were very unsanitary—bad air and everything. Now it shows you how you can be in a nice tunnel under the ground where the air is good. You know it's good because there have been hundreds using it before you got a hold of it.

June 17, 1923

New York, that city from which no weary traveler returns without drawing again on the home town bank.

May 25, 1924

★ ★ ★

New York is getting like Paris. Its supposed devilment is its biggest advertisement. The rest of the country drops in here and thinks if they don't stay up till four A.M., that New Yorkers will think they are Yokels, when as a matter of fact, New Yorkers have been in bed so long they don't know what the other half is doing.

New York lives off the out-of-towner trying to make New York think he is quite a fellow.

January 13, 1929

★ ★ ★

I see where an Alderman in New York City was robbed.

I thought it was an unwritten law that crooks did not bother each other.

January 16, 1926

★ ★ ★

I see where New York City is going to make their night clubs close at 3 in the morning and the people there are kicking about it.

Well, I say, they ought to close 'em. Anybody that can't get drunk by 3 A.M. ain't trying.

1926

★ ★ ★

New York is so situated that anything you want, you can get in the very block you live in. If you want to be robbed, there is a robber living in your block; if you want to be murdered, you don't have to leave your apartment house; if you want Pastrami or Gefillter Fish, there is a delicatessen every other door; if it's feminine excitement you crave, your neighbor's wife will accommodate you.

Notes

★ ★ ★

There is only one trouble with New York, and that is it is the most self-centered place in the world, outside an Englishman's London.

It feels like it is the biggest place in the world and ought to run everything, but it just don't.

October 29, 1927

★ ★ ★

The Ku Klux Klan couldn't get much of a footing in New York. If there was some man they wanted to take out and tar and feather, they wouldn't know where he lived. People move so often here, their own folks don't know where they live.

And even if they found out, the elevator man in the apartment building wouldn't let 'em up.

December 31, 1922

NEWSPAPERS

All I know is just what I read in the papers.

The New York Times advertises "All The News That's Fit To Print." I believe the news that's NOT fit to print is what makes the newspapers.

August 2, 1925

The old newspaper in the morning is my breakfast. 'Course I don't entirely depend on it. I like it accompanied by some ham and eggs and a few biscuits, a series of cups of coffee, a few wheat cakes to help get your mind off the editorials.

November 27, 1927

You have to read your newspaper in the morning to find out who you're sore at. I don't know who I am sore at. I ain't sore at nobody but when I get my newspaper in the morning, I'll have it in for somebody.

January 27, 1935

Good papers will always last, and tabloids will continue to do a big business for those that can't read.

May 10, 1931

In New York I spoke for the Newspaper Publishers Association. That's a gang that gathers in from all over the country once a year to help better each other's conditions, then go home and write editorials against unionism. Not all of 'em, but some do.

May 10, 1931

Everything in the world, and everyone in the world that is worth while, has been photographed. We know how they look.

The Police Gazette was the originator of it. They used to print actresses' and chorus girls' pictures in tights and people thought it was terrible. Now our newspapers have taken the tights off them and people think it's artistic.

December 21, 1924

Today excitement is everywhere. Nations furnish the news nowadays and not just society and crooks. So let's all read the newspapers and be merry, for tomorrow the paper may not have enough ads to come out.

March 6, 1932

I tell you, you got to be an awful careful and close reader to see much that is much, nowadays. You got to wade through many a gruelling murder, a few ransoms, a bevy of kidnappings, and auto deaths till they read like a telephone directory.

But every once in a while you run onto some little item that's sorter put in to keep the reader from becoming blood soaked.

June 17, 1934

O

OCEAN FRONTAGE

I have been putting what little money I had in ocean frontage, for the sole reason that there was only so much of it and no more, and that they wasn't making any more.
April 13, 1930

OHIO

Ohio claims they was due a President as they haven't had one since Taft.

But look at the United States; it hasn't had one since Lincoln!
1920

OIL

The difference between good times and bad times is gasoline, and what goes with it.
March 3, 1935

★　★　★

At the hearing in Washington, all the big oil men were there, and that, of course, meant a big poker game. Any time two oil men meet, they don't open a filling station, they open a poker game. Then an oil man never travels without his big lawyer, and in another room the lawyers have a crap game.

In the poker game for the first time it was all cash on the table, no checks. They didn't trust each other. That's their new code.

The lawyers used the same old code—cash. They had never trusted each other.
August 20, 1933

★　★　★

John D. Rockefeller says: "Love is the greatest thing in the world."

You take a few words of affection and try and trade them to him for a few gallons of oil, and you will discover just how great love is.

January 27, 1924

OKLAHOMA

What a great territory we had before we struck oil and Republicans, followed by mortgages, foreclosures and impeachments.

September 18, 1928

★　★　★

There is a good deal in the paper about giving my native state of Oklahoma back to the Indians. Now I am a Cherokee and very proud of it, but I doubt if you can get them to accept it—not in its present state.

When the white folks come in and took Oklahoma from us, they spoiled a happy hunting ground.

January 27, 1924

★　★　★

I can remember as a kid the payment we had when the Government paid out the money to the Cherokees for the Cherokee Strip. We had it for hunting grounds, but we never knew enough to hunt oil on it. I think the Government only gave us about a dollar an acre for it. There was something over three million dollars as there was that many acres and we got about $320 apiece.

The Cherokees are supposed to be the highest civilized tribe there is and yet, that's all we ever got in all our lifetime and we sold a fortune in oil and wonderful agricultural land to get that little $320 apiece.

Yet there was the Osages lived right by us, and they get that much before breakfast every morning, and they are supposed to be uncivilized.

May 4, 1930

★　★　★

No wonder comedians come from Oklahoma. Did you read our Constitution? It says: "A Governor is to be duly elected and seated and serve till duly found out and unseated."

It's the one state where a Lieutenant Governor always gets a break—if you can call it that.

March 21, 1929

★　★　★

Oklahoma and Texas have an original primary system. They always have so many seeking office that the first primary is only to find out how many are desirous of living off the state. The second primary is to eliminate 50 per cent of these. The third is to get rid of half of what is left. The fourth is to eliminate any good man or woman that might have crept in by mistake.

Now you have just politicians left, so the fifth primary is to leave in the two worst ones and they run it off against each other.

July 30, 1930

★ ★ ★

Our new Governor is going to help out Oklahoma's unemployment problem by not releasing any more prisoners. If we had everybody back in jail that was in, and that ought to be in, why, we would have to borrow hands from other states.

January 13, 1931

OLYMPIC GAMES

Jesse Owens breaks world records as easy as the rest of us break Commandments.

June 12, 1935

★ ★ ★

I see where we are holding the American Olympic trials. Nearly every great runner and jumper is here.

Nearly every state has sent one or more athletes, yet in the big games that's held in Washington every year, not a single state seems to be able to send a statesman.

June 22, 1934

★ ★ ★

I begin to think this athletic racket is a pretty tough thing, at that. There is about as many disappointments as successes. And you can't just let it go and make up for it at the next meet. The next Olympics is four years away and four years is a long time in an athlete's career.

I think us fellows that can't do anything are just as well off. We are never disappointed.

August 7, 1932

★ ★ ★

Only test of endurance at the opening of the Olympic Games was a 10,000 meter prayer and speech. A man with a short prayer and speech could get a booking for life just at these international events.

July 31, 1932

OPTIMISM

I must tell you the past year was a year of "under-and over-estimation."

Nothing was guessed right all year. Optimism was overrated and pessimism was underrated.

February 8, 1931

★   ★   ★

My idea of an optimist is a near-sighted man in a five dollar seat at the big prizefight.

September 14, 1927

ORANGES

I would not have left California, but I do love a No. 1 good California orange. So I am going back to New York to get them.

I had survived for a whole year on seconds.

May 25, 1924

ORIENT

The biggest difference between the Oriental and the Occidental is that one looks into the past, where they know what's happened, the other looks into the future where they don't know any more what's going to happen than a Weather Bureau Man.

April 2, 1932

P

PACIFIC OCEAN

We say we have to have Hawaii to protect the Pacific. Why don't we have to have the Azores to protect the Atlantic?

May 1, 1932

★　★　★

We had some terrible weather. One whole 24 hours we only made 50 miles—and most of that was up and down.

March 5, 1932

★　★　★

There ought to be a law against making an ocean this wide.

December 2, 1931

PACIFISTS

I've been reading all day in the papers about all these bright young boys and girls marching—marching to keep from going to war.

These students learning to march in these Peace Parades, that would give them just about the training we give our soldiers in a regular war. They'll be just about ready for it then.

April 14, 1935

PALM SPRINGS, CALIFORNIA

They advertise this place: "If you are troubled with investigations and Republicans, come to Palm Springs for a tan that when you get home they can't tell who you are."

May 7, 1931

PANAMA CANAL

A bunch of Congressmen landed in New York from the Panama

213

Canal, where they had been at Government expense, I guess to see if it really connected the two oceans, or was it just propaganda.
April 7, 1929

PAN AMERICAN DAY

I see where tomorrow is Pan-American Day. We are celebrating it by rushing two cruisers to Nicaragua.
April 13, 1931

★   ★   ★

The best thing to do about these countries is to get out, let 'em alone then sell things cheaper and better than any other nation. Then we don't have to worry about relations and goodwill.
April 13, 1931

PARACHUTES

I never forget the first time I put on one of those parachutes. I asked: What do you do if . . . ?

"Oh, you just jump, count to five, and then reach for this ring at your left side and pull. The idea is that the ring is over your heart and you would always remember your heart and reach there to find the ring."

Well, I told them: "If I ever jumped and reached for where my heart is, I will choke myself to death."
December 25, 1927

★   ★   ★

I wish there was some kind of parachute invented to use in automobile accidents. The only thing they have ever invented when it looks like an automobile crash, is to throw both hands over your eyes and scream.
December 25, 1927

PARDONS, CRIMINAL

In a Los Angeles bank robbery last week, two were killed and four captured. Well, I wish you could read the crime and jail records of those six men. They had been paroled from every institution in the state at least once a month for the last fifteen years. They wasn't prisoners; they were traveling men, making hotels out of jails, and that's not an unusual case in any state.
August 31, 1932

★   ★   ★

Pardoning has been one industry that hasn't been hit by recession.
August 31, 1932

PARENTS

Take the Chinese. Parents are a tradition with them and not just a means of arriving on earth.

April 2, 1932

PARKING

Politics ain't worrying this country one-tenth as much as finding a parking space.

January 6, 1924

PEACE

I have a scheme for stopping war. It's this—no nation is allowed to enter a war till they have paid for the last one.

August 29, 1928

Peace is kinder like prosperity. There is mighty few nations that can stand it.

November 12, 1930

★　★　★

If we pulled together as much to put over a siege of peace as we do a spell of war, we would be sitting pretty. But we can hardly wait for a war to end to start taking it out on each other.

November 12, 1930

★　★　★

I have a plan that will stop all wars. When you can't agree with your neighbor, you move away; or with your wife, she either shoots you or moves away from you. Now that's my plan—move nations away from each other. Take France and Germany, they never can agree with each other. Take France and trade places with Japan. Let Japan live there by Germany. They may fight, but at least it would be something new.

1923

★　★　★

The greatest contribution to peace in the world would be an international clause: "Any nation can have a nice local revolution, any time it sees fit without outside aid or advice from America or England."

August 20, 1933

PEACE CONFERENCE

The nations in this world that get along and never have any

trouble are the ones that never meet in conference at all.
July 27, 1930

The first few days of the Peace Conference they are just complimenting each other. Wait till they go to dividing up something.
1919

At this Peace Conference there are ten nations there but only four are speaking to each other.
191923

I have often said it is cheaper for America to go to war than it is for us to confer with anybody. It's funny, but we can talk our heads off until it comes to a time when it means something and then we are as dumb as an oyster.
February 1, 1925

★   ★   ★

Remember that the more nations you create, the more chances you have of war. That's self-disintegration of small nations.
October 2, 1926

PEACE TREATY

You know, these so-called peace treaties are a funny thing. You ask 'em: "Does it prevent war?"

"No!"

"Does it ensure peace?"

"No!"

"Is it for anything?"

"No!"

"Is it against anything?"

"No!"

I think the whole thing is just to find out if we can write.
January 8, 1929

★   ★   ★

You can't get nothing without trying, and if no effort is made toward peace, why, we can't expect any.
October 20, 1929

PEDESTRIANS

I represent what is left of a vanishing race, and that is the pedestrian. While traffic officers have been directing traffic in the big cities, I know more about it than they do—I have been dodging it. That I am able to be still here, I owe to a keen eye and a nimble pair of legs.

But I know they'll get me some day. I am not as young as I used to be and they are missing me closer every day.

1923

PERSONAL

When *The New York Times* started negotiations for me to write and tell America's secrets during the war, well, as we had none, there was no demand from Washington for me to keep them.

October 21, 1923

Owing to this Wall Street boom only having reached us by newspaper reports, I been buying some fifty-cent blue working shirts, and you know, I found out something. They haven't got any pins in 'em. No, sir, they are made so solid they don't have to pin 'em up till you get 'em home.

Pins in shirts have caused more profanity than putting in golf has.

August 26, 1932

I can applaud a winner as loud as anybody, but somehow a loser appeals to me.

October 9, 1934

I am just an old country boy in a big town, trying to get along. I've been eating pretty regular and the reason I have been is because I've stayed an old country boy.

August 30, 1924

I sure used to envy General Grant and Jesse James when they had smokeless cigars named after 'em, but here I am, sitting in the brand new, most up-to-date hotel in the Southwest, the Will Rogers Hotel in Claremore, Oklahoma.

I know now how proud Christopher Columbus must have felt when he heard they had named Columbus, Ohio, after him.

February 16, 1930

PHILADELPHIA, PENNSYLVANIA

Philadelphia is trying to raise money to advertise itself and become known outside of somnambulistic circles.

May 19, 1929

I have been in old Philadelphia for a couple of weeks and you would be surprised at the life the old Girl is showing. It's been fairly well established that Washington slept here in not only one, but various beds.

Washington crossed the Delaware (with everybody rowing but him) somewhere near here (wherever the Delaware is). I don't remember whether he crossed it to get to, or away from Philadelphia.

May 19, 1929

★   ★   ★

The old Liberty Bell is here in Philadelphia; in fact I think the Constitution in its original form (without Amendments) was cooked up and signed here. The place is practically saturated with our early scandal.

May 19, 1929

★   ★   ★

Philadelphia, it's a great old town, in a great old state, the cradle of political corruption.

May 19, 1929

PHILIPPINE ISLANDS

I did want to meet Aguinaldo, the Philippine revolutionary leader. I have always been an admirer of that old hombre. We used to call him a bandit. Any man is a bandit if he is fighting opposite you and licking you most of the time; but if you are fighting against him, why, that's patriotism.

The difference between a bandit and a patriot, is a good press agent.

April 30, 1932

PHILOSOPHY

It's a great world, even if you are just looking at it for comedy purposes.

January 28, 1932

★   ★   ★

The Chinese think that what you have never had and never been used to, you will never miss. We think what we haven't got we ought to have, and will miss if we don't get it.

April 2, 1932

★   ★   ★

We are always yapping about the "Good Old Days," and how we look away back and enjoy it, but I tell you, there is a lot of hooey to it.

There is a whole lot of all our past lives that wasn't so hot.

September 2, 1934

★   ★   ★

It's great to be great, but it's greater to be human.

February 28, 1930

★   ★   ★

If we must sin, let's sin quick and don't let it be a long, lingering sinning.

Notes

★   ★   ★

Lead your life so you wouldn't be ashamed to sell the family parrot to the town gossip.

Notes

PHOTOGRAPHY

I think the camera has done more harm for politics than any other one faction. Everybody would rather get their picture than their ideas in the paper.

July 8, 1928

★   ★   ★

We are getting to be a nation that can't read any more. If the thing hasn't got a picture of it, why, we are sunk. Instead of reporters nowadays we use photographers. Newspapers are advertising themselves as having "20 pages of advertising and 278 cameramen."

December 21, 1924

PILGRIMS

Provincetown, Massachusetts, officials sent me a lot of official data that when the Pilgrims landed, they found some corn that the Indians had stored and that the Pilgrims were about starved and that they ate this Indian corn. You see, the minute the Pilgrims landed, they got full of corn and they shot the Indians, probably because they hadn't stored more corn.

April 14, 1935

★   ★   ★

Of course, Pilgrims would always pray. That's one thing about a Pilgrim, he would pray—mostly for more Indian corn. I bet you never in your life have seen a picture of one of those old Pilgrims praying when he didn't have a gun right by the side of him. That was to see that he got what he was praying for.

April 14, 1935

New England has got to pacify the rest of America and tell why were the Pilgrims allowed to land anywhere? I hope my Cherokee blood is not making me prejudiced. I want to be broad minded but I am sure it was only the extreme generosity of the Indians that allowed the Pilgrims to land.

Suppose we reverse the case. Do you reckon the Pilgrims would have ever let the Indians land? Fat chance! The Pilgrims wouldn't even let the Indians live after the Indians went to the trouble of letting 'em land.

April 14, 1935

They were very religious people that came over here from the old country. They were very human. They would shoot a couple of Indians on the way to every prayer meeting.

June 10, 1934

PIONEERS

We're always talking about Pioneers and what great folks they were. Well, if we stopped and looked history in the face, the Pioneer wasn't a thing in the world but a guy that wanted something for nothing. He was a guy that wanted to live off everything that nature had done. He would cut a tree down that didn't cost him anything, but he never planted one and he plowed up land that should have been left to grass.

April 14, 1935

PLANS

Plans get you into things, but you got to work your way out.

June 24, 1931

Now Republican presidents—that's one thing about Republican presidents—they never went in much for plans. They only had one plan. It says: "Now boys! My head is turned; just get it while you can!"

I am like everybody else. I could sit by the hours and tell of plans that have been tried that have maybe not only looked foolish, but were foolish—but all that criticism wouldn't do any good. It would just add up to the yell of the pack.

I could sit from now till morning and tell you what the President should not have done, but if you give me five minutes continuous time, I couldn't tell you what he should have done, and neither can any of the rest of them.

There ain't but one place that a plan is any good and that it would really work and that's on paper. But the minute you get it off the sheet of paper and get it out in the air, it blows away, that's all.

So plans just don't work. If they are milk and honey to you, they are poison ivy to somebody else.

So let's all just call a moratorium on plans. If the Republicans would forget their plan, which is to get into the White House, and the Democrats would forget their main plan to stay in there, and if all these various third parties would just look at their history which shows that none of them ever did get in there, why, we'd all recover overnight.

April 21, 1935

PLUMBERS

One of my free feeds during the week was at a big banquet for eleven hundred rug manufacturers and dealers. There was a fine den to go in amongst, but I was glad, as in building a home, I had encountered two troops of brigands.

I thought, when I paid the plumbers the height of highway-manship had been reached. But boy, when my wife commenced to try and get those floors covered to try and hide the dirt, I wanted to rush back and kiss the plumbers and apologize. So it was just my good fortune that I should be able to speak to these rug people. They couldn't find anyone else that would say even as much good about them as I did.

April 25, 1923

POKER

We played some poker—a game which any of my friends know, they never even saw me attempt. Well, I livened the trip up a bit for the boys by paying their passage and incidental expenses. I contributed very little humor, but something much more substantial to the trip.

Now I know no one will ever see me play it again.

March 19, 1932

POLICE

Pity the police; the poor fellows can't catch many criminals as our towns have them too busy handing out tickets to cars that have been parked too long.

February 29, 1928

★   ★   ★

Policemen used to carry a club that they used to crack over

crook's heads. Now they have discarded that and they have a whistle. That's why there is so much crime. Whistling at a crook is not near as effective as to crack him on the bean with a hickory stick.

May 31, 1925

In Memphis today, over 25 Policemen went to a hospital and volunteered to give blood transfusions to a kid that was near death.

I know that I am out of order in speaking of the good things that cops do, but I am one of the old-fashioned people who believe if someone pounces on me, I could holler for a policeman and he would come and help me out without me having to pay him anything.

February 29, 1928

Police Chiefs

They are holding a convention of International Police Chiefs here in New York this week. So yesterday, I was asked to address the convention. I had never caught a crook, but neither had they, so we had a mutual feeling.

May 13, 1923

At the convention of International Police Chiefs the big Scotland Yard man from England lost his watch and return ticket the first day in the convention room. New York certainly did entertain them royally and made them feel at home. They put on robberies and murders for them every day they were here.

May 13, 1923

New York just appointed a new police chief. The murderers just wouldn't surrender to the other one.

December 13, 1928

We got a new police chief in New York and he has arrested most of the population and over half the police force.

He has the cops so scared that they are arresting traffic instead of directing it.

It would be a good joke on this town if he did clean it up.

January 13, 1929

Police Commissioner

The New York Police Commissioner appointed a crime committee of twenty, to help him keep a list of crimes.

If they hear of any crimes that he don't, then they report those crimes to him. Then at the end of the year, the one that has heard the most crimes, gets a prize.

May 16, 1929

★ ★ ★

New York's Police Commissioner has rounded so many crooks up and put 'em in jail, that it's interfering with theater attendance.

December 26, 1928

POLITICS

All politics is applesauce!

December 31, 1922

★ ★ ★

If you ever injected truth into politics, you would have no politics.

July 15, 1923

★ ★ ★

In politics nowadays, it's about as big a crime to be dumb, as it is to be dishonest.

February 3, 1929

★ ★ ★

Politics sure is a gentleman's game. Everybody is of a high type, till the time comes when there is something worth while to be little over.

October 12, 1928

★ ★ ★

Politics ain't nothing but reciprocity, you know. Congress will vote for anything if the thing they vote for will turn around and vote for them.

June 2, 1935

★ ★ ★

Politics started on these shores in 1612. And in 323 years—the short span of 323 years—it has grown in leaps and bounds until it's now become America's leading racket.

May 5, 1935

★ ★ ★

The more I see of politics the more I wonder what in the world any man would ever want to take it up for.

Then some people wonder why the best men of a community are not the office holders.

September 27, 1925

★ ★ ★

Politics is a business where most of the men are looking for glory and personal gratification more than they are for money.

October 10, 1928

Times have only proven one thing, and that is that you can't ruin this country, even with politics.

November 4, 1928

★   ★   ★

It sure is a bad time for a man to get ambitious and want to go into politics. There never was a time when respect for public office was at such a low ebb.

December 28, 1930

★   ★   ★

In England, politics is an obligation; over here, it's a business.

June 5, 1929

★   ★   ★

Our politics is just a revolving wheel. One Party gets in, and through a full stomach and a swelled head it oversteps itself, and out they go. And then the other one gets in and that's all there is to it.

So that about concludes the bedside story of the two great political Parties which we work night and day to support.

June 24, 1934

★   ★   ★

There is very little dignity, very little sportsmanship, or very little anything in politics. It's only: "Get The Job and Hold It!"

November 2, 1932

★   ★   ★

Politics is not the high class, marvelous thing that lots of you picture. Our whole government workings are crammed with baloney.

But with all the hooey, it's the best system there is in the world, and the honesty of our men in big jobs is very high—there is many dumb ones get in there, but no downright dishonest ones.

November 10, 1932

★   ★   ★

There is no more independence in politics than there is in jail.

November 11, 1928

★   ★   ★

Politics is a great character builder. You have to take a referendum to see what your convictions are for that day.

May 29, 1930

★   ★   ★

Politics has got so expensive that it takes lots of money to even get beat with nowadays.

June 28, 1931

Political Candidates

No elective candidate is ever as bad, or as good, as we expect him to be.

September 16, 1934

Political Machines

Party politics is the most narrow-minded occupation in the world. A guy raised in a straight jacket is a corkscrew compared to a thick-headed Party politician.

March 29, 1925

There is a hundred things to single you out for promotion in party politics, besides ability.

October 14, 1928

Political Parties

How often do politicians say: "I don't have to tell you what our great Party stands for! You know the facts!

The Supreme Court with all its divided knowledge can't tell you what either Party stands for. About the only thing that you can safely say is that both Parties stand for re-election.

September 21, 1928

Political Speeches

It's too bad there is not some machine or way of registration just how many votes a political speech gets, or loses. I claim if we had some way of finding out, it would do away with political speeches.

September 21, 1928

Politicians

America has the best politicians money can buy.

Notes

★   ★   ★

A politician is not as narrow-minded as he forces himself to be.

October 30, 1932

★   ★   ★

Our system has been that when a man is defeated at election, he is appointed to a bigger job than the one he was defeated for.

November 16, 1930

★   ★   ★

Politicians are like the rich—they're always with us.

September 21, 1924

A politician is just like a pickpocket; it's almost impossible to get one to reform.

March 25, 1923

The trouble with you politicians is you see, but you don't see far. You wear reading glasses when you are looking into the future. You got a putter in your hand when you should have your driver.

October 29, 1927

If more men in politics would raise children instead of issues, we would have a bigger and better country.

October 26, 1928

Now about politicians! The least said the best. They haven't the social standing of the diplomats. All their damage is done internally. Where the Ambassador generally winds up with a decoration of red ribbon, the politician generally winds up with an indictment staring him in the face.

June 9, 1928

★   ★   ★

With politicians horning in, our comedian business is overcrowded.

January 8, 1933

★   ★   ★

I am just like a politician—the less I know about anything, the more I can say.

January 27, 1935

★   ★   ★

A politician is just like a spoiled kid. If he feels that his stick of candy is not the longest, why, he will let out a yap that will drown out the neighborhood.

August 17, 1930

★   ★   ★

We cuss our elected officials and we joke about 'em but they are all good fellows at heart and if they wasn't in politics, why, they would be doing something else against us that might be worse.

May 18, 1926

Nowadays people are taking their comedians seriously and the politicians as a joke, when it used to be vice versa.

November 22, 1932

Did you ever know a politician that was not facing the "most critical time in the world's affairs" every time he spoke in public?

January 13, 1924

Look at these politicians! They are a bunch of local bandits, sent by their local voters to raid the public treasury; and if they come home with enough public loot, they are known as statesmen.

January 12, 1928

You fellows in politics, you-all have generally been able to detect a voting prospect through a brick wall with no windows.

June 8, 1926

Children, what was the first thing you learned about politics at school? It was that Politics was business, wasn't it? That it was advertised under the heading of idealism, but it was carried on under the heading of business, and the bigger the business, the bigger the politician.

October 20, 1929

To get into politics, there is no qualifications. If you had a bad night the night before and wake up feeling that there is nothing left in life for you, that you are no good to yourself, the world or your friends, why, one day later finds your name on a ballot, running for something.

April 2, 1932

Politics is the best show in America. I love animals and I love politicians, and I like to watch both of 'em at play, either back home in their native state, or after they've been captured and sent to a zoo, or to Washington.

Notes

★ ★ ★

It's surprising in a state how many people will vote for a rascal. Let him think up enough things in his platform to promise, and he would make 'em believe it.

Our system of nominating, where we let anybody run that can write his name down, is wrong. There should be some way, maybe a high-class committee of men that would pass on the qualifications and decide which men would even be eligible to run. You will no more get on a plane unless you know the pilot is a recognized pilot but you will live in a state when the governor maybe has

never had one hour's instructions at the wheel of the ship of state.
June 17, 1934

POLLS, PUBLIC OPINION

Course, who ever wins in these polls, it won't mean anything, only another argument. I don't know who they are mailing these ballots to. I haven't seen any, or any one that has.
March 30, 1930

★   ★   ★

Everyone is watching the various polls. It's like a rehearsal for the election every time, and in case the poll vote is over before the election, I doubt if they even hold the election at all; they will just take this poll and inaugurate the winner on that.
October 21, 1928

POLO

They call Polo a gentleman's game for the same reason they call a tall man "Shorty."
Notes

★   ★   ★

Polo is played by us lazy ones, because the horse does all the work and we love to just go for the ride.
April 17, 1934

★   ★   ★

I play a little polo, just enough to get hit in the mouth.
April 22, 1923

POMPEII, ITALY

Pompeii, that was at one time the Beverly Hills of Italy, was caught in a landslide. It covered the city with a second mortgage. Now if you like buried cities, you can't beat this one, personally I don't care for buried cities. But it is a very good example of early buried architecture. Every tourist is "so surprised" to find the houses and rooms "just as they were before" Vesuvius' ashtray run over. I don't know why they should be "so surprised." How was it going to change after they were all snowed under? There has been some scandal unearthed as well as art. It seems some of the "Boys about Town" didn't reach the right house before the visitation of providence. You should see Pompeii.

Philadelphia comes nearer approaching it than any big city I know of.
May 25, 1926

POOR, THE

I represent a new class of people in this country, the newly poor.
Notes

★   ★   ★

We'll hold the distinction of being the only nation in the history of the world that ever went to the Poorhouse in an automobile.
October 18, 1931

POPE

I guess our country holds the record for dumbness. The Pope spoke to the world this morning in three languages and we didn't understand a one of 'em.

But the minute he finished and the local radio stations got back to selling corn salve and pyorrhea tooth paste, we were right up our intellectual alley again.
May 15, 1931

PORK BARREL PROJECTS

We are sure getting sucked into a lot of things for the sole benefit of a local community, to be paid for by everybody.
February 5, 1933

★   ★   ★

Congress always wants the Government to spend the taxpayers' money to build something, then don't want 'em to run it.
February 5, 1933

★   ★   ★

Just think of an old bird owning a farm away out in the country in most any out of the way place, no paved road, no dam, no rural delivery, yet through his taxes he is paying for every dam, every road, and every other dam thing that he is not using.
February 5, 1933

PORTUGAL

Portugal is having a revolution.
Good joke on us. We haven't any more Marines to cover that one.
February 8, 1927

★   ★   ★

Portugal discovered the whole world and when there was no new world for the Portuguese to find, they just folded up and went out of business.
April 2, 1933

When I was in Europe last year Portugal had three revolutions and three different Presidents, all in 24 hours. They only worked eight hour shifts.

February 6, 1927

POSTERITY

Posterity means, people, two weeks later.

October 13, 1929

PRAYER

The trouble with our praying is, we just do it as a means of last resort.

May 11, 1930

★   ★   ★

We just pray for anything whether we got any dope on it, or not.

May 11, 1930

PREDICTIONS

This apostle of doom at Patchogue on Long Island, near New York City, says the world is coming to an end tonight.

This is happening at a very inopportune time for me, because I have a payment to meet on some land out in California. I have tried all day to have the payment postponed until tomorrow. I don't know which would be the greater disappointment—having to pay or having to die.

February 15, 1925

PREPAREDNESS, MILITARY

This is a time in the history of the world when you better be pretty well prepared or you won't get anywhere.

December 23, 1931

★   ★   ★

Now if you thought there wasn't going to be any war, you should have seen some of those nations preparing. They are not the people who will go to work and learn a trade that they are not going to work at.

When I told that to the President, I said that these are only tips. I was like the old rooster when he brought out the ostrich egg and showed it to all the hens and said: "I am not criticizing but I just want you to know what others are doing!"

December 4, 1926

PRESIDENCY

The only way to keep a Governor from becoming Senator is to sidetrack him off into the Presidency.

June 8, 1920

An Emperor is bigger than a President; he is what a President would be if he didn't have any Congress or Senate to see that he does nothing.

April 30, 1932

It's a tough life, this thing of being President and trying to please everybody—well, not exactly everybody, but enough to be re-elected.

September 22, 1929

There is only one way to get even with the President now, and that is to leave him in there another term.

March 18, 1923

You don't have to listen to some fellow telling you how bad things are going for the President, or what's to become of the Constitution. They all seem to forget that those nine old gentlemen in kimonos will look after the Constitution, and the President will just have to look after himself.

He has to do our worrying, but we don't have to do his.

July 21, 1935

No President can be as bad as the men that advise him. We don't need a different man as bad as we need different advisers for the same man.

August 21, 1932

Your personal habits, Mr. President, your looks, your dress, whether you are a good fellow, or not, with the Boys, the old assumed Rotary or Kiwanis spirit, why, they don't mean a thing. You can shut up and never say a word for the entire four years; you can go out and talk yourself deaf, dumb and blind so it's only when you are asleep that you are quiet; you can be a teetotaler; you can have a drink when ever you like; in all these things, and a million others, you can be either on one side or the other, and it won't make the least bit of difference in the world, that is, it won't if the country has enjoyed prosperity, over which you had no personal control.

September 12, 1926

The minute it's not raining enough and we can't raise anything, or it's raining too much and we raise too much, why, we throw our President out and get a new one.

February 27, 1932

★   ★   ★

All I know is just what I read in the papers or what I hear as I prowl around the nation's joke factory. I was up to the White House today.

"Do you want me to tell you the latest political jokes, Mr. President?" I asked him.

"You don't have to, Will," he said, "I know 'em already. I appointed most of them."

1921

★   ★   ★

Funny thing about us, we will listen to any old shyster politician that comes along to advise us, but we won't trust any of our Presidents when we think they are trying to tell us who to elect.

September 27, 1930

★   ★   ★

An awful lot of people are predicting the President's downfall—not only predicting, but praying.

We are a funny people. We elect our Presidents, be they Republicans or Democrats, then go home and start daring 'em to make good.

April 1, 1935

★   ★   ★

We are wonderful with our Presidents. When the sun shines we cheer 'em, but let it start raining and if they don't furnish us with an umbrella and galoshes, we give 'em the boot right then.

April 30, 1933

★   ★   ★

A President-elect's popularity is the shortest-lived of any public man. It only lasts till he picks his Cabinet.

December 26, 1928

★   ★   ★

No matter what a President does, he is wrong according to some people.

September 22, 1929

★   ★   ★

We are a good natured bunch of saps in this country.
When the President is wrong, we charge it to inexperience.

June 30, 1930

You know, our President is like a magician in a vaudeville

show. He's arrived at the theater, only his special properties and luggage ain't arrived yet. So he's got to borrow somebody else's magic hat. Well, he goes ahead and does his tricks.

But when he reaches in the hat to draw out a rabbit, he doesn't know himself whether he is drawing out a rabbit or a skunk. That's like most of these new schemes. He's got to hold 'em up for public view, regardless how the ideas turn out.

August 8, 1935

When the President appoints some judge, or someone to some prominent position, he should send out the names of the fellows who wanted that person appointed. That's to stop these politicians from endorsing every applicant that comes along.

Some of them were so promiscuous with their endorsements that they must have been working on a commission basis. Now a lot of these politicians are going to kick on this new plan. But for every politician the President loses, he will gain two more friends.

April 19, 1929

I can't see the advantage of having one of your own party in as President. I would rather be able to criticize a man than to have to apologize for him.

March 18, 1923

They talk about how the President is doing. He has only been in just over a year and it all depends on how we do the last year of a presidency, not the first year. A voter—you can give him three years of prosperity and then, the last year he goes to the polls and if he has got a dollar, you stay in, and if he ain't got a dollar you go out. The memory of a voter is about as long as a billy goat's.

April 20, 1930

★ ★ ★

Even a glider aeroplane is not subject to as many conditions as a United States President. The cold winter was against him, the wet spring was against him, the Senate was against him, the House of Representatives was against him, and to add to his other hard luck, the fish wasn't biting.

We shouldn't elect a President; we should elect a magician.

May 26, 1930

★ ★ ★

If our President does nothing else but keep our army and navy at home, we can forgive him for not giving us rain, lower taxes and an inflated stock market.

September 8, 1930

The President goes on the air tonight. Even if he is good, there's plenty of 'em won't like it. He can speak on the Lord's Supper, and he will get editorials against it.

April 28, 1935

Just sitting here and reading in all parts of the papers where "So-and-So appealed to the President." Is there nothing that anybody in our country can do by themselves anymore?

If you must appeal to somebody, appeal to the Supreme Court. That's all they are paid for.

November 25, 1934

Presidential Cabinets

Cabinets are picked—not on ability, but what they have done for the Party.

January 14, 1923

★   ★   ★

That list of new Cabinet members shows us that three of 'em escaped from the Senate!

That's like going to the Old Men's Home to get an athlete.

February 23, 1933

★   ★   ★

Lots of times a cabinet attracts more attention between the time they are announced and the time they take seats, than they ever do afterwards.

February 19, 1929

PRIMITIVISM

Something ought to be done about those "primitive" people who live in various parts of the world, and don't know a thing but to live off what nature provides.

You would think they would learn to live off each other like us civilized folks do.

September 10, 1933

PRISON

Our big problem is this discontent in our prisons. Hardly a day passes that prisoners don't show some little outward signs of uneasiness, such as shooting a few guards, burning some buildings and giving a hint publicly that they want to participate in this era of prosperity through which we are struggling to make both ends meet.

It just looks like the boys in there don't appreciate how fortunate they are to have no installment payments to meet.

August 7, 1929

Some new plan has got to be worked out in our prison system.

Of course, this may be a radical suggestion but couldn't they fix it some way where the guards carried the weapons instead of the prisoners?

December 12, 1929

Here is the usual daily A.P. dispatch from Indiana: "Michigan City; Four Prisoners, three serving life terms, escaped from prison today."

A sentence from a judge reads: "You are sentenced to prison as long as it's made comfortable for you, and you desire to remain. In checking out, kindly let the warden know, so he will know how many there will be there for supper."

April 23, 1934

PROFESSION

The best a man can do is to arrive at the top of his chosen profession. I have always maintained that one profession is deserving of as much honor as another, provided it is honorable.

If a man takes up painting and becomes only a mediocre painter, why should he be classed above the brick layer, who has excelled every other brick layer?

If you are the best taxi driver, you are as much an artist as Kreisler.

August 17, 1924

PROHIBITION

I have always claimed America didn't want a drink as bad as they wanted the right to take a drink if they did happen to want one.

April 7, 1933

★　★　★

Congress has cost us more talking about Prohibition than it has trying to enforce it.

June 8, 1930

Statistics have proven that listening to Prohibition lectures has driven more people to drink than any other cause.

March 25, 1923

★   ★   ★

Here is my plan. Have the Government pass a law making it compulsory for everybody to drink. People would rebel against it so that they would stop drinking.

That's a funny thing about American people; tell 'em they have to do something and they will die twice before they do it.

August 27, 1928

★   ★   ★

The silver pocket flask has supplanted the Xmas card as our national gift; nothing is more welcome when full, or more bungle-some when empty.

January 18, 1923

★   ★   ★

In the Bible, right in the start of Genesis, the ninth Chapter, the twenty-first verse, it says: "Noah drank the wine and was drunk." Now you see Noah, our forefather, drank and he didn't drink water and he was a man who knew more about water than practically any man of his time. And this wine had such ill effects on Noah that he only lived to be 950 years old.

June 8, 1930

★   ★   ★

Prohibition is never an issue in the South, their habits and their votes have nothing in common. They feel they are the origi-nators of the still, and any legislation to permit large breweries would be unfair competition and would perhaps destroy the entire revenue of hundreds of thousands of small still owners who have no other visible means of support. Corn likker is their product, and I can't blame them for wanting to protect its life.

We would be a fine liberty-loving country if we allowed a few Yankees to dictate to us what we could make and what we could drink.

October 16, 1926

PROSPERITY

We are told that indirectly, prosperity trickles down.
Now you tell one.

August 9, 1931

★   ★   ★

Prosperity is based on just what you produce, and if you don't

produce much, you are just out of luck.
October 10, 1926
★   ★   ★

There is nothing that sets a nation back as far in civilization as prosperity.
April 2, 1933
★   ★   ★

We would all be mighty prosperous in this country; all we need is just some money to practice it with.
May 9, 1930
★   ★   ★

We never will have any prosperity that is free from speculation till we pass a law that every time a broker or person sells something, he has got to have it sitting there in a bucket, or a bag, or a jug, or a cage, or a rat trap, or something, depending on what it is he is selling.

We are continually buying something that we never get from a man that never had it.
September 24, 1930

PUBLIC SPEAKERS

Nothing in the world exposes how little you have to say as making a speech.
March 30, 1929
★   ★   ★

At the Newspaper Publishers Association convention, Amon G. Carter, owner of the Ft. Worth *Star Telegram*, was the Toast Master. He knows the newspaper business and he knew the shape they were in, and he knew the shape the guests were in, and he just shaped his remarks accordingly.
May 10, 1931

PUBLICITY

We are living in an age of publicity. It used to be only saloons and circuses that wanted their names in the paper, but now it's corporations, churches, preachers, scientists, colleges and cemeteries.
June 23, 1931

Q

QUALITY OF LIFE

Trying to live past our parents, and not "up to them" is one of our drawbacks.

The old Chinese got the right idea along that line.

July 31, 1932

QUINTUPLETS, DIONNE

Those triplet—quin—well, I don't know how many there is, there's a mess of them, they've been a great boon for motherhood. It's put motherhood on a mass production basis.

It's made the mother of only one chick practically discouraged.

May 12, 1935

R

RAILROADS

The nearest the trains ever came to being on time was the day they turned the clock back one hour.

1920

★　★　★

Railroads are waking up now. They are speeding up and giving great service, and getting their rates down, finally competing with the bus and truck now, instead of just cussing 'em.

March 12, 1934

RANCHES

You see we call 'em ranches in California. It sounds big and don't cost any more on the lien. Mine is called "Rancho Premiro Y Segundo Mortgages." The literal translation of that is "The Ranch of the First and Second Mortgage"—and there would be a third if these old bankers were more liberal-minded.

September 17, 1933

★　★　★

Buy a ranch somewhere in the West. Every man has wanted to be a cowboy. Why play Wall Street and die young, when you can play cowboy and never die?

July 10, 1931

★　★　★

In California everything big enough to spread a double mattress on is called a "Ranch." Well, up here in the mountains at Bishop, California, where there is lots of fishing, why, every house you pass they sell fishing worms, and it's called a "Worm Ranch."

I always wanted to own a Ranch, so I am in the market for a good Worm Ranch. I never was so hot as a cowboy, but I believe I

239

would make a good "Worm Herder."

August 30, 1932

I bought my Worm Ranch. The man is to turn over two thousand yearling worms, two thousand two-year olds, five hundred bull worms and the rest a mixed herd.

Now I find in these Sierra Nevadas they are fishing with grasshoppers, so I got a Grasshopper Ranch adjoining.

September 4, 1932

REAL ESTATE

Real estate is the greatest game I ever saw. You can't lose. Everybody buys to sell and nobody buys to keep. What's worrying me is who is going to be the last owner. It's just like an auction; the only one stuck is the last one.

July 1, 1923

In a real estate man's eye, the most exclusive part of the city is wherever he has a house to sell. The Dog Pound may be on one side and the City Incinerator on the other, but it's still exclusive.

And it is, too, for it will be the only house in the world so situated.

April 1, 1923

★   ★   ★

You just try to call one a "real estate agent" and he won't sell you anything. He is a "Realtor;" it's the same as what the old-fashioned real estate agent used to be, only the commission is different.

July 1, 1923

★   ★   ★

Real estate ads read: "This house is located on the shady banks of a beautiful stream." Say, if there is a beautiful stream anywhere now, the railroad runs along it.

April 1, 1923

RED CROSS

We are so used to the things that the Red Cross does, that we sometimes just forget to praise them. But this time, in this flood, they outdid themselves feeding and housing and caring for as many as six hundred thousand.

Lord, what a blessing an organization like that is. I would rather have originated the Red Cross than have written the Constitution of the United States.

June 19, 1927

Today I got my official document from the Red Cross head-quarters of being made a life member. Well, sir, I am crazy about it for two reasons. One, of course, is that it is one of the greatest organizations in the United States (including the world). I think it is greater than the Republican Party.

The other reason is it looks like a diploma. You know I never had any kind of diploma; I never finished from anything. I always wanted something that looked important. I never even had an oil share.

July 14, 1927

REFORMERS

These reformers are always wanting to save you, and if it wasn't for them, people wouldn't need saving.

1919

RELIEF, GOVERNMENTAL

We have ways and means of gathering any sort of information, how much money you earned to a nickel, how many rabbits were born in the Dakotas, how much rainfall between here and Honolulu, but yet, we just can't seem to get even a fairly reliable count of who really needs government helping, and who don't.

April 7, 1935

The whole idea of Government Relief was to loan somebody more money so they could get further into debt.

November 27, 1932

RELIGION

The church is in Politics more than the Politicians.

February 17, 1929

★　★　★

These big wars over commerce, they kill more people, but one over religion is really the most bitter.

September 8, 1929

★　★　★

Americans don't fear the Lord as much as they do the next payment.

July 30, 1929

★　★　★

There is no argument in the world that carries the hatred that a religious belief does. The more learned a man is, the less consideration he has for another man's belief.

January 20, 1924

★ ★ ★

Church people all over the country are divided and arguing over where we come from. Never mind where we come from, Neighbor! Woman living next door to you will find out where you come from, and all about you, better than all the Preachers.

Just let the Preachers make it their business where you are going when you leave here.

May 27, 1923

★ ★ ★

Can you imagine our Savior dying for all of us, yet we have to argue over just whether He didn't die for us personally and not for you. Sometimes you wonder if His lessons of sacrifice and devotion was not pretty near lost on a lot of us.

April 7, 1935

★ ★ ★

Do anything in this world but monkey with somebody else's religion. What reasoning of conceit makes anyone think theirs is right?

1926

★ ★ ★

It's better to let people die ignorant and poor, believing in what they have always believed in, than to die prosperous and smart, half believing in something new and doubtful.

1926

★ ★ ★

If I am broad minded in any way (and I hope I am in many) I am broad minded in a religious way. There has been times when I wished there had been as much real religion among some of our creeds as there has been vanity, but that's not in any way a criticism.

January 8, 1933

REPUBLICANS

Don't blame all the things that have happened to us lately on the Republicans—they're not smart enough to have thought 'em up.

Notes

★ ★ ★

With the election coming on, you are going to be fed up with a lot of hooey about a lot of things. Naturally the Republicans are to put their best side forward.

They are just trying to figure out which side is their best.

May 29, 1932

You keep a Republican broke and out of office and pretty near anybody can get along with them.

November 11, 1923

★   ★   ★

In the South, a Republican is the fellow that knows enough to stop planting cotton.

November 9, 1926

★   ★   ★

Why do you laugh any time anybody says "The Republican Party?" Say, that's no laughing matter, being a Republican in these perilous times. Anyone can be a Republican when the stock market is up, but when stocks are selling for no more than they're worth, I tell you, being a Republican—it's a sacrifice.

October 14, 1934

★   ★   ★

From now on I am going to lay off the Republicans. I have never had anything against them as a race. I realize that out of office they are just as honest as any other class, and they have a place in the community that would have to be taken by somebody.

So I want to apologize for all that I have said about them and henceforth will have only a good word to say of them. Mind you, I am not going to say anything about them for a while, but that is not going to keep me from watching them.

July 8, 1927

Republican National Conventions

The Convention opened with a prayer, a very fervent prayer. If the Lord can see his way clear to bless the Republican Party, the way it's been carrying on, the rest of us ought to get it without even asking for it.

June 12, 1928

★   ★   ★

They commenced to pray. The prayer was very long, but of course the parson may have known his audience and their needs better than me.

June 10, 1924

★   ★   ★

I see where the California delegation to the Convention are taking a carload of California poppies to scatter. They figure on catching the dope addict vote, which is very large this year.

June 6, 1920

An alternate is the lowest form of political life there is. He is the parachute in a plane that never leaves the ground.

June 12, 1932

I hate to say it, but the women that spoke were all terrible—they were pretty near as bad as the men, and that will give you an idea how bad they were.

June 15, 1928

The President and the Vice-President were both nominated last night. The Presidential candidate early in the evening at the Convention, and the Vice-Presidential candidate later at the hotel.

June 15, 1928

The Convention's Resolution Committee just got a dictionary apiece and found all the possible phrases and words that don't mean anything, then got 'em together and called it a Resolution. It offers no solutions, but will prolong the argument.

June 17, 1932

I am being paid to write something funny about this Republican Convention. That's funny. All a fellow has to do to write something funny on a Republican Convention is just write what happened.

June 1920

Men who yesterday wouldn't even speak to a Vice-President, are now trying to be one.

June 12, 1928

A bank was robbed just before the Republican National Convention opened this morning. The Chicago and Indiana delegations are under surveillance. If there is enough banks to rob, there is no telling when this Convention will adjourn.

June 14, 1928

★   ★   ★

They adjourned till tomorrow for the sake of the hotels. They could have finished this Convention today.

June 12, 1928

★   ★   ★

Now, that the Conventions are over and I sit and think of the amount of apple sauce and hooey that was spilled there, you wonder that we are even doing as well as we are as a nation.

July 10, 1932

If these delegates vote the way they were instructed to vote back home, they will be the first politicians that ever did what the people told them to do.

June 9, 1924
★   ★   ★

I am leaving tonight with New York's delegation of unnecessary delegates. Boy, they preach economy and here are hundreds of thousands of dollars being wasted to ship all these destructive delegates to a place to announce something that everybody in the United States knew six months ago. The President could have been nominated by post card. Why didn't somebody suggest taking the money they are spending to tell him he is nominated and give it to the poor in each state?

Don't say there is no poor. There must be some Democrats in every state.

June 9, 1924
★   ★   ★

The lobbyists have taken over the whole Convention. They give you a badge and a drink. Lot of us don't know what to do with all the badges.

June 14, 1932
★   ★   ★

If all the money spent on political badges and political literature was spent on Farm Relief, we would have the most prosperous country east of the Alleghenys.

June 12, 1924
★   ★   ★

The alternates are camped on the edge of town and are being cared for by the Salvation Army. They say they are going to stay till they get badges as big as the ones the delegates have.

June 13, 1932
★   ★   ★

The loudspeaker system didn't work and half of 'em couldn't hear the keynote speech. They got mad and got to leaving—but not as quick as those that was sitting near and could hear it.

June 14, 1932
★   ★   ★

Listening to a keynote speech is like listening to a Chautauqua lecture when you could have gone to the Ziegfeld Follies.

June 14, 1932
★   ★   ★

This is the day of the keynote speech. A keynote speech is press notices for the Republican Party, written by its own members. The keynote speaker has the toughest job of any of them. If he points to

the accomplishments, he is sunk, and if he views with alarm, he is
sunk; so we are liable to get two solid hours on the weather.

June 13, 1928

★   ★   ★

Listening to the keynote speech, here are just a few things that
I bet you didn't know the Republicans were responsible for: radio,
telephone, baths, automobiles, savings accounts, law enforcement,
workmen living in houses and a living wage for Senators.

The Democrats, on the other hand, had brought on war, pestilence, disease, boll weevil, suspenders, floods and droughts.

June 13, 1928

★   ★   ★

In the old days it was not: "Who will we nominate for Vice-
President?" It was: "Who can we get to take the thing?"

June 10, 1924

★   ★   ★

It took six months and about 50 million dollars to nominate a
Republican candidate for President.

They nominated the Vice Presidential candidate while they
were putting on their hats.

1920

★   ★   ★

They have weeded the Vice-Presidential candidates down
now to just the following: ninety-six Senators, 435 Congressmen
and forty seven Governors.

June 13, 1928

★   ★   ★

There is really no difference in the two Platforms. How could
there be? They are both catering to the same voters.

August 23, 1928

★   ★   ★

They read the Platform.

It is now six hours later and everybody has forgotten what the
Platform was.

June 13, 1924

★   ★   ★

The poor delegate will be allowed to sit and sweat and finally
vote on something that he thinks is a Platform, but when he gets
home it will be found to have a "trick floor," one of those things
that you can raise or lower without the audience ever seeing you do
it. It will have a false bottom, and when you think you're standing
on it, you won't be at all, you're over it, not on it.

June 3, 1928

You can take any one of our Party Platforms that they promise before election and they promise anything. The same fellows that make them, make out these insurance policies. That is, what they say on one page they can deny on the other.

May 5, 1923

The speeches will be the same ones delivered for forty years but never listened to. And as for the Platform, it will be the same they have read for forty years, but have never used.

April 20, 1932

The Republicans built their Platform not only to stand on, but it's in such shape that they can hide behind it or run clear around it, or even crawl under it.

1920

RESIGNATIONS

It's awfully hard to get a Democrat to resign. It's pretty near as hard to get one to resign as it is to get him elected.

June 21, 1928

REVOLUTIONS

It had just become almost impossible for a country to have a nice, home-talent little revolution among themselves without us butting in.

Everywhere an American went to invest some money in the hope of making 100 percent, why, there would be a gunboat to see that he had all the comforts to which he had become accustomed.

January 7, 1934

We used to have a rule that our Government wouldn't recognize any new Government that had come into power by force and revolution. Then somebody that had accidentally read our history, happened to ask: "Well, how did our Government come into power?"

So now we recognize 'em no matter who they shot to get in. All you have to promise is that you will buy something from us, even if it's only guns for the next revolution.

September 19, 1930

It does seem good to be able to read of revolutions in some of these Central and South American nations, and not to read where "U.S. Marines have landed and have the situation well in hand."

September 8, 1930

Won't it be wonderful if we ever live to see the day when any country can have its own revolution, and even a private and congenial war with a neighboring nation, without uninvited guests?

September 8, 1930

RICH, THE

All these big moneyed people, they are just like the underworld—they all know each other and kinder work together.

June 2, 1928

There's as much money in the country as there ever was. Only fewer people have it.

October 18, 1931

That is the unfortunate thing about this country, we have rich people over here who would pay to get into Purgatory, if they knew they were not wanted in there.

April 29, 1923

The whole viewpoint of the people in regard to our rich men has been changed in the last few years. Now we judge a man's greatness on how he has spent his money.

June 11, 1929

ROBBERS

The toughest part of robbing nowadays is to find somebody that has something.

June 7, 1931

As soon as there is a man that has a dollar, there is a robber to take it.

August 28, 1926

Do you know what caused this wave of robberies? It's the business recession. The poor robbers have to rob more people nowadays just to make the same amount that they used to. Just give us good times again and the robber will get what he needs that day out of the very first man he robs.

December 1, 1930

★   ★   ★

Robbery statistics from all cities were published the other day. They can show you the statistics but not the robbers. We go to great lengths to keep track of what a robber did, but do nothing to find out where he went.

December 1, 1930

Robbing is one profession that certainly has advanced in this country. And the remarkable thing is that there is no school or anything to learn you to rob. No other line, outside of drinking, can show the progress that robbing has had in the last five years.

We spend billions of dollars on education and we're no smarter today, and we spend nothing to foster robbing, and here it is one of our most skilled industries we have.

April 25, 1926

I see where the courts are going to be more strict with burglars. One robber was caught twice on the same block and they took his license away from him. From now on, when they catch 'em, they are going to publish their names.

1920

ROME, ITALY

Rome wasn't built in a day. It's not a Miami Beach by any means.

June 5, 1926

Rome has more churches and less preaching in them than any city in the world.

1926

Rome, it's the oldest uncivilized town in the world. New York is just as uncivilized, but it is not as old as Rome.

1926

I didn't know it before I got here, and they told me all this, that Rome had Senators. Now we know why it declined.

June 5, 1926

Rome has more Art and less bathtubs than any city outside Moscow.

1926

The Colosseum is a great old building. That's where the Romans held their games. You see, Romans loved blood. What money is to an American, blood was to a Roman. A Roman was never as happy as when he saw somebody bleeding.

June 5, 1926

★   ★   ★

The whole of Rome, Italy, seems to have been built, painted and decorated by one man, that was Michelangelo.

If you took everything out of Rome that was supposed to have been done by Michelangelo, Rome would be as bare of Art as Los Angeles.

June 5, 1926

ROOSEVELT, FRANKLIN D.

This fellow Roosevelt never gets through surprising us. We just find out now that he speaks French fluently. That's the second linguistic surprise he has handed us. He is the only guy who can talk "Turkey" to the Senate.

March 31, 1933

Say, this Roosevelt is a fast worker. Even on a Sunday—when all a President is supposed to do is to put on a silk hat and have his picture taken coming out of church—why, this President closed all the banks and called Congress in extra session, and that's not all he is going to call 'em either, if they don't get something done.

March 6, 1933

A lot of people are kidding Mr. Roosevelt about having college professors as his advisors. They say that the men that advise him are three inmates of Columbia University.

That's all right. We have had Presidents that acted like they were advised by the inmates of Matawan, the Institution for the Criminally Insane.

May 7, 1933

Tonight I am on the radio with President Roosevelt. I am on ahead of Mr. Roosevelt. Generally at big affairs, where I have been fortunate enough to speak, I follow those big men, because they always have a lot of theories and everything, and somebody has to come along and offset them with facts.

But not with Mr. Roosevelt.

May 7, 1933

ROOSEVELT, THEODORE

Teddy Roosevelt was a man who wouldn't even waste hatred on nothing.

August 9, 1925

★ ★ ★

If we can spare men like Teddy Roosevelt and Woodrow Wilson, there is no use in any other politician ever taking himself seriously.

February 22, 1925

RULES

There is one rule that works in every calamity, be it pestilence, war or famine—the rich get richer and the poor get poorer. The poor even help arrange it.

October 31, 1929

RUMORS

Rumor travels faster, but it don't stay put as long as truth.

March 9, 1924

★ ★ ★

I flew into Washington, the old Fountain of Rumors, to watch the hired boys work out under perspiration.

August 17, 1933

★ ★ ★

The Stock Market operates not on only on O.P.M. (Other People's Money) but O.P.R. (Other People's Rumors).

October 24, 1933

RUSSIA

Russia's made great strides since I visited the place eight years ago, and most of it has been by eliminating Communism.

September 16, 1934

★ ★ ★

Russia hates everybody so bad it would take a week to pick out the one she hates the most.

August 26, 1926

★ ★ ★

Russia is a country that is burying its troubles. Your criticism is your epitaph.

November 25, 1930

Russia is a country that looks like it was invented for arguments' sake.

Notes

★   ★   ★

It's really not, or ever has been a nation—it's a dispute.

Notes

★   ★   ★

Russia is the boarding house hash of nations.

1926

★   ★   ★

Suppose nobody could write you a composite article on America, how are they going to do it on Russia, a country that is so much bigger than us that we would rattle around in it like a good idea in Congress?

November 6, 1926

★   ★   ★

I went to the races in Moscow and the grandstand had all the men of the Party, and over in center field stood the mob in the sun.

Well, there was Bourgeoisie and Proletariat distinction for you.

December 4, 1926

★   ★   ★

They claim they have done away with illiteracy, but you can't go into a book store and buy any book you want.

December 4, 1926

★   ★   ★

I read that Russia wants to discuss debt payments with us. Wise guys, those Russians! You see, if you promise to repay America it will loan you twice as much as you promise to repay. Wise guys, those Russians.

September 1, 1926

★   ★   ★

Didn't you see the headlines in this morning's papers, saying that "Russia is going to extract snow from clouds before those clouds reach Moscow." Now that sounded silly, don't it? But then, in the next column, it says "President and Congressional Committee propose to take 200 million dollars from Government expenditures."

Well, I'll bet you the Russians get the snow out of the clouds before the President and Congress get any Government employees out of their swivel chairs.

April 10, 1932

★   ★   ★

There has been more said and written about Russia than there has been about Honesty in Politics, and Farmers' Relief, and there has been just as little done about either of those two.

November 6, 1926

★   ★   ★

Has Russia changed much and is it better off? Say, that is the one answer that you can go and bet on. Most of their people live on the land and their existence wouldn't change even if the Populists or the Democrats run Russia. It wouldn't be nothing but Russia. You see, people don't change under governments, governments change but the people remain the same.

December 4, 1926

★   ★   ★

Over there, in Russia, everybody gets what he can get, and where he can get it, and it takes two to watch one, and then four to watch those two.

November 6, 1926

★   ★   ★

You see, Russia, she don't do as much harm to the rest of the world as she just worries 'em. She just loves to put a thumb in the soup and lets the guests see it's there. The whole world's nerves are jumpy anyhow, right now. Anybody with a sheet over their head could run the world home and under the bed.

May 19, 1931

★   ★   ★

I see where somebody has started a movement to "unrecognize" Russia. I guess we didn't sell 'em as much as we thought we would.

I guess their recognizing us hasn't turned out so hot for them, either.

December 16, 1934

★   ★   ★

If I wanted to start an insane asylum that would be 100 per cent cuckoo, I would just admit applicants that thought they knew something about Russia.

September 14, 1930

★   ★   ★

In Moscow I met a guy today that could remember back to the time when there was a Czar in Russia, Trotsky was pressing pants in New York, and governments paid their debts.

August 31, 1934

Russian Language

No English speaking person living today can remember a single Russian name. The Russians were told they could have only so many letters in their alphabet. Well, they took fifteen of these they didn't want and traded them for fifteen extra K's and Z's. So the alphabet consists of twenty-six letters: seventeen K's and Z's and nine other letters.

That is the thing that has made Lenin and Trotsky famous outside Russia. They were the only ones that the outside world could pronounce their names.

November 6, 1926

S

SAFETY PINS

You can have all your Einsteins, your Edisons and your Robert Fultons, but yesterday somebody invented a safety pin that flies shut, instead of open, and you can feed it to your babies with oatmeal.

If that's not a contribution to the world, there never was one.

July 21, 1935

ST. LOUIS, MISSOURI

You see, every guy thinks that the first time he sees anything, that that is the first time it ever existed. I will never forget the first time I went to St. Louis. I thought sure I was the first one to find it.

March 13, 1927

ST. PAUL, MINNESOTA

St. Paul is the town where no one can remember whether it is in Wisconsin or Minnesota, and it acts more like North Dakota. Climatically it's the capital of Siberia. Somebody with a sense of humor built it, and Minneapolis right close together and then moved away to watch the fun. If either city could find him, his life wouldn't be worth as much as a bank messenger's in Chicago.

November 8, 1925

ST. PETER

Everybody wants to see where St. Peter was buried, but nobody wants to live like him.

1926

ST. PETERSBURG, RUSSIA

St. Petersburg, or Petrograd, or Leningrad is much more modern and European than Moscow. Winter starts the first week in July and ends the last week in June. Spring, Summer and Fall are not what you would call long, but they are comfortable—all three days are very pleasant.

December 4, 1926

You have to move twice a day in Leningrad—at low tide you live downstairs and at high tide you move back upstairs. Peter the Great settled it, but that is not why he is called Peter the Great.

December 4, 1926

I am in this town they used to call St. Petersburg. Then, when the war came along with Germany, and they got afraid Germany would capture it, they changed the name to Petrograd so it would fool the Germans and they wouldn't know what town they were capturing. And just when the Czar was gloating over the clever strategy, a fellow named Lenin found out where it was and he had never had a town named after him.

December 4, 1926

From what I could gather, St. Petersburg used to be quite a place—a kind of cross between Hollywood, St. Louis and Chicago. It had the drab night life of Hollywood, the color, dash and brilliance of St. Louis, and the pistol and rifle fire of Chicago.

December 4, 1926

The Hermitage Museum

St. Petersburg is much the most beautiful city in Russia. It has some of the most wonderful art treasures in the world in the Hermitage. But after looking over Russia, I believe there is a hundred things I could think of to improve them with beside Art. Russians need meat right now worse than they do naked statues. Russia don't need to develop so many men who can paint or sculpture a beautiful, well-rounded human body. What they need is somebody who can provide the wherewith to fill out that well-rounded body.

December 4, 1926

SALT LAKE CITY, UTAH

Salt Lake City is the only town in the world that saw far

enough ahead and predicted the forthcoming traffic jam, and made wide streets.

March 28, 1926

SALVATION ARMY

If we spent as much with the Salvation Army as we do with the Post Office every Christmas, why, the poor would be fat all Winter.

December 25, 1928

SAN FRANCISCO, CALIFORNIA

Summertime anywhere, there is not a lot of difference—only San Francisco at night; then it snows.

August 26, 1934

In San Francisco children are taught two things; one is to love the Lord, and the other is to hate Los Angeles.

1920

I bet that San Francisco was a city from the very first time it had a dozen settlers. Cities are like Gentlemen, they are born, not made.

You are either a city, or you are not. Size has nothing to do with it. New York is "Yokel" but San Francisco is "City" at heart.

April 30, 1934

★   ★   ★

Frisco is the place that keeps this end of the state in the Union. It's to California what the Cherokee Nation is to Oklahoma, it's the aristocracy of the Commonwealth.

June 14, 1931

★   ★   ★

When a Los Angeles guy comes up here to Frisco, it's just a country boy going to town. You have to take your spurs off here; you can't explain Frisco. It's just the Greta Garbo of the West.

June 1, 1932

★   ★   ★

We in Los Angeles have the numbers down there, but San Francisco has got the class.

This town is going through a wild orgy of bridge building. You know how a town is when it decides to pave. Well, San Francisco is that way with bridges. You daren't leave a few buckets of water out overnight, or somebody will build a bridge over it by morning.

August 5, 1935

San Francisco Bay

Did you ever see the Bay of Naples that you have heard and read so much about? Did you ever see the harbour in San Francisco?

Well, it makes the Bay of Naples look like the Chicago Drainage Canal—and I am from Los Angeles.

May 25, 1926

SANTA BARBARA, CALIFORNIA

All the news in the eastern papers has been this earthquake in Santa Barbara. At first they reported hundreds killed and thousands wounded. Of course it was mighty nice, the sympathy they showed, but it was kind of like: "I told you it would happen if you insisted on going out there!"

July 12, 1925

SARAJEVO, YUGOSLAVIA

Did you know that almost all over Europe they celebrate St. Vitus Day? That was the day when a young student shot that Austrian Archduke Ferdinand in a town called Sarajevo, and started the World War.

Down the street, ahead of the parade, another companion had thrown a bomb at him, too, but missed. And the young kid that started the whole thing was named Princip. And the funny part about it is that we can pronounce it, and that's unusual in that part of the world.

July 22, 1934

SAVING

Everybody is talking and preaching "Economy," but the only ones that are practicing it are the ones that ain't got anything.

October 4, 1925

SAVOIR-FAIRE

When you have to be told what to say when you meet anyone, you are not the one to meet them.

January 8, 1927

SCANDALS

I know more scandal than a White House cook.

October 4, 1925

In politics practically everything you hear is scandal, so a thing has got to be mighty scandalous to be worth repeating.

October 12, 1928

SCANDINAVIA

All those Scandinavian countries are great countries. I think they are the smartest and cleanest and mind-their-own-business countries in the world—the Scandinavian countries. They make fine citizens when they come over here. We never had a Scandinavian gangster.

November 4, 1934

Americans will never become civilized enough to tell a Swede from a Dane, or a Norwegian from a Swede. I know the difference means a lot to them, but it just means another tall blonde to us.

April 3, 1933

SCIENTISTS

It's a funny thing about those scientists, they can tell you just to the minute when something is going to happen ten million miles away, and none of them has ever been smart enough to tell you what day to put on your long underwear.

February 1, 1925

Those scientists are always studying out what some other world and planets are doing. Better find out what this one is doing; it's been acting mighty crazy lately.

February 1, 1925

Scientists, I expect, have more fun out of us than we do out of them. Neither really knows when the other is kidding.

May 28, 1933

SEASICKNESS

My Dear President: Will you kindly find out for me through our Intelligence Department who is the fellow that said a big boat didn't rock? Hold him till I return.

July 17, 1926

★　★　★

I get seasick before the boat unties from the dock.

January 3, 1932

SELFISHNESS

All we hear is "What's the matter with the country?" "What's the matter with the world?"

There ain't but one thing wrong with any of us in the world, and that's Selfishness.

March 10, 1935

SHAKESPEARE, WILLIAM

Shakespeare is the only author that can play to losing business for a hundred years and still be known as an author.

April 21, 1927

SHANGHAI, CHINA

Shanghai was a knockout! It's Brooklyn gone English.

January 1, 1932

SHAW, GEORGE BERNARD

George Bernard Shaw has more original ideas on any subject you name than any man in the world. Now he is an Irishman but he lived in England all these years and they don't know yet whether he is "for or against 'em."

July 27, 1930

★   ★   ★

Here is one of George Bernard Shaw's observations to me: "America and Russia are the only two countries left in the world with any scheme of life. Russia is trying an experiment and America is trying everything."

July 27, 1930

SHREWDNESS

Shrewdness in public life all over the world is always honored while honesty in public men is generally attributed to dumbness and is seldom rewarded.

November 30, 1924

SLOGANS

The prize slogan of all is: "Two can live as cheap as one!" That, next to "Law Enforcement" is the biggest bunk slogan ever invented. Why, two can't even live as cheap as two, much less one.

April 12, 1925

You see a fool slogan can get you into anything. But you never heard of a slogan getting you out of anything. It takes either bullets, hard work or money to get you out of anything.

April 12, 1925

★   ★   ★

Even political campaigns are run and won on slogans. Years ago some fellow ran on "The Full Dinner Pail" and after he was elected and they opened it, there was nothing in it.

We got into the War on a slogan that was supposed to keep us out. After we got in we were going to "Make The World Safe for Democracy!"

And maybe we did—you can't tell because there is no nation tried Democracy ever since. Our Boys went over singing: "Over There" and come back singing "I am always chasing Rainbows."

April 12, 1925

★   ★   ★

You shake a slogan at an American and it's just like showing a hungry dog a bone. We even die by slogans. I saw an undertaker's sign the other day which read: "There is a satisfaction in dying if you know the Woodlawn Brothers are to bury you."

April 12, 1925

SLOT MACHINES

What would you say was the biggest and most prosperous convention held in Chicago? It's not the autos, steel or bankers. The only industry that has never asked for Government's relief. Frank Behringer, manager at the big Sherman Hotel, says it's the only convention that paid their room rent since 1929: It's the Slot Machine convention, manufacturers and operators.

Those games where you put in a nickel, pull the lever and play marbles with yourself. It's replaced golf, bridge, and the N.Y. Stock Exchange for exercise and gambling.

February 20, 1935

SNOW

I see where the weather bureau predicts more snow for the Northwest. Good joke on the weather bureau. They can't have any more. They haven't got any place to put it.

February 25, 1923

SOCCER

After a football game in Lima, Peru, five were killed. They only kill ten in a revolution down there, so two football games equal one revolution.

Up here we don't kill our football players. We make coaches out of the smartest ones and send the others to the Legislature.

January 5, 1931

SOCIETY

On the Riviera in France, they found a bunch of people wearing no clothes and not particularly caring who they were married to, and they call it a cult.

Over here we call it society.

October 26, 1927

SOUTH, THE AMERICAN

The South has gone Republican and the North has gone Democratic. Why? Both have done it because it looked like there was money in it.

April 21, 1935

SOUTH AMERICA

"Was you ever in South America?"
"I was."
"Was you trusted?"
"Yes, as long as I paid in advance."

January 31, 1926

★　　★　　★

Why did America want to settle something in South America? Didn't we have anything to settle here at home?

January 31, 1926

★　　★　　★

Why did the President think we were trusted in South America? He had never been there.

January 31, 1926

SPAIN

That's the trouble with traveling in Spain. The high-ups all speak English, but nobody else.

How are you going to get to the high-ups?

June 26, 1926

Spain is trying to get a republic. They think one is great, so that shows their ignorance.

October 16, 1930

★　★　★

Did you ever spend a lonesome hour in a strange town? You all think you have, but you haven't. The lonesomest hour in the entire world is in Mexico or Spain on Sunday afternoon between the hours of 4 and 5, when everyone has gone to the bull fights.

I am not against it. Every nation for their own affairs and own sports. Some nations like to see blood, and some like to see their victims suffer from speculation. It's all in your point of view.

They kill the bull very quick. Wall Street lets you live and suffer.

November 1, 1931

★　★　★

Spain is so far off to herself that she can't afford to pay transportation to any country she could lick.

April 2, 1933

Spanish Language

Spanish is the language! This old gag of having the children take up French, because it's fashionable, is the baloney. You don't see anybody in France but Americans, so you don't get any chance to try out your French, anyway.

But just look at the dozens of countries that speak Spanish, in addition to Spain. It's the only one to learn, for you can use it commercially for the rest of your life.

December 9, 1928

SPEED

There never was such a demand for speed, for less reason. There is not a one of us that couldn't walk where we are going and then get there earlier than we have any business.

April 28, 1933

★　★　★

The trouble with American transportation is that you can get somewhere quicker than you can think of a reason for going there.

What we need now is a new excuse to go somewhere.

March 12, 1934

SPORTS, AMATEUR

Modern College football has some queer customs. The heroes can have all the girls they want, but they are not allowed to marry one

of 'em. They can play for their tuition, board and room, and a moderate salary but they are not allowed to do it "for the wife and kiddies."
November 18, 1930

★　★　★

The poor old professional in all our sports now just prays for the day when he can afford to be an amateur.
August 23, 1929

SPRING

Spring is coming; I can tell by the poetry and the real estate ads.
April 1, 1923

STANDARD OF LIVING

Brother, we are just riding mighty, mighty high in this country. For every automobile we furnish an accident. For every radio we put on two murders. Three robberies for every bathtub installed. Building two golf courses to every church. Our bootleggers have manicures and our farmers have mortgages. Our courts are full, our politicians are full.

Truly Rome never saw such prosperity.
April 24, 1930

★　★　★

To us, Progress is to work ourselves up to a 6-cylinder Buick, have a dinner jacket, belong to six lunch clubs and wear knee breeches on Sunday. Then we go out and tell the world how the Standard of Living has raised. And start telling the world we are the only ones with the right idea.
April 10, 1927

★　★　★

You know, I think we put too much emphasis and importance and advertising on our so-called "High Standard of Living." I think that "High" is the only word in that phrase that is really correct. We sure are a-living HIGH.
June 2, 1928

★　★　★

Every official in the Government and ever prominent manufacturer is forever bragging about our "High Standard of Living."

Why, we could always have lived this high, if we had wanted to live on the installment plan.
December 9, 1926

STATE LEGISLATURE

There is nothing that will upset a state's economic condition like a legislature. It's better to have termites in your house than the legislature.

March 31, 1935

STATES

What's the size of a state got to do with how good it is? I heard of a fellow that was satisfied with Rhode Island—and part of his garage lopped over into Connecticut and half his yard was in Massachusetts.

May 29, 1926

The rest of America have sat patiently by for years and listened to Florida and California argue. America couldn't pick up a magazine without looking at a picture of somebody hitting a golf ball in sunny California, or balmy Florida. To read the ads, you would think those were the only places where golf ball were being missed. They have both howled about their climate till you would think the rest of the states of the Union kept their inhabitants alive by artificial respiration.

May 29, 1926

STATESMEN

A statesman is a man that can do what the politician would like to do but can't, because he is afraid of not being elected.

July 5, 1934

STATISTICS

This thing called 'Statistics' was the worst thing that was ever invented.

May 14, 1933

We are always reading statistics and figures. Half of America does nothing but prepare propaganda for the other half to read.

February 24, 1929

We have eleven million unemployed, counting the four million that do nothing but keep statistics on things we would be better off if we didn't know.

April 2, 1932

STATUS QUO ANTE

Status Quo Ante, it's an old Indian word that means: "This thing has gone far enough; let's go back to where we started from and next time we will watch each other closer."

February 27, 1932

STOCK SWINDLES

Just been talking today to the Senators investigating these stock swindles and over-capitalizations.

There ought to be some form of guardianship for people who buy all this junk. Education won't do it. Most sales are made to the ones we have educated up till they are just smart enough to fall for anything that comes along.

November 12, 1933

The California committee who were looking into receiverships and fake stock schemes (which are one and the same) they found out that Californians will buy anything in the way of stock if it's phoney enough.

November 17, 1933

STRIKES

I can think of nothing more unpopular than a strike, a strike of anything.

September 24, 1933

A strike should be the very last means, for it is like war. It always falls on those who had nothing to do with calling it.

August 6, 1933

The hard thing in this British strike from an American standpoint, is to look at an Englishman and judge from the way he is working whether he is on strike, or not.

There is not an American that wouldn't say England is on strike. But they wouldn't be at all; it would only be tea time.

May 16, 1926

If American Labor would work while their case is being arbitrated, instead of striking, they would have the gratitude of the President and the sympathy of everybody.

October 13, 1933

Both sides in this steel strike seem anxious to strike. Well, if they would only strike each other, it wouldn't be so bad.

But don't it look like there ought to be some civilized way of finding out what the employee and the employer owed to each other?
June 7, 1934

SUBMARINES

The one thing these old Boys with a big navy are scared of, and that's submarines. They are always claiming they are inhuman and not a civilized form of warfare.

It would be rather interesting to see published the name of the weapons that are considered a pleasure to be shot by.
April 30, 1935

SUCCESS

I am no believer in this "Hard Work, Perseverance and Taking Advantage of your Opportunities," that these magazines are fond of writing some fellow up in.

The Successful Ones don't work any harder than the Failures. They get what is called in baseball "the breaks."
November 15, 1925

SWIMMING

I've heard a lot of people say: "Why do these young American girls want to swim the English Channel for, anyway?"

Well, I will tell you why! These girls at some time in their life crossed on a boat and that's why they decided that if she ever had to cross it again, she would prefer swimming it. I know, I crossed it one time in a boat.
August 30, 1925

SWITZERLAND

Look at Switzerland! There is an example of a country minding its own business. No wars, no notes—just tending to its own business.
June 28, 1925

★   ★   ★

Switzerland just sits there in the middle of it all and hopes for a war so they can take care of the rich refugees from both sides. Switzerland is just like one of these board things they have in a bull ring where you can run when the bull gets after you.
April 2, 1933

T

TARIFFS

The tariff is an instrument invented for the benefit of those who "make" to be used against those who "buy." As there is more "buyers" than there is "makers," it is a document of the minority. But what a minority.

June 28, 1929

In Washington, our arguments are over tariffs. It's what started politics. It's what started Parties. It split Washington and Jefferson. There is no answer to it.

Why, twenty men can enter a room as friends and someone can bring up the Tariff and you will find nineteen bodies on the floor with only one living that escaped.

September 8, 1929

Arguing tariff is like arguing religion—there just ain't an answer. If a business thrives under a protective tariff, that don't mean that it has been a good thing. It may have thrived because it made the people of America pay more for the object than they should have, so a few got rich at the cost to the many.

June 1, 1930

Some of the smartest and most conscientious men in our national life have been divided on this new tariff bill question. It's not all politics, a lot of it is a matter of real opinion, based on long study.

It's all right to help out the folks back home and bring every voter some kind of relief, but those Boys in Washington, they are up against something that is above them. It's a smart man's business; it's not just for mere politicians to mess with.

June 1, 1930

TAXES

It's a great country, but you can't live in it for nothing.
February 5, 1934

★   ★   ★

If you make any money, the Government shoves you in the creek once a year with it in your pockets, and all that don't get wet, you can keep.
January 28, 1914

★   ★   ★

This would be a great world to dance in if we didn't have to pay the fiddler.
June 27, 1930

★   ★   ★

Taxes is more important to every individual than the name of any man that will ever be in the White House.
November 2, 1924

★   ★   ★

Every politician is talking about taxes. Now in the early days of this country they used to pay their whole year's taxes with a few sacks of tobacco they raised on their farm. Now, the same farm, you put another mortgage on every time a tax comes due.

But mind you, in those early days there was only 26 Senators and about 50 Congressmen to support. It's a good thing we haven't any more states to add on, for we would go broke. As it is, it will only take a few more years and we will all be on an allowance from the government.
October 19, 1924

★   ★   ★

It ain't taxes that is hurting this country, it's interest. There is more mortgages in this country than there is votes.
January 6, 1924

★   ★   ★

The nearest thing we have to a 'non-kick' tax, has been the gasoline tax, because they knew the money was going for roads. What would be the matter with using every cent from a liquor tax for charity and unemployment relief? And make the tax very high, even as high as 100 per cent. If it was a 100 per cent tax, and it went to charity, you wouldn't be drinking alone. Some poor family would be drinking with you. You get a beer, somebody gets a loaf of bread. Anybody give a big champagne party and spend hundreds of dollars, not even a Communist could kick on it, for the needy get half of it.
July 20, 1933

I don't believe any of us really know what our obligation is to our fellow man. That should be established, as I say, you can't go by conscience for they vary too much. So find the needy and tax us exactly our proportionate share to keep 'em, and you won't run up this tremendous national debt. We pay as we go, and if it's done fair and equal like this, you won't hear many kicks.

January 6, 1935

★　★　★

When will they quit taxing farmers' land, regardless of whether it made anything? Or selling people's homes for taxes?

Not till they get a sales tax—small on necessities and large on luxuries. A tax paid on the day you buy is not as tough as asking for it the next year, when you are broke. It's worked on gasoline—it ought to work on Rolls-Royces, cigarettes, lipstick and Coca-Cola.

September 7, 1931

★　★　★

People are getting smarter nowadays; they are letting lawyers, instead of their conscience, be their guide.

April 8, 1923

★　★　★

I read where there is some talk of lowering income tax, and they will have to. People are not making enough to pay it.

April 8, 1923

★　★　★

Our financial ills will never be settled till you fix it so every man will pay an income tax on what he earns, be it a farm, grocery store or municipal or government bonds.

March 21, 1933

★　★　★

No slick lawyers, or income tax experts can get you out of a national sales tax. It's so much on the dollar on every luxury you buy. Then, if you like to live in luxury, the poor fellow knows you are paying for it and he will even encourage you to buy more so it will help out the government.

November 2, 1924

★　★　★

The income tax has made more liars out of the American people than golf has.

November 2, 1924

★　★　★

People don't mind spending their money if they know it's not going for taxes.

June 26, 1926

Taxation is about all there is to Government. You know, people don't want their taxes lowered near as much as the politicians try to make you believe. People want just taxes more than they want lower taxes.

November 2, 1924

I bet you, tomorrow if you started a political party and had this as its platform: 'No taxes are to be paid at all! We will borrow money on our national resources for all current expenses! Remember the slogan: No taxes as long as we can borrow!' Well, I bet you, you would have the biggest political party in America.

January 10, 1926

By the way, did you charge off money given to the Democratic campaign? You could, it's a legitimate charity—not organized, but a charity nevertheless.

March 15, 1929

This is Income Tax paying day. There is going to be no attempt at humor, for it would be mighty forced. No two can agree on what is deductible. When it's made out, you don't know if you are a crook or a martyr.

March 15, 1929

★   ★   ★

As it is now, Congress is taxing everybody without a lobby.

February 29, 1932

★   ★   ★

Every time Congress starts to tax some particular industry, it rushes down to Washington with its main men and they scare Congress out of it.

February 29, 1932

★   ★   ★

The crime of taxation is not in the taking of it, it's in the way it's spent.

March 20, 1932

★   ★   ★

Congress, with an eye not on the budget, but on the election in November, talks about putting a tax as high as 72 per cent on some incomes. That's almost three fourth. Why, even the Communists only asked for half.

March 20, 1932

★   ★   ★

Where is all the money coming from that the government

plans to throw away? Well it just sorter looks like it might come from the ones that have got it.

April 7, 1935

TAX-EXEMPT BONDS

Tax exempt bonds is the biggest thing in the world the matter with our tax system. It's the most unjust law we have. Every one of you that own or make anything, pays some sort of tax on it, yet there is a way that a man could draw millions from our government and never pay a cent of it out in taxes.

March 19, 1933

Nothing in our country should be tax exempt, so write to your Congressman and tell him to do away with tax exempt bonds. Even if he can't read, write to him.

March 19, 1933

TAXPAYERS

I am in Washington, D.C., today. Everybody is on a trip somewhere if they work for the government.

I wonder when the taxpayers take their trip?

July 8, 1923

It looks like the taxpayers in the United States are the only folks hiring any help nowadays. A private business, when it don't do any business, don't use anybody. But the less business the public has, the more we hire to tend to it.

July 5, 1932

The big yell comes nowadays from the taxpayers. I bet you, when the Pilgrims landed on Plymouth Rock, and they had the whole of the American continent, and all they had to do to get an extra 160 acres was to shoot another Indian, well, I bet you anything they kicked on the price of ammunition. I bet you they said—like we're doing now: "What's this country coming to that we have to spend a nickel for powder?"

April 7, 1935

TECHNOCRACY

What do you think of Technocracy?
Nothing you can't spell will ever work.

January 3, 1933

We thought Technocracy was a tough bird to get the lowdown on, but it's only a first reader compared to hearing a guy explain "Inflation."
May 2, 1933

TEMPERAMENT

I'll tell you about temperament. Temperament is liable to come with a little success, especially if you haven't been used to success. The best cure in the world for temperament is hunger. I have never seen a poor temperamental person.
August 30, 1925

<u>TEXAS</u>

I see where a woman was elected governor in Texas. I know she was just nominated, but when I say elected, I mean elected. For when they nominate a Democrat in Texas, they stay nominated. You don't catch them wasting any nominations.
September 7, 1924

Texas is a great state. It's the "Old Man River" of states. No matter who runs it, or what happens to it politically, it just keeps rolling along.
August 30, 1932

★   ★   ★

I tell you, that Texas is a great state. It's the biggest thing you ever saw and has the most variety of products. It will get so big that it will become an empire all its own, like it was one time. Don't you remember that time when Mexico won the war from the U.S. and made us take Texas back?
November 5, 1933

★   ★   ★

Just got a beautiful pamphlet of the "Big Bend Country" down in Texas on the border between El Paso and San Antonio. I doubt if America holds a more interesting place, and for you guys that like to hunt, my goodness, there is your star spot.

You talk about some wild, old country. Well, that is about the wildest of the wild we got left—outside of the cities.
January 15, 1933

★   ★   ★

For any guy that can run Texas, running America ought to be a pipe cinch.
November 29, 1927

If you think this Texas ain't some size, you just try to drive from one part of it to another in a car.

January 27, 1931

THANKSGIVING

Thanksgiving Day! In the days of our founders, they were willing to give thanks for mighty little, for mighty little was all they expected.

But now, neither Government or nature can give enough but what we think it's too little. Those old boys in the Fall of the year, if they could gather a few pumpkins, potatoes and some corn for the Winter, they was in a thanking mood.

But if we can't gather in a new car, a new radio, a tuxedo and some Government relief, we feel like the world is agin us.

November 28, 1934

THOUGHTS

A young man, he just thinks; but an old man, when he's sitting and thinking, he's supposed to be pondering.

October 7, 1934

TOKYO, JAPAN

This Tokyo is quite a capitol. Got everything but Senators, which really may be responsible for their tremendous advancement.

No matter what you do in Japan, you must first have tea; then, after you do what you was going to do, you have tea again.

January 24, 1932

TOUPEES

Figure out a toupee that the hair won't stay combed the same way all the time, and you will go down in history.

December 21, 1924

TOURISTS

There is nothing the American tourist won't carry off. The Grand Canyon is the only thing they haven't carried away, and that's only because it's a hole in the ground.

Notes

★ ★ ★

The greatest thing that the Petrified Forest has demonstrated to the world is that there is nothing that the American tourist won't carry off. The wayside is strewn with cars that tried to get out with too much.

I have often wondered why the Government goes to the expense of tearing down any public building. All they have to do is let the report get out that Washington slept there and then put up a sign "Please Don't Touch!" then have a guard stand there with his back turned and in two days the entire house will be in the back end of Fords, being transplanted to Iowa and Kansas.

Notes

★   ★   ★

That's one thing the tourists have done anyway—they have improved Europe's plumbing!

1926

★   ★   ★

I had visited some strange places in the world, but it was always so full of tourists by the time I got to it, that the tourists were stranger than the place.

April 14, 1929

★   ★   ★

A tourist is one of the worst, if not the worst, investment there is. He knocks everything and buys nothing. He don't know where he is going, only that he wants to get away from his own home. He is sore at his wife and a family that are in the car, and he takes it out on your part of the country.

A tourist contributes nothing but empty tin cans and profanity to the upbuilding of your state.

September 22, 1929

★   ★   ★

Americans spent $700 million to be insulted in Europe last summer and they could have got it done for half the money here.

January 8, 1927

TRADITION

That thing "Tradition," has held more things back in this world than a red traffic light.

March 30, 1929

★   ★   ★

Tradition is nothing more than saying "The Good Old Days," and what you mean by anybody's "good old days," is the days they can remember when they was having more fun than they are having now.

March 30, 1929

Tradition? It's the thing we laugh at the English for having, and we beat 'em practicing it.

May 26, 1928

TRAFFIC, VEHICULAR

I see where everybody is trying to solve the traffic problem here in Los Angeles. Well, if the prices of automobiles keep on going up, that will solve the traffic problem itself.

1920

★　★　★

I have a solution to the traffic problem and that is to raise the speed limit to 75 miles an hour, and make everybody go that fast or be arrested. That would eliminate the slow and kill off the fast.

1920

★　★　★

The only way to solve the traffic problems of this country is to pass a law that only paid-for cars are allowed to use the highways.

That would make traffic so scarce we could use our boulevards for children's playgrounds.

January 6, 1924

★　★　★

Suggestions to solve traffic problems:

Everybody traveling west, go Monday; east, Tuesday; north, Wednesday; south, Thursday.

Sundays reserved for weekend drivers alone, Sunday night—caring for the injured.

1920

★　★　★

Eliminate what few street cars there are, as they only get in people's way who are in a hurry walking home.

1920

★　★　★

Why do they call it a traffic problem? When it ceases to move, it's not traffic.

1920

TRAVEL

It's getting so you can travel cheaper than you can stay at home.

March 24, 1935

★　★　★

I left home as a kid and worked my way all through the Argentine, South Africa, Australia and New Zealand and I was three years getting enough money to get home on. I never found it necessary to have my "American Rights" protected.

Nobody invited me into those countries and I always acted as their guest, not as their advisor.

June 28, 1925

"TRICKLE DOWN" ECONOMIC THEORY

Money was appropriated in the hopes that it would trickle down to the needy. Herbert Hoover was an engineer. He knew water trickled down. Put it uphill and let it go and it will find the driest little spot. So money was appropriated for the top in the hope that it would trickle down to the needy.

But he didn't know that money trickled up! Give it to the people at the bottom and the people at the top will have it before night, anyhow. But it will at least have passed through the poor fellow's hands.

November 27, 1932

TRUTH

When somebody calls you "names" and there is no truth in it, and you know that everybody knows there is no truth in it, why, you naturally don't pay any attention to it. You just laugh it off.

But, if what they call you is hitting at the truth and kinder getting you in your weak spot, why you start hollering and denouncing at once.

December 14, 1930

★   ★   ★

Nothing makes a man, or a body of men, as mad as the truth. If there is no truth to it, they laugh it off.

September 17, 1931

★   ★   ★

A remark generally hurts in proportion to its truth. If it's so untrue as to be ridiculous, why, nobody pays any attention to it.

March 31, 1935

TURKEY

The Turk never saw the day when he was held in as low esteem by even an Armenian, as the Republican is held by the Southern Democrat.

November 2, 1928

★   ★   ★

There is nothing that irks a Turk so much as peace.

October 19, 1930

TUXEDOS

I drag out the old blue serge suit, double breasted, that has fooled many a one, if you don't watch it too close, into thinking maybe it's a quarter-breed tuxedo.

'Course, the soft shirt and collar look kinder negligee, but the black bow tie and the old blue serge looking black by lamplight, why, it looks within the requirements of "dress formal."

November 26, 1933

U

UNEMPLOYMENT

What we got is substantial unemployment and that's the thing that needs fixing, never mind World Court and Disarmament, and all that hooey!

December 14, 1930

The unemployment situation is lightening up. California, to help relieve unemployment has decided as its contribution to charity to take on nine more Congressmen.

November 19, 1930

The reason there wasn't much unemployment in the last ten years was that every man that was out of a job went to work for the Government—federal, state, or city.

March 27, 1932

★ ★ ★

We had enjoyed special blessings over other nations, and we couldn't see why they shouldn't be permanent. We was a mighty cocky nation, we originated mass production and mass produced everybody out of a job with our boasted labor-saving machinery. It saved labor, the very thing we are now appropriating money to get a job for. They forgot that machinery don't eat, rent houses, or buy clothes. We had begun to believe that the height of civilization was a good road, bath tub, radio and automobile.

I think the Lord just looked us over and decided to set us back where we belonged.

December 30, 1930

★ ★ ★

Every paper every morning tells of a big gathering and prominent men who have spoken on "Better Times." If every Chamber of Commerce would give workers a job, instead of some speakers a dinner, there would be no unemployment.

October 24, 1930

There has been more optimism talked and less practiced than at any time during our history. Every millionaire we have has offered a speech instead of offering a job. Our optimism is all at a banquet table, where everybody has already more than he can eat.

October 24, 1930

Everybody kinder tries to explain the cause of this recession, and that's where they all fall down.

If a snake bites you, you ain't going to stop and study where he come from—you want to start figuring on what to do with yourself right then. What we got now is "substantial" unemployment and that is the thing that needs fixing.

December 14, 1930

There is not one unemployed man in the country that hasn't contributed to the wealth of every millionaire in America. Every one of us that have anything, got it by the aid of these very people.

October 18, 1931

★   ★   ★

If you live under a government and it don't provide some means of you getting work when you really want it, and will do it, then there is something wrong. It should be arranged that if you could in no way find a job, you could go to some state or national public work, that would give you, say, four hours a day work. Instead of dole being handed out as charity, you work for it.

January 18, 1931

UNITED STATES OF AMERICA

That's what makes us a great nation. We take the little things serious, and the big ones as a joke.

September 15, 1933

★   ★   ★

You can diplomat America out of almost everything she has, but don't try and bluff her.

May 4, 1924

★   ★   ★

All we have to do to get in bad, is just to start out on what we think is a Good Samaritan mission, that's when we wind up in the pesthouse.

October 2, 1926

What's the matter with us? No country ever had more and no country ever had less. Ten men in our country could buy the whole world, and ten million can't buy enough to eat.
August 16, 1931

★   ★   ★

We are not only the richest nation in the world, but we are the poorest; we got more than any of them, but we owe more, too.
January 11, 1925

★   ★   ★

Nobody is going to spoil the country but the people. No one man can do it, and all the people are not going to do it, so it's going to run in spite of all the mistakes that can happen to it.
October 30, 1932

★   ★   ★

We are the champion yap nation of the world for swallowing propaganda. You can take a sob story and a stick of candy and lead America right off into the Dead Sea.
December 2, 1923

★   ★   ★

We will never get things righted in our country till every line of sport, industry, profession or trade have some system of everybody contributing while working to the welfare of the old and unemployed in his own line. I don't mean to put all ball players, for example in an old ball players' home; I mean a system of help where it's done and they retain their respect and courage and self-esteem.
April 10, 1932

★   ★   ★

People ask: "What's the matter with this country?" Nothing, only there is millions got a putter in their hand when they ought to have a shovel.
August 5, 1930

★   ★   ★

America invents everything, but the trouble is we get tired of it the minute the new is wore off.
December 28, 1924

★   ★   ★

There is no country in the world where a person changes from a hero to a goat, and a goat to a hero, or vice versa, as they do with us. And all in no change in them. The change is always in us.
Notes

★   ★   ★

Oh, boy, I am glad to set my old big feet on American soil,

even if it has got a second mortgage on it.

February 9, 1932

Remember we got two great friends you can always depend on, the Atlantic and the Pacific oceans—three thousand miles wide and a mile deep. No nation ever had two better friends!

April 9, 1933

All I know is just what I read in the papers. We seem to get involved all over the world. You know, it will always seem funny to me that we are about the only ones that really know how to do everything right. I don't know how a lot of these other nations have existed as long as they have till we could get some of our people around and show 'em how really to be Pure and Good like us.

February 27, 1932

America has just been musclebound from holding a steering wheel. The only callused place on an American is at the bottom of his driving toe.

October 25, 1931

What I want to know is what the devil business is it of ours how some country runs their business? How do we know what THE EYES OF THE WORLD are on? As a matter of fact, THE EYES OF THE WORLD are on a dollar bill, and especially if somebody else has it. The rest of the world's eyes don't even know this country exists!

June 28, 1925

We can get hot and bothered quicker over nothing and cool off faster than any nation in the world.

February 13, 1930

America has a great habit of always talking about protecting American interests in some foreign country. PROTECT 'EM AT HOME! There is more American interests right here than anywhere.

June 28, 1925

We're possessed with a great curiosity, the greatest curiosity in the world to horn in on somebody else's business. We've always had that!

June 10, 1934

Why, they didn't discover America until 1492, and by that time the world had 1492 wars, 1492 peace and economic conferences—all before we was ever heard of. England controlled all the oceans, half the land and half the world's international commerce; France is no Babe in Arms, Japan and Russia are of age; yet it is always America that they kid into thinking she is the whole cheese.

June 22, 1933

UNITED STATES CONGRESS

There is an old legend that years ago there was a man elected to Congress who voted according to his own conscience.

1919

★   ★   ★

Congress meets tomorrow morning. Let us all pray. Oh, Lord, give us strength to bear that which is about to be inflicted upon us.

Be merciful with them, oh, Lord, for they know not what they are doing. Amen.

December 5, 1926

★   ★   ★

If we took Congress serious we would be worrying all the time.

February 28, 1926

★   ★   ★

Washington, D.C., papers say: "Congress is deadlocked and can't act!" I think that is the greatest blessing that could befall this country.

January 27, 1924

★   ★   ★

Of course Congress is not doing the best they can, but they are doing the best they know how.

May 29, 1932

★   ★   ★

Did you ever figure it out? Congress is the only people in the world that are paid to do one job and do every other one there is but that. If businessmen strayed as far from their actual business, we would have the prosperity of India.

March 26, 1928

★   ★   ★

The Senate is a body of men that can talk for two weeks on the duty on hair pins, even if women ain't using them, but that don't matter.

April 27, 1930

You may ask: Isn't the Presidency higher than Senator? Well, no! The Senate can make a sucker out of any President, and generally does.

June 8, 1920

Congress even has slogans:

"Why sleep at Home, when you can sleep in Congress?"

"Join the Senate and investigate something!"

"It is easier to fool 'em in Washington than it is at home, so why not be a Senator?"

"Come to Washington and vote to raise your own pay!"

"Work for Uncle Sam, it's just like a pension."

April 12, 1925

They do love publicity. Talk about actors basking in the limelight! Say, an old Senator can make an actor look like he is hid under a barrel.

November 11, 1929

I did everything in the Circus, Wild West Show, the Follies, the Movies, and even a real play where you had to remember lines, and everything.

There is one amusement line I haven't been in and that's go to the Senate. But I ain't going to try that; I've got some pride left.

July 1, 1934

You see, the class of help a President gets in the Senate and the House, is restricted and you can't treat 'em with kindness. A Congressman or a Senator is not used to kind treatment—even at home—you have to be rough with those birds.

June 3, 1923

★   ★   ★

The bad part about the whole structure of paying our Congressmen is that we name a sum and give them all the same, regardless of ability. If some efficiency expert would work out a scheme where each Congressman would be paid according to his ability, I think we would save a lot of money.

March 22, 1925

★   ★   ★

Distrust of the Senate started with Washington, who wanted to have 'em court martialled. Jefferson proposed life imprisonment for 'em; old Andy Jackson said "To Hell with 'em" and got his wish; Lincoln said: "The Lord must have hated 'em, for he made so few of 'em." Teddy Roosevelt whittled a big stick and beat on 'em for six years. They drove Wilson to an early grave and Coolidge never let 'em know what he wanted, so they never knew how to vote against him. Hoover took 'em serious, thereby making his only political mistake.

November 2, 1929

Anything that has to pass that Senate is just like a rat having to pass a Cat Convention—it's sure to be pounced on, and the more meritorious the scheme is, the less chance it has of passing.

May 11, 1930

I have to go to Washington every so often to see what the Senators are doing. I can't just leave 'em, they wouldn't do a thing—or, if they did, it would be the wrong thing. I got to go down there and kinder prod 'em up every once in a while, same as the President has to bring 'em in and pat 'em on the back every so often.

February 11, 1934

★ ★ ★

Say, did you know that Washington, D.C., has an underground tunnel running from the Government offices to the Capitol? This tunnel is the place where legislators have been hiding when they didn't want to be put on record with a vote on any important subject.

When the Senators and Congressmen receive their pay checks every month, they need this secret passage to get to their homes without someone arresting them for robbery.

October 5, 1924

★ ★ ★

It's hard to get money out of the Senate for anything but for politics.

January 23, 1929

★ ★ ★

I suggested a plan one time to shorten Senate debates. Every time a Senator tells all he knows, make him sit down. That will shorten it. Some of them wouldn't be able to answer roll call.

April 27, 1930

★ ★ ★

They are a pretty tough bunch of hyenas, those Senators, but they are likeable rascals and every time we let one of 'em out, a worse one gets in. So I am in favor of keeping this same bunch we got now.

April 27, 1930

The fellows from New England, or the Pacific Coast, or Texas, or the South, all have some scheme in their district that they want to get done and they are looking for an appropriation so the vote trading will start in Congress: "You help me dig out the Missouri and I will help you gyp the Treasury out of enough to put in a new post office building for your constituents."

At the finish every state will get something it don't need and the politician gets re-elected, thereby everybody getting something they don't want.

November 8, 1925

Spent the afternoon in Washington, D.C. (Don't Complain), Congress was in session and I was in the Speaker's office. I asked him why he wasn't in the Chamber and he said: "I am Speaker, not Listener."

"What are they talking about?" I asked. He said: "Taxes."

I said: "Why, that ought to be a good lively subject. I am going in there and hear it." He replied: "Go ahead; you do it at your own peril!"

I went in. I was all alone in the gallery. Somebody was talking, but there was only four members in their seats. Oh, it was a lonesome place. It reminded me of the night I played Madison, Wisconsin.

December 27, 1925

Now you mind my words and watch what will happen. This being an election year for a lot of these "statesmen" (in the making), they will go home and run on "I didn't raise your tax!" Then they will come back next year and find the huge deficit and they will have to dig up something else to raise the money on.

February 28, 1926

If we didn't have to stop to play Politics, any administration could almost make a Garden of Eden out of us. You could transfer Congress over to run Standard Oil or General Motors, and they would have both things bankrupt in two years. No other business in the world could afford to carry such deadwood.

November 11, 1928

★   ★   ★

All voters in all states are hereby asked to pass the following resolution, addressed to their Senators and Congressmen:

We want you to help our particular district as far as it is legitimately possible, without, of course, expense or injury to any other part of our country. But please keep in mind that even should the President be of your opposite political faith, or not of your particular and personal branch of your same faith, be it understood that it won't be necessary for you to shoot his dog, or question his integrity. In fact, you can act like gentlemen, and while it will be a surprise, we won't hold it against you at the next election.

May 9, 1929

Let's see what we got to be thankful for?

Congress adjourned! I know that will be the first thing that comes into your mind. But that blessing will be short-lived, for they are soon to meet again.

November 27, 1929

★   ★   ★

The Senate just sits and waits till they find out what the President wants, so they know how to vote against him. Be a good joke on 'em if he didn't let 'em know what he wants.

That's the way Mr. Coolidge used to do it. He would keep 'em guessing so long that they voted his way accidentally part of the time.

June 29, 1930

★   ★   ★

We are a good natured bunch of saps in this country.

When Congress is wrong we charge it to habit.

When the Senate is right, we declare a National Holiday.

June 30, 1930

★   ★   ★

Did you know that one hundred years ago we only had 36 Senators and look how that evil has grown. There was no golf in this country then and there was no unemployment in those days. If a man wasn't working, he sat in front of the grocery store and whittled.

May 14, 1933

★   ★   ★

This is a very momentous Congress that is in session. They have appropriated more money than any Congress ever did, but I guess that is all right—we are not paying our national debt, anyhow. We just keep on adding to it, so it don't matter how much it is, anyway.

June 11, 1933

★   ★   ★

Watched Congress open in Washington around noon today, then I realized I couldn't do anything about it. So I left.

February 2, 1934

★   ★   ★

All I know is just what I read in the papers. Well, Congress thought they knew more about how to run a country than the President, so the President decided to go fishing. The trouble is the wrong one went fishing.

March 28, 1934

★   ★   ★

To show you that we get along better without 'em, since Congress adjourned last Monday, business has jumped up like it's been shot. Honest, the Stock Market and everything went up. Everybody is feeling better.

If Congress had adjourned before they had met, I expect we'd have been the most prosperous nation in the world.

June 24, 1934

★   ★   ★

I am anxious to see how they will classify these newly elected Senators and Congressmen. Some are Republicans, but Liberals; some are Democrats, but not Liberal. Some are Democrats and just use the label; some are Republicans, just to try and keep an old custom alive.

This next Congress is sure going to be a pack of mongrels.

November 6, 1934

Congressional Hearings

What does the Senate do with all the knowledge they demand from other people? They never seem to use it.

June 12, 1930

★   ★   ★

These hearings have been a fine thing for Washington. The hotels are crowded. Every time a guest registers the clerk asks him: I suppose you will be here until you testify?

March 2, 1924

★   ★   ★

They ought to pass a rule in this country that in any hearing, if a man couldn't tell the truth the first time, he shouldn't be allowed to try again.

March 2, 1924

Congressional Lame Ducks

A "Lame Duck" is a Senator or Congressman who has had his official position shot from under him by the excellent judgment of the voters back home.

March 11, 1928

★   ★   ★

An awful lot of people are confused as to just what is meant by a "Lame Duck Congress."

It's like where some fellows worked for you and you let 'em out, but after you fired 'em, you let 'em stay long enough so they could burn your house down.

December 8, 1932

★   ★   ★

A Lame Duck is a politician who is still alive, but the Government paymaster has been notified that he is about to become totally disabled.

December 3, 1928

★   ★   ★

The Lame Ducks met today, and why are they Lame Ducks? Because their constituents were thinking faster than they was.

December 1, 1932

Congressional Record

Senator Reed Smoot of Utah: "This stuff you are talking here costs the people of the United States $44 a page. That's beside what it costs to ship it to the Asylums where it's read!"

March 21, 1926

★   ★   ★

Well, all I know is just what I read in the Congressional Record. They have had some awful funny articles in there lately. As our Government deteriorates, our humor increases. They been arguing over taxes and that gives 'em all a chance to get some original views on where they was going to raise those billions of bucks that they are overdrawn.

June 5, 1932

★   ★   ★

One Senator objected to the remarks of a "professional joke maker" being included in the Congressional Record! Taking a dig at me, see? They didn't want any outsider contributing. Well, he had me wrong. Compared to them, I'm an amateur, and the things about my jokes is they don't hurt anybody. You can take 'em or leave 'em. You know what I mean. But with Congress, every time they make a joke, it's a law. You know. And every time they make a law, it's a joke.

May 12, 1935

★   ★   ★

A Congressional Record, a dictionary and a political platform is the three least-used things in existence today.

March 30, 1929

★   ★   ★

A foreigner coming here and reading the Congressional Record, would say that the President of the United States was elected solely for the purpose of giving a Senator somebody to call a horse thief.

December 19, 1930

UNITED STATES CONSTITUTION

You see, the old founders of the Constitution made it so it didn't matter who was in office, things would drag along about the same.
October 29, 1927

The Constitution of the United States gives the right to every free man to get all he can for whatever he has. That Constitution wisely allowed every person freedom, and bargaining power; so what has the ordinary man got? Nothing but his vote.

If I want to sell it, I will sell it, if I want to keep it and not use it at all, that is my inestimable right by the Constitution. If I want to even give it away for free, the only thing I have to look out for is the Insane Asylum.
May 20, 1926

★   ★   ★

I haven't seen a copy of the Constitution in years (I guess they are out of print), but I don't remember anything in there about what IT was to do if you raised too much, or if you manufactured too much, or if you went into debt too much, or if you drove your automobile too much, or if you bathed too much.

In fact, if I remember right, we owed more to the Constitution than it did to us.
October 23, 1933

★   ★   ★

As for changing the Constitution, that's done every day. They have juggled it around till it looks like a moving picture version of a popular book—it's so different from the original. But when those Boys that blue-printed the first Constitution decided that a man can believe what he likes in regard to religion, that's one line that is going to stay put.
July 19, 1925

Amendments to the Constitution

The nineteenth Amendment, I think that's the one that made women humans, by Act of Congress.
July 27, 1924

★   ★   ★

There is no use getting excited over a little thing like an amendment to our Constitution, because if you don't like this one, wait till next year and they will have some more.

It is pitiful when you think how ignorant the founders of the Constitution must have been. Just think what a country we would have if the men in those days had the brains and forethought of our men today!
December 28, 1924

One side says: "We got where we are as a great nation by this set of laws that we're living under, so why change them? Let the Constitution alone." And that's mighty good logic, too, I want to tell you.

But there is something they forget. You, or I, can rightfully say we got where we are by these laws, but there is a lot of folks that haven't got anywhere under 'em, you know. And the prospects ain't any too bright for 'em to get any further. So they might not be averse to some small change in the Constitution. They might say: "Yes, give us what you've got, and we'll say it's a perfect Constitution, too." See?

June 9, 1935

UNITED STATES DEPARTMENT OF STATE

Most of our Secretaries of State I ever heard of, gained fame by sending Diplomatic Notes to some of the nations. Why can't the present Secretary of State send one too?

Why don't he send a Diplomatic Note demanding protection of our American tourists in France? They have been skinned alive there for years.

June 28, 1925

That's a tough baby, the Secretary of State thing. You come in there labelled a statesman, and limp out headed for the ash can of political hopes.

February 3, 1929

UNITED STATES GOVERNMENT

It's no harder to work for the Government than it is to vote for it. In fact, most jobs is not as hard.

September 1926

Even the Government is in on it. It has slogans:

"Get in the Cabinet, you won't have to stay long!"

"If you are a lawyer and have never worked for a Trust, we can get you into the Cabinet!"

"Be a Politician, no training necessary."

All such slogans are held up to the youth of this country.

April 12, 1925

Maybe that's what has been the matter with our Government in Washington. Everybody seems unanimous that something is the matter. Well, maybe it has been too cheap.

I am a great believer in high-priced people. If a thing costs a lot, it may not be any better, but it adds a certain amount of class that the cheap thing can never approach. In the long run, it's the high-priced things that are the cheapest.

May 20, 1926

★ ★ ★

Of course we know our Government is costing us more than it's worth, but do you know of any other, cheaper Government that's running around? If you do, they'll sell you a ticket there anytime. You can try Russia; there is no income tax in Russia—but there is no income.

April 7, 1935

★ ★ ★

Sure, the Government can help us on everything—if we just furnish 'em the money to do it with.

Notes

★ ★ ★

The more men that have anything to do with trying to right a thing, why, the worse off it is. The Government has not only hundreds, but literally thousands in Washington to see that no man can personally tend to his own business. They go there to do it for him.

April 17, 1932

★ ★ ★

Our Government is not a business, it's a charity organization.

Notes

★ ★ ★

Lord, the money we do spend on Government and it's not one bit better than the Government that we got for one third the money twenty years ago.

March 27, 1932

★ ★ ★

People ask me: "Will, where do you get your jokes?" I just tell 'em: "Well, I just watch the Government and report the facts, that is all I do, and I don't even find it necessary to exaggerate."

June 11, 1933

★ ★ ★

You can't believe a thing you read in regard to official statements. The minute anything happens connected with official life, why, it's just like a cold night back home—everybody is trying to cover up.

October 4, 1925

★ ★ ★

We are going on the assumption that nothing in public life (or out of it, for that matter) is any good. Now what we have set out to do, is to find the worst.

It's no trouble to pick out the bad, but I tell you, when you sit

down to pick out the worst, you have set some task for yourself.
January 6, 1924

We got a long-sighted government. When everybody has got money, they cut taxes, and when they're broke, they raise 'em.

That's statesmanship of the highest order.
March 27, 1932

I tell you, this finding out how to govern a country, or state, or even a town, has got the whole world licked. There is not a type of government that can point with complete pride and say: "There, this is the best that can be had!"
June 17, 1934

If there is one thing that we want to inculcate into the minds of the youth of this country, it is that honesty and fair dealing with our own Government is the foundation of this nation.

Our history honors many names whose morals would not stand the acid test, but our history honors no man who betrayed, or attempted to betray, a Government trust.
February 10, 1924

On account of us being a Democracy, and run by the people, we are the only nation in the world that has to keep a Government for four years, no matter what it does.
February 21, 1930

There is not a man in this country that can't make a living for himself and his family. But he can't make a living for them AND his Government, too, not the way this Government is living.

What the Government has got to do is live as cheap as the people.
December 20, 1932

I bet you that many a public man wishes there was a law to burn old records.
July 30, 1928

Government Waste

Our Government is the only people that just love to spend money without being compelled to, at all.

But the Government is the only people that don't have to worry where it is coming from.
April 21, 1935

Everybody's asking: "What about all this money the Government is spending?"

It's pleasing the fellow that's receiving it, but it's driving the guy who thinks he's going to have to pay for it about nuts.

February 4, 1934

★ ★ ★

We say the Government is nutty and throwing away money. But any time any is thrown our way, we have never dodged it. Well, if the Government is throwing money away, the only thing I see for the ones that they are throwing it to, have 'em refuse to take it.

Just say: "It's Government money and it's tainted, and I don't believe in the Government spending all this money, and hence I don't take any part of it!"

But you haven't heard that, have you? So don't be so critical of the present plans as long as you are living on the loot from them.

April 7, 1935

★ ★ ★

Just reading of a fund the Government has, called the "Conscience Fund." If you feel that you have cheated the Government, you send them money.

Say, how about the Government having a "Conscience Fund?" They have skinned us many a time.

May 6, 1935

UNITED STATES MILITARY

United States Army

We would send soldiers anywhere that could get ten signers to a petition that said they wanted us. We was in the humanity business and we was going to do it right.

March 19, 1932

United States Army Air Corps

We ought to have the greatest air defence in the world, we got more air.

Notes

★ ★ ★

They was putting this parachute on me. It didn't look right to be telling me there was no danger and at the same time cinching one of those up on me, but it's Army regulation, and a good rule too.

I asked him if the thing worked. He said: "We have never had a complaint. If it don't work, bring it back and we will give you another one. It's the one thing in the Army that is absolutely guaranteed with a replacement."

I tell you, any experiment that is being made in the air is not a waste of time or money. Our defense, offense and all, have got to come from the air!

May 29, 1932

Aviation is sort of like the old .45 pistol, which made little men as dangerous as big men. It's sort of an equalizer. You could give little Switzerland enough airplanes and she would worry the Old Ned out of the big ones. There is no end to how many we ought to have. But about fifty thousand.

December 14, 1934

United States Marine Corps

You can't pick up a paper without reading where our Marines have landed to keep some nation from shooting each other, and if necessary we shoot them to keep them from shooting each other.

July 5, 1925

I don't think people have realized yet the most important thing about these ocean flights have brought out, and that is the quicker transportation of our Marines to other people's wars.

In the last year transportation has held us back, sometimes we were a week or so late. But with airplanes there is no excuse. So our slogan will be now: "Have your civil wars wherever and as far away as you want, but on opening day we will be there!"

June 12, 1927

Did you ever notice how much more peaceful it is all around when our Marines are at home instead of prowling around?

Why, if we keep 'em at home a while, we are liable to get out of the habit of wanting to send 'em away off, every time we heard of some little nation was about to pull off a local amateur revolution.

May 5, 1929

I am way out here in Peking, and say, if I didn't run onto another batch of U.S. Marines here! Marines are not soldiers; they are tourists. I find 'em all over. I have gotten out of maybe an airplane in the oddest places in the world, not thinking there was any civilization in a thousand miles, and there would be six or eight companies of Marines there.

They are likeable cusses; been everywhere, seen everything—but America. Some of them spoke pretty fair English.

March 19, 1932

Most of the Marines are back in America. It's the first time in years. Some of the boys like it here—they think this is a great country and a lot of them are going to take out citizenship papers.

January 27, 1935

Ever since I can remember telling jokes on the stage, and years before I started writing for any papers, I have used kidding stuff about us going into somebody's country. And it's always been tremendously popular stuff, for not a soul wanted us to be sending Marines out over the world like a big city would send policemen to places where they hear there was trouble.

January 7, 1934

United States Navy

I believe that if they didn't scrub brass and paint on a ship, they would run it with about one man.

August 9, 1934

Get our naval forces to be the biggest one. Second money with a fleet is sorter like running second in a Presidential election. It's better to spend more money and have the best fleet, just like it is better to spend money and get the most votes.

June 9, 1928

The Navy has a slogan: "Join the Navy and see the World!" You join and all you see for the first 4 years is a bucket of soap suds and a mop, and some brass polish. You spend the first 5 years in Newport News. On the sixth year you are allowed to go on a cruise to Old Point Comfort. So there is a slogan gone wrong.

April 12, 1925

Everybody is always advising the Government not to go into business, yet the Navy football team played to 125,000 in Chicago Saturday. That's not bad business, even for a Government.

I propose they keep them playing every Saturday the year round, and make 'em buy their own battleships.

October 15, 1928

UNITED STATES SUPREME COURT

Supreme Court decisions will always remain the same, five against four.

When it's six to three, that's called unanimous.

February 5, 1930

★   ★   ★

When Congress passes a law, or a President exceeds his authority, have some person notify the Supreme Court and get them to examine the medicine and see if it's poison BEFORE it's given to the patient, and not at the funeral. This would make the Supreme Court a preventive, and not an autopsy jury.

May 28, 1935

★   ★   ★

One time the Supreme Court of the United States prohibited the sale of anything in which liquor might be held or transported— bottles, jugs, barrels, buckets, gourds, flasks, corks, labels, boxes and burlap sacks. You couldn't sell any of these, but you could sell the wheat and corn that liquor is supposed to be made with. In other words, according to that Supreme Court decision you were allowed to make it, but not allowed to have anything to hold it in.

You see, it's on account of decisions like that why they got to be careful the type of men they put on the Supreme Court bench.

May 6, 1930

UNITED STATES TREASURY DEPARTMENT

By the way they are raiding the Treasury now, there don't look like it will do anybody any good to be elected in the future. What's the use of running your head off to get to the table where the food has just been all eaten up?

If I was an office seeker, I would kinder be doubtful whether there was enough in the Treasury left to pay my salary, much less what I wanted to run for the office for in the first place.

May 13, 1928

★   ★   ★

The Secretary of the Treasury informed all the Treasury Department people to keep out of politics!

There wouldn't be any such luck to have that spread to other departments?

June 8, 1934

V

VACATIONS

If we could ever get vacations down to where you wasn't any more tired on the day one was over than on our regular work day, it would be wonderful.

September 4, 1933

★ ★ ★

This busy man's vacation is a lot of "baloney" anyhow. The bigger he is the less he enjoys a vacation. It's always the bird that never does anything that enjoys a vacation.

There is nothing in the world as hard as playing when you don't want to.

February 14, 1929

VANITY

Talk about women being vain and always primping, why, say, men will make a sucker out of any woman when it comes to thinking he is about the grapes; a corset manufacturer told me that if it was not for men's corsets, they would have to go out of business.

May 20, 1928

★ ★ ★

Did you see the figures issued by the Department of Commerce about the amount men spend on cosmetics to beautify themselves? Didn't I tell you they are getting vainer over their look than women?

The spent over one billion dollars and there is more bald-headed ones and more ugly ones and more funny looking ones than we ever had before.

April 30, 1929

298

VENICE, ITALY

Say, what a fine swamp that Venice turned out to be. I stepped out of the wrong side of a Venice taxicab and they were three minutes fishing me out.

June 7, 1926

★　★　★

I got seasick crossing an alley.

June 7, 1926

★　★　★

If you love to have someone row you in a boat, you will love Venice. But don't try to walk, or they will be searching for you with grappling hooks.

June 7, 1926

VERMONT

Vermont has more hills in what they call their valleys, than Dakota can produce on top of their hills.

June 12, 1927

★　★　★

A Vermont farm don't lay, it hangs. When your corn grows up big enough to gather, you go up on the farm and shake the ears off and they fall into the barn.

June 12, 1927

★　★　★

Vermont is, what you would call, a "hard-boiled" state. The principal ingredients are granite, rock salt and Republicans—the last being the hardest of the three.

March 29, 1925

VETERANS

The most popular joke I had after the war in New York, when the Boys were coming back from Europe, and parading every day, was: "If we really want to honor our Boys, why don't we let THEM sit in the reviewing stands and make the people march by? They don't want to parade, they want to go home and rest. But they won't discharge a soldier as long as they can find a new street in a town that he hasn't marched down yet. If the money spent on stands and parades would be divided up amongst the soldiers, they would have enough to live comfortably on until the next war."

August 19, 1923

Us letting the veterans entirely alone, and not caring what his wants are, now that we don't need him (or think we don't), is like lots of people we have who allow their old parents, or grand parents, to be sent to a sanatorium because they were getting to be too much trouble and too much in the way for them to take care off at home.

July 25, 1927

★   ★   ★

We have kind of lost our pep and enthusiasm for our Boys. I thought, maybe, America might be interested in the Boys that fought the last war. If you are not interested, you better grab up your tabloid and start looking at the picture of your favorite murderer just as he is being released on bond.

But remember, the best insurance in the world is to take care of the ones that fought in the last war. You see, I am not so sure myself of no more wars, and there is the barest possibility that we might want to use these soldiers again!

July 24, 1927

★   ★   ★

I will never joke about old soldiers who try to get to reunions to talk over the war again. To talk of old times with old friends is the greatest thing in the world.

March 7, 1926

★   ★   ★

The Harvard College paper says the American Legion convention in Boston was just "one wild party."

Poor Harvard paper; they have a habit that just borders on genius for saying the wrong thing. Imagine any college paper criticizing somebody else for giving a wild party. Wait till another war comes and let the Harvard editorial staff fight it, and then they can show how a convention should be conducted.

Where the mistake was made was in not asking our boys when recruited if they ever took a little nip, and if they did, why, not allow 'em in our army. In that way we could have had a respectable war—and lost it.

October 13, 1930

VETERINARIANS

Personally I have always felt that the best doctor in the world is the veterinarian. He can't ask his patients what is the matter— he's got to just know.

November 5, 1927

If your hog has the cholera, the whole state knows it and everybody is assisting in stamping it out. You can have 5 children down with the infantile paralysis, more deadly ten times over than any foot and mouth disease, and see how many doctors they send out from Washington to help you.

May 11, 1924

VICE PRESIDENTS, UNITED STATES

We have certain things in America that we can always get a laugh on such as: "What is the name of our Vice President?"

June 14, 1925

★ ★ ★

I think the Vice President answers about the same purpose as a rear cinch on a saddle. If you break the front one, you are worse off than if you had no other.

Notes

★ ★ ★

I had lunch with the Vice President. I only did it on condition that we ate alone. I didn't want it to get out that I ate with a Vice President.

July 10, 1926

VIRGINIA

I wrote the other week about the Natural Bridge in Virginia. Why, if Europe had that, Americans would withstand any insults and ridicule in traveling to get to go and see it.

March 13, 1927

★ ★ ★

Am down in Old Virginia, the mother of Presidents when we thought Presidents had to be aristocrats.

Since we got wise to the limitations of aristocrats, Virginia has featured their ham over the Presidential timber.

January 31, 1927

VODKA

Vodka. It's a deceptive fluid. It's as harmful a looking thing as a nice gourd full of branch water, but when you start sampling it, your eyes begin expanding. It's the only drink where you drink and try to grit your teeth at the same time. It gives the most immediate results of any libation ever concocted. By the time it reaches the Adam's apple, it has acted.

December 3, 1933

Vodka is a time saver. It should especially appeal to Americans as it pays quicker dividends than any libation ever assembled. A man stepping on a red-hot poker could show no more immediate animation.

December 3, 1933

VOTERS

All you have to do to vote is just to check your brain on the way to the poll and then cast your ballot—just like the rest of us.

April 29, 1923

In most places it's awful hard to get folks to go and register to vote, but out here in Los Angeles, where we do everything "big," why, each qualified voter is allowed to register himself and ten dead friends. If he hasn't got ten dead friends, why, he is allowed to pick out ten live ones, just so they don't live in this state.

The Republicans are kicking on this arrangement, as they claim that system of registration gives the Democrats the best of it, as very few Republicans have ten friends.

October 17, 1934

Napoleon said one time an Army traveled on its stomach. I don't know what soldiers do, but I know what voters do in regard to their stomach. They go to the polls and if it's full, they keep the guy that's already in; and if the old stomach is empty, they vote to chuck him out.

March 30, 1929

★   ★   ★

No voter in the world ever voted for nothing; in some way he has been convinced that he is to get something for that vote. His vote is all that our Constitution gives him and it goes to the highest bidder. He jumps the way his bread looks like its buttered the thickest.

March 30, 1929

★   ★   ★

They talk about a man not being a good citizen if he don't vote. If everybody didn't vote then none of them would get elected and that would be the end of politics, and we would just go out and hire some good man to run the country, the same as we should now.

November 9, 1928

WALL STREET

Don't gamble! Take all your savings and buy some good stock and hold it till it goes up, then sell it.

If it don't go up, don't buy it.

October 31, 1929

On Wall Street there are more commissions paid out to stock salesmen, than profit is ever collected by stock buyers.

October 14, 1923

We are a good-natured bunch of saps in this country. When the Market drops fifty points, we are supposed not to know that it's through manipulation.

June 30, 1930

★ ★ ★

The Senate passed the bill to regulate Wall Street. The Government is going to put traffic lights on it; it has always been a hit-and-run street.

May 13, 1934

★ ★ ★

It's not a bad Thanksgiving at that. Wall Street stocks are about down to where the suckers can start buying again.

November 27, 1929

★ ★ ★

I tell people that this country is bigger than Wall Street, and if they don't believe it, I show 'em the map.

December 1, 1929

WAR

You can have all the advanced war methods you want, but, after all, nobody has ever invented a war that you didn't have to have somebody in the guise of soldiers to stop the bullets.

May 12, 1928

I am a peace man. I haven't got any use for wars and there is no more humor in 'em than there is reason for 'em.

December 4, 1931

When you get into trouble 5,000 miles from home, you've got to have been looking for it.

February 9, 1932

Wars strike me as being the only game in the world where there is absolutely no winner—everybody loses.

August 26, 1926

Wars are not fought for Democracy's sake—they are fought for land's sake. And we are the only country that ever went to war and come home with nothing.

November 4, 1934

When you can be killed just as dead in an unjustified war, as you can in one protecting your own home.

May 26, 1929

WAR PREVENTIONS

Somebody is always telling us in the papers how to prevent war. There is only one way in the world to prevent war and that is for every nation to tend to its own business. Trace any war and you will find some nation was trying to tell some other nation how to run their business. All these nations are interfering with some other nation's personal affairs but with an eye to business. Why don't we let the rest of the world act like it wants to?

June 28, 1925

If the world knew that we had the greatest Air Force in the world, you can bet no one would be coming over here and pouncing on us.

June 5, 1927

WASHINGTON, D.C.

Washington, D.C. You know, this is the only place where our public men can do foolish things and they look kinder plausible at the time?

Notes

If you could just get these lobbyists out of Washington, it would be as good as almost any city.

March 8, 1925

They say hot air rises. And I guess it does. An airplane flying over the Capitol the other day caught fire from outside sources.

January 27, 1924

WASHINGTON, GEORGE

George Washington was a surveyor in his younger days. He was a good surveyor. He took the exact measure of the British, and surveyed himself out about the most valuable piece of land in America at that time, Mount Vernon.

George not only could tell the truth, but he could tell land values.

February 13, 1927

★ ★ ★

We are about to celebrate the birth of George Washington. George was not only the father of our country, but he was the most celebrated woodsman that ever lived. He gained more fame with his hatchet than Lincoln did with his axe.

February 22, 1925

★ ★ ★

George Washington was the most versatile President we ever had. He was a farmer, civil engineer and gentleman.

He made enough with civil engineering to indulge in both the other luxuries.

December 23, 1928

★ ★ ★

It was really the first real estate promotion scheme. Washington and Jefferson landed on two of the best hills in the country and the Government got the swamps.

February 10, 1929

You know, America celebrating for Washington—a man who was so truthful—seems kinder sacrilegious. A lot of lying Americans get together and celebrate. Americans celebrating a truthful man's birthday always reminds me of a snake charmer celebrating St. Patrick's Day.

February 22, 1925

They will tell you how George Washington's farsightedness is exemplified in the width of Pennsylvania Avenue in Washington, D.C.; that he knew that some day the merry Fords and the frolicsome Chevrolets would be flitting hither and thither.

They credit this to the foresight of Washington, when as a matter of fact the width of the Avenue was determined to give a Senator or a Congressman room to stagger to his lodgings without bumping into a building.

February 10, 1929

WEST, THE AMERICAN

Ah, to be out in the wide open spaces, where men are men and farms are mortgaged. Where the government showed them every way in the world where they could borrow money and never yet introduced an idea of how to pay any of it back. Where women are women and only get to town when they have to go to endorse a note with their husband.

June 12, 1927

WEST VIRGINIA

West Virginia had seceded from Virginia when they got tired of listening to nothing but ancestry and smoked ham. 'Course, West Virginians could have bragged about their ancestors, too, only they weren't such big liars as the Virginians were.

West Virginia is, what you might call, the truthful end of the Virginias. Two feuds is about as far back as a West Virginian can ever trace any of his ancestors.

May 25, 1930

WHITE HOUSE

Funny thing about the White House. It wears down the most hardy of our menfolks, but the women seem to thrive on it.

October 11, 1934

If there is one thing that this country has been especially happy about, it's been the fact that we have been continually blessed with some fine, charming women in the White House.

Some of the men might have been able to stand a little over-hauling, but I tell you, there has never been a chirp of regret out of any one about the female occupants.

June 30, 1929

I guess you been reading in all the papers about the President's other "White House." The one where the President can get to and be far enough away so Congressmen and Senators couldn't come to eat breakfast off him.

Years ago some fellow in Baltimore left 200 thousand dollars for this very thing. But in his will, he left only eighteen months for Congress to accept or reject it. Well, Congress can't get the roll called in eighteen months, much less accept or reject anything. Then, besides, 200 thousand dollars wouldn't hardly be enough to pay for the Senatorial investigation to find out where that man got the money that he gave to the country.

December 23, 1928

WINTER

Winter is coming and tourists will soon be looking for a place to mate.

October 27, 1932

WOMEN

Women are not the weak, frail, little flowers that they are adver-tised. There has never been anything invented yet, including war, that a man would enter into, that a woman wouldn't too!

December 17, 1933

The women can well feel proud of their record at this last Democratic Convention. They made better and shorter speeches, didn't sell out, looked better, dressed better, stayed awake better and had they been running it, we would all been home earlier.

July 17, 1924

I don't suppose there is any country, unless it be India, where the wife is more downtrodden than they are in the United States.

May 23, 1932

What's this generation coming to? I bet you the time ain't far off when a woman won't know any more than a man.

April 29, 1923

Although the gamest women can keep back tears in sorrow, they can't keep them back in happiness.

July 27, 1924

The female of the human race has retained her beauty, but the male has been a throw-back. He has retained none of the springy movements and the grace and beauty of form and skin.

Our only salvation is to raise just females.

June 5, 1932

Women promised us that they would clean up politics. But the women themselves—you talk to them—they admit that about all they have added to the whole voting and political thing is just more votes and more bookkeeping. But it ain't the women's fault—politics is bigger than any race or sex. Why, even if we gave the children the vote, it ain't going to clean up politics.

June 2, 1935

WOMEN'S CHRISTIAN TEMPERANCE UNION

The women Drys here in Houston have a regular hall where they go and pray that no Wet shall enter the Kingdom of Heaven.

They forget that when women enter politics their prayers don't mean any more to the Lord than men's.

June 25, 1926

WOMEN'S MARKSMANSHIP

The past week 9 women in various parts of the U.S. shot and killed their husbands. In no line of modern scientific advancement has progress been more marked than in the marksmanship of the weaker sex.

Remington and Smith and Wesson have done more to advance the cause of woman's suffrage than all the arguments of its millions of believers. Man used to be bigger than woman, but now woman carries the difference in her vanity case, neatly oiled and loaded.

January 13, 1924

WOMEN'S RIGHTS

A band of women hailed me yesterday and wanted me to write something about helping them get "Equal Rights." So I told them I thought myself that they had too many, and it was mighty nice of them to want to split some of them with the men.

June 25, 1928

WORLD SERIES

My idea of the height of conceit would be a political speaker that would go on the air when the World Series is on.

October 3, 1928

These announcers of the World Series did a great job. I got a radio in my stable. Well, they made it seems so real that half a dozen times I started into a box stall to buy a hot dog and a bottle of beer.

I liked the way they announced where the batter come from, his home town, his weight, age, batting average and who he had been keeping company with.

October 3, 1933

There was twenty million baseball fans that listened to the World Series that knew every play made, and why, and how it was made, but still don't know whether Harvard is a town or a mouth wash, whether Yale is a yell or a lock, and think all Notre Dames are churches.

So viva baseball. It's for us unfortunates who have no alumni.

October 14, 1929

WRESTLING

Went down last night to a world's championship wrestling match. Us movie actors are advised to go there by our producers, so we can learn how to act.

It was a fine show, everybody enjoyed it, but wrestling management are overlooking an extra big revenue, for folks would pay even more to see them rehearse with each other before the match.

July 25, 1935

WRITERS

Everybody is writing something nowadays. It used to be just the literary, or newspaper men who were supposed to know what they were writing about that did all the writing.

But nowadays, all a man goes into public office for is so he can try to find out something, then write about it when he comes out.

December 31, 1922

Y

YOUTH

Some criticize today's youth, but I think that that criticism is unwarranted. Youth must have its fling, and because we are too old to fling, we must be tolerant with those that are flinging.

December 1928

★   ★   ★

Youth must sow its wild oats, and oat seed hasn't changed since the day Eve planted the first crop.

Youth today is no worse than we were, only the publicity is greater today. Long skirts hid more in your mother's day, but the provocation was there. We had no automobiles by the roadside in those days, but horses would stop, too. We covered more space in our dances and didn't use the huddle system. The kiss was shorter, but there were more of them.

December 1928

★   ★   ★

Even back in my time, when I was going good, I have come dragging in from a dance horseback by daylight. We wasn't making payment on so many things, but we was making some mighty nifty "whoopee."

August 24, 1930

★   ★   ★

Your mother gets mighty shocked at you girls nowadays, but in her day her mother was just on the verge of sending her to a reformatory; so we just got to live and let live and laugh the thing off.

August 24, 1930

YUGOSLAVIA

That Yugoslavia, they just seem to want to fight anyhow. Be a good joke on them if nobody prevented 'em.

December 18, 1934

You see, you can't just sit down and cut out a nation on the map. You don't know how many people in any country are pulling for a revolution for they have a great amount of dissatisfied people in them. The more nations you create, the more chances you have of war. That's self-disintegration of small nations.

August, 26, 1926

★   ★   ★

Those little Balkan nations, they are like a mess of stray Terriers anyhow, they just as well be fighting as like they are.

I remember when I was over in those countries in the summer of '26, why, they were growling at each other like a couple of fat prima donnas on the same opera bill. And Serbia, she don't want to lose her reputation, they want to go down in history as having started all the wars. You see, the whole mess of 'em, they have no more love for each other than a litter of hyenas, they either lost or gained territory during the last war and they feel—those that did gain—that in another war they would grab off even more; and those that lost, can't see how they could possibly make that mistake again, and that if given a chance to play the same hole over again, they could make it in par the next time.

If we keep our nose clean and don't start yapping about somebody else's honor, or what our moral obligations are, we might escape it.

But it's going to take better statesmanship than we have been favored with heretofore.

October 19, 1930

Z

ZIEGFELD, FLORENZ (FLO), JR.

I started with Ziegfeld in 1924 as a child prodigy. I was just a little feller and went into the Follies first on account of chewing gum. I chewed gum for Mr. Ziegfeld for twelve years and never dropped a cud, or anything. I was better than a cow that way.

April 6, 1930

ZIEGFELD FOLLIES

I am to go and perform in the Ziegfeld Follies and I have no act. So I thought I'll run down to Washington and get some material. Now most actors appearing on the stage have some writer write their material, but I don't do that; Congress is good enough for me. They have written my material for years and I am not ashamed of the material I have had. You see, there is nothing so funny as something done in all seriousness.

June 8, 1928

★ ★ ★

I have met most of you bankers as I come out of the stage door of the Follies every night. I want to tell you that any of you that are capitalized under a million dollars needn't hang around there. Our girls may not know their Latin and Greek, but they certainly know their Dun and Bradstreet.

1923

When I die, my epitaph, or whatever you call those signs on gravestones, is going to read: "I joked about every prominent man of my time, but I never met a man I dident like."

I am so proud of that, I can hardly wait to die so it can be carved. And when you come to my grave you will find me sitting there, proudly reading it.

Will Rogers
June 16, 1930

Index